# CIVIL LIBERTIES AND CIVIL RIGHTS

## IN THE

# UNITED STATES

By

HARRIET POLLACK

Professor of Government
John Jay College of Criminal Justice

and

ALEXANDER B. SMITH

Professor Emeritus of Sociology
John Jay College of Criminal Justice

ST. PAUL, MINN.
WEST PUBLISHING CO.
1978

50356

**Library of Congress Cataloging in Publication Data**

Pollack, Harriet, 1925–
    Civil liberties and civil rights in the United States.

    Includes index.

    1.  Civil rights—United States.  I.  Smith, Alexander B., 1909– joint author.  II.  Title.
KF4749.P63        342'.73'085        78-5892

**ISBN** 0-8299-2003-x

To our mentors, with gratitude
and affection

Ruth G. Weintraub, Dean Emeritus, Hunter College,
City University of New York

and

Wellman J. Warner, Professor Emeritus,
New York University

*

# PREFACE

President Carter in his 1976 electoral campaign repeatedly referred to the essential decency of the American people. He spoke constantly of bringing America back to where she had once been, a force for good and a leader in the struggle for freedom and justice for mankind. His theme struck a responsive chord in the public, and from all parts of the country came evidence that in the United States there is a widespread underlying vein of idealism, of a patriotism that expresses itself not in flag waving or saber rattling, but in pride in our heritage as a nation "conceived in liberty and dedicated to the proposition that all men are created equal."

Much of this struggle has taken place in the courts, especially the U.S. Supreme Court. This book deals with some of the major issues in civil liberties and civil rights that have been adjudicated by our highest tribunal. Generally these cases fall into three categories: 1) those involving the freedoms protected by the First Amendment—speech, press, assembly and religion; 2) criminal procedure cases arising under the 4th, 5th, 6th, and 8th amendments; and 3) equal protection cases stemming from racial or sexual discrimination and involving interpretation of the 14th Amendment. In each area, we have tried to select those cases which best illustrate the constitutional issues in question, and to place them in historical and sociological context. We have tried to make the text as readable as possible, and if we have failed the failure is ours alone, for our subject matter is truly one of the grand dramas of human history.

Many colleagues and friends have helped us, not least by patiently accepting the role of sounding boards for our monologues on the themes of this book. John Jay College gave us a congenial environment in which to work and the services of a devoted library staff, in particular Chief Librarian Eileen Rowland and Professor Antony Simpson. Sylvia Rothberg, our typist for this as well as for our previous books, has our profound grati-

## PREFACE

tude for her efficiency and resourcefulness. Betty Goldstein and Gertrude Schwortz, our incomparable departmental secretaries were, as always, cheerful and helpful, and performed innumerable tasks which made our work easier. Above all, we wish to thank our students from whom we have learned so much.

HARRIET POLLACK
ALEXANDER B. SMITH

New York, N. Y.
April, 1978

# TABLE OF CONTENTS

Page

CHAPTER V.  EQUALITY BEFORE THE LAW

CHAPTER VI.  PRESSURE GROUPS, LAWYERS AND
THE SUPREME COURT

# THE CONSTITUTION OF THE UNITED STATES

## PREAMBLE

---

We the People of the United States, in Order to form a more perfect Union, establish Justice, insure domestic Tranquility, provide for the common defence, promote the general Welfare, and secure the Blessings of Liberty to ourselves and our Posterity, do ordain and establish this Constitution for the United States of America.

# CONSTITUTION OF THE UNITED STATES

## Article I

Section 1. All legislative Powers herein granted shall be vested in a Congress of the United States, which shall consist of a Senate and House of Representatives.

Section 2. [1] The House of Representatives shall be composed of Members chosen every second Year by the People of the several States, and the Electors in each State shall have the Qualifications requisite for Electors of the most numerous Branch of the State Legislature.

[2] No Person shall be a Representative who shall not have attained to the Age of twenty five Years, and been seven Years a Citizen of the United States, and who shall not, when elected, be an Inhabitant of that State in which he shall be chosen.

[3] Representatives and direct Taxes shall be apportioned among the several States which may be included within this Union, according to their respective Numbers, which shall be determined by adding to the whole Number of free Persons, including those bound to Service for a Term of Years, and excluding Indians not taxed, three fifths of all other Persons. The actual Enumeration shall be made within three Years after the first Meeting of the Congress of the United States, and within every subsequent Term of ten Years, in such Manner as they shall by Law direct. The Number of Representatives shall not exceed one for every thirty Thousand, but each State shall have at Least one Representative; and until such enumeration shall be made, the State of New Hampshire shall be entitled to chuse three, Massachusetts eight, Rhode Island and Providence Plantations one, Connecticut five, New York six, New Jersey four, Pennsylvania eight, Delaware one, Maryland six, Virginia ten, North Carolina five, South Carolina five, and Georgia three.

[4] When vacancies happen in the Representation from any State, the Executive Authority thereof shall issue Writs of Election to fill such Vacancies.

[5] The House of Representatives shall chuse their Speaker and other Officers; and shall have the sole Power of Impeachment.

Section 3. [1] The Senate of the United States shall be composed of two Senators from each State, chosen by the Legislature thereof, for six Years; and each Senator shall have one Vote.

[2] Immediately after they shall be assembled in Consequence of the first Election, they shall be divided as equally as may be into three Classes. The Seats of the Senators of the first Class shall be vacated at the Expiration of the Second Year, of the second Class at the Expiration of the fourth Year, and of the third Class at the Expiration of the sixth Year, so that one third may be chosen every second Year; and if Vacancies happen by Resignation, or otherwise, during the Recess of the Legislature of any State, the

Executive thereof may make temporary Appointments until the next Meeting of the Legislature, which shall then fill such Vacancies.

[3] No Person shall be a Senator who shall not have attained to the Age of thirty Years, and been nine Years a Citizen of the United States, and who shall not, when elected, be an Inhabitant of that State for which he shall be chosen.

[4] The Vice President of the United States shall be President of the Senate, but shall have no Vote, unless they be equally divided.

[5] The Senate shall chuse their other Officers, and also a President pro tempore, in the Absence of the Vice President, or when he shall exercise the Office of President of the United States.

[6] The Senate shall have the sole Power to try all Impeachments. When sitting for that Purpose, they shall be on Oath or Affirmation. When the President of the United States is tried, the Chief Justice shall preside: And no Person shall be convicted without the Concurrence of two thirds of the Members present.

[7] Judgment in Cases of Impeachment shall not extend further than to removal from Office, and disqualification to hold and enjoy any Office of honor, Trust, or Profit under the United States: but the Party convicted shall nevertheless be liable and subject to Indictment, Trial, Judgment, and Punishment, according to Law.

Section 4. [1] The Times, Places and Manner of holding Elections for Senators and Representatives, shall be prescribed in each State by the Legislature thereof; but the Congress may at any time by Law make or alter such Regulations, except as to the Places of chusing Senators.

[2] The Congress shall assemble at least once in every Year, and such Meeting shall be on the first Monday in December, unless they shall by Law appoint a different Day.

Section 5. [1] Each House shall be the Judge of the Elections, Returns, and Qualifications of its own Members, and a Majority of each shall constitute a Quorum to do Business; but a smaller Number may adjourn from day to day, and may be authorized to compel the Attendance of absent Members, in such Manner, and under such Penalties as each House may provide.

[2] Each House may determine the Rules of its Proceedings, punish its Members for disorderly Behavior, and, with the Concurrence of two thirds, expel a Member.

[3] Each House shall keep a Journal of its Proceedings, and from time to time publish the same, excepting such Parts as may in their Judgment require Secrecy; and the Yeas and Nays of the Members of either House on any question shall, at the Desire of one fifth of those Present, be entered on the Journal.

# CONSTITUTION OF THE UNITED STATES

[4] Neither House, during the Session of Congress, shall, without the Consent of the other, adjourn for more than three days, nor to any other Place than that in which the two Houses shall be sitting.

Section 6. [1] The Senators and Representatives shall receive a Compensation for their Services, to be ascertained by Law, and paid out of the Treasury of the United States. They shall in all Cases, except Treason, Felony and Breach of the Peace, be privileged from Arrest during their Attendance at the Session of their respective Houses, and in going to and returning from the same; and for any Speech or Debate in either House, they shall not be questioned in any other Place.

[2] No Senator or Representative shall, during the Time for which he was elected, be appointed to any civil Office under the Authority of the United States, which shall have been created, or the Emoluments whereof shall have been increased during such time; and no Person holding any Office under the United States, shall be a Member of either House during his Continuance in Office.

Section 7. [1] All Bills for raising Revenue shall originate in the House of Representatives; but the Senate may propose or concur with Amendments as on other Bills.

[2] Every Bill which shall have passed the House of Representatives and the Senate, shall, before it become a Law, be presented to the President of the United States; If he approve he shall sign it, but if not he shall return it, with his Objections to the House in which it shall have originated, who shall enter the Objections at large on their Journal, and proceed to reconsider it. If after such Reconsideration two thirds of that House shall agree to pass the Bill, it shall be sent together with the Objections, to the other House, by which it shall likewise be reconsidered, and if approved by two thirds of that House, it shall become a Law. But in all such Cases the Votes of both Houses shall be determined by yeas and Nays, and the Names of the Persons voting for and against the Bill shall be entered on the Journal of each House respectively. If any Bill shall not be returned by the President within ten Days (Sundays excepted) after it shall have been presented to him, the Same shall be a Law, in like Manner as if he had signed it, unless the Congress by their Adjournment prevent its Return in which Case it shall not be a Law.

[3] Every Order, Resolution, or Vote, to Which the Concurrence of the Senate and House of Representatives may be necessary (except on a question of Adjournment) shall be presented to the President of the United States; and before the Same shall take Effect, shall be approved by him, or being disapproved by him, shall be repassed by two thirds of the Senate and House of Representatives, according to the Rules and Limitations prescribed in the Case of a Bill.

Section 8. [1] The Congress shall have Power To lay and collect Taxes, Duties, Imposts and Excises, to pay the Debts and provide for the common Defence and general Welfare of the United States; but all Duties, Imposts and Excises shall be uniform throughout the United States;

[2]   To borrow money on the credit of the United States;

[3]   To regulate Commerce with foreign Nations, and among the several States, and with the Indian Tribes;

[4]   To establish an uniform Rule of Naturalization, and uniform Laws on the subject of Bankruptcies throughout the United States;

[5]   To coin Money, regulate the Value thereof, and of foreign Coin, and fix the Standard of Weights and Measures;

[6]   To provide for the Punishment of counterfeiting the Securities and current Coin of the United States;

[7]   To Establish Post Offices and Post Roads;

[8]   To promote the Progress of Science and useful Arts, by securing for limited Times to Authors and Inventors the exclusive Right to their respective Writings and Discoveries;

[9]   To constitute Tribunals inferior to the supreme Court;

[10]   To define and punish Piracies and Felonies committed on the high Seas, and Offenses against the Law of Nations;

[11]   To declare War, grant Letters of Marque and Reprisal, and make Rules concerning Captures on Land and Water;

[12]   To raise and support Armies, but no Appropriation of Money to that Use shall be for a longer Term than two Years;

[13]   To provide and maintain a Navy;

[14]   To make Rules for the Government and Regulation of the land and naval Forces;

[15]   To provide for calling forth the Militia to execute the Laws of the Union, suppress Insurrections and repel Invasions;

[16]   To provide for organizing, arming, and disciplining, the Militia, and for governing such Part of them as may be employed in the Service of the United States, reserving to the States respectively, the Appointment of the Officers, and the Authority of training the Militia according to the discipline prescribed by Congress;

[17]   To exercise exclusive Legislation in all Cases whatsoever, over such District (not exceeding ten Miles square) as may, by Cession of particular States, and the Acceptance of Congress, become the Seat of the Government of the United States, and to exercise like Authority over all Places purchased by the Consent of the Legislature of the State in which the Same shall be, for the Erection of Forts, Magazines, Arsenals, dock-Yards, and other needful Buildings;—And

[18]   To make all Laws which shall be necessary and proper for carrying into Execution the foregoing Powers, and all other Powers vested by

this Constitution in the Government of the United States, or in any Department or Officer thereof.

Section 9. [1] The Migration or Importation of Such Persons as any of the States now existing shall think proper to admit, shall not be prohibited by the Congress prior to the Year one thousand eight hundred and eight, but a Tax or duty may be imposed on such Importation, not exceeding ten dollars for each Person.

[2] The privilege of the Writ of Habeas Corpus shall not be suspended, unless when in Cases of Rebellion or Invasion the public Safety may require it.

[3] No Bill of Attainder or ex post facto Law shall be passed.

[4] No Capitation, or other direct, Tax shall be laid, unless in Proportion to the Census or Enumeration herein before directed to be taken.

[5] No Tax or Duty shall be laid on Articles exported from any State.

[6] No Preference shall be given by any Regulation of Commerce or Revenue to the Ports of one State over those of another: nor shall Vessels bound to, or from, one State be obliged to enter, clear, or pay Duties in another.

[7] No money shall be drawn from the Treasury, but in Consequence of Appropriations made by Law; and a regular Statement and Account of the Receipts and Expenditures of all public Money shall be published from time to time.

[8] No Title of Nobility shall be granted by the United States: And no Person holding any Office of Profit or Trust under them, shall, without the Consent of the Congress, accept of any present, Emolument, Office, or Title, of any kind whatever, from any King, Prince, or foreign State.

Section 10. [1] No State shall enter into any Treaty, Alliance, or Confederation; grant Letters of Marque and Reprisal; coin Money; emit Bills of Credit; make any Thing but gold and silver Coin a Tender in Payment of Debts; pass any Bill of Attainder, ex post facto Law, or Law impairing the Obligation of Contracts, or grant any Title of Nobility.

[2] No State shall, without the Consent of the Congress, lay any Imposts or Duties on Imports or Exports, except what may be absolutely necessary for executing it's inspection Laws: and the net Produce of all Duties and Imposts, laid by any State on Imports or Exports, shall be for the Use of the Treasury of the United States; and all such Laws shall be subject to the Revision and Controul of the Congress.

[3] No State shall, without the Consent of Congress, lay any Duty of Tonnage, keep Troops, or Ships of War in time of Peace, enter into any Agreement or Compact with another State, or with a foreign Power, or engage in War, unless actually invaded, or in such imminent Danger as will not admit of delay.

# CONSTITUTION OF THE UNITED STATES

## Article II

Section 1. [1]  The executive Power shall be vested in a President of the United States of America. He shall hold his Office during the Term of four Years, and, together with the Vice President, chosen for the same Term, be elected, as follows:

[2]  Each State shall appoint, in such Manner as the Legislature thereof may direct, a Number of Electors, equal to the whole Number of Senators and Representatives to which the State may be entitled in the Congress; but no Senator or Representative, or Person holding an Office of Trust or Profit under the United States, shall be appointed an Elector.

[3]  The Electors shall meet in their respective States, and vote by Ballot for two Persons, of whom one at least shall not be an Inhabitant of the same State with themselves. And they shall make a List of all the Persons voted for, and of the Number of Votes for each; which List they shall sign and certify, and transmit sealed to the Seat of the Government of the United States, directed to the President of the Senate. The President of the Senate shall, in the Presence of the Senate and House of Representatives, open all the Certificates, and the Votes shall then be counted. The Person having the greatest Number of Votes shall be the President, if such Number be a Majority of the whole Number of Electors appointed; and if there be more than one who have such Majority, and have an equal Number of Votes, then the House of Representatives shall immediately chuse by Ballot one of them for President; and if no Person have a Majority, then from the five highest on the List the said House shall in like Manner chuse the President. But in chusing the President, the Votes shall be taken by States the Representation from each State having one Vote; A quorum for this Purpose shall consist of a Member or Members from two thirds of the States, and a Majority of all the States shall be necessary to a Choice. In every Case, after the Choice of the President, the Person having the greater Number of Votes of the Electors shall be the Vice President. But if there should remain two or more who have equal Votes, the Senate shall chuse from them by Ballot the Vice President.

[4]  The Congress may determine the Time of chusing the Electors, and the Day on which they shall give their Votes; which Day shall be the same throughout the United States.

[5]  No person except a natural born Citizen, or a Citizen of the United States, at the time of the Adoption of this Constitution, shall be eligible to the Office of President; neither shall any Person be eligible to that Office who shall not have attained to the Age of thirty five Years, and been fourteen Years a Resident within the United States.

[6]  In case of the removal of the President from Office, or of his Death, Resignation or Inability to discharge the Powers and Duties of the

said Office, the Same shall devolve on the Vice President, and the Congress may by Law provide for the Case of Removal, Death, Resignation or Inability, both of the President and Vice President, declaring what Officer shall then act as President, and such Officer shall act accordingly, until the Disability be removed, or a President shall be elected.

[7]  The President shall, at stated Times, receive for his Services, a Compensation, which shall neither be increased nor diminished during the Period for which he shall have been elected, and he shall not receive within that Period any other Emolument from the United States, or any of them.

[8]  Before he enter on the Execution of his Office, he shall take the following Oath or Affirmation: "I do solemnly swear (or affirm) that I will faithfully execute the Office of President of the United States, and will to the best of my Ability, preserve, protect and defend the Constitution of the United States."

Section 2.  [1]  The President shall be Commander in Chief of the Army and Navy of the United States, and of the militia of the several States, when called into the actual Service of the United States; he may require the Opinion, in writing, of the principal Officer in each of the Executive Departments, upon any Subject relating to the Duties of their respective Offices, and he shall have Power to grant Reprieves and Pardons for Offenses against the United States, except in Cases of Impeachment.

[2]  He shall have Power, by and with the Advice and Consent of the Senate to make Treaties, provided two thirds of the Senators present concur; and he shall nominate, and by and with the Advice and Consent of the Senate, shall appoint Ambassadors, other public Ministers and Consuls, Judges of the supreme Court, and all other Officers of the United States, whose Appointments are not herein otherwise provided for, and which shall be established by Law; but the Congress may by Law vest the Appointment of such inferior Officers, as they think proper, in the President alone, in the Courts of Law, or in the Heads of Departments.

[3]  The President shall have Power to fill up all Vacancies that may happen during the Recess of the Senate, by granting Commissions which shall expire at the End of their next Session.

Section 3.  He shall from time to time give to the Congress Information of the State of the Union, and recommend to their Consideration such Measures as he shall judge necessary and expedient; he may, on extraordinary Occasions, convene both Houses, or either of them, and in Case of Disagreement between them, with Respect to the Time of Adjournment, he may adjourn them to such Time as he shall think proper; he shall receive Ambassadors and other public Ministers; he shall take Care that the Laws be faithfully executed, and shall Commission all the Officers of the United States.

Section 4.  The President, Vice President and all civil Officers of the United States, shall be removed from Office on Impeachment for, and Conviction of, Treason, Bribery, or other high Crimes and Misdemeanors.

# CONSTITUTION OF THE UNITED STATES

## ARTICLE III

Section 1. The judicial Power of the United States, shall be vested in one supreme Court, and in such inferior Courts as the Congress may from time to time ordain and establish. The Judges, both of the supreme and inferior Courts, shall hold their Offices during good Behaviour, and shall, at stated Times, receive for their Services a Compensation, which shall not be diminished during their Continuance in Office.

Section 2. [1] The judicial Power shall extend to all Cases, in Law and Equity, arising under this Constitution, the Laws of the United States, and Treaties made, or which shall be made, under their Authority;—to all Cases affecting Ambassadors, other public Ministers and Consuls;—to all Cases of admiralty and maritime Jurisdiction;—to Controversies to which the United States shall be a Party;—to Controversies between two or more States;—between a State and Citizens of another State;—between Citizens of different States;—between Citizens of the same State claiming Lands under the Grants of different States, and between a State, or the Citizens thereof, and foreign States, Citizens or Subjects.

[2] In all Cases affecting Ambassadors, other public Ministers and Consuls, and those in which a State shall be a Party, the supreme Court shall have original Jurisdiction. In all the other Cases before mentioned, the supreme Court shall have appellate Jurisdiction, both as to Law and Fact, with such Exceptions, and under such Regulations as the Congress shall make.

[3] The trial of all Crimes, except in Cases of Impeachment, shall be by Jury; and such Trial shall be held in the State where the said Crimes shall have been committed; but when not committed within any State, the Trial shall be at such Place or Places as the Congress may by Law have directed.

Section 3. [1] Treason against the United States, shall consist only in levying War against them, or, in adhering to their Enemies, giving them Aid and Comfort. No Person shall be convicted of Treason unless on the Testimony of two Witnesses to the same overt Act, or on Confession in open Court.

[2] The Congress shall have Power to declare the Punishment of Treason, but no Attainder of Treason shall work Corruption of Blood, or Forfeiture except during the Life of the Person attainted.

## ARTICLE IV

Section 1. Full Faith and Credit shall be given in each State to the public Acts, Records, and judicial Proceedings of every other State. And the Congress may by general Laws prescribe the Manner in which such Acts, Records and Proceedings shall be proved, and the Effect thereof.

Section 2. [1] The Citizens of each State shall be entitled to all Privileges and Immunities of Citizens in the several States.

[2] A Person charged in any State with Treason, Felony, or other Crime, who shall flee from Justice, and be found in another State, shall on demand of the executive Authority of the State from which he fled, be delivered up, to be removed to the State having Jurisdiction of the Crime.

[3] No Person held to Service or Labour in one State, under the Laws thereof, escaping into another, shall, in Consequence of any Law or Regulation therein, be discharged from such Service or Labour, but shall be delivered up on Claim of the Party to whom such Service or Labour may be due.

Section 3. [1] New States may be admitted by the Congress into this Union; but no new State shall be formed or erected within the Jurisdiction of any other State; nor any State be formed by the Junction of two or more States, or Parts of States, without the Consent of the Legislatures of the States concerned as well as of the Congress.

[2] The Congress shall have Power to dispose of and make all needful Rules and Regulations respecting the Territory or other Property belonging to the United States; and nothing in this Constitution shall be so construed as to Prejudice any Claims of the United States, or of any particular State.

Section 4. The United States shall guarantee to every State in this Union a Republican Form of Government, and shall protect each of them against Invasion; and on Application of the Legislature, or of the Executive (when the Legislature cannot be convened) against domestic Violence.

## ARTICLE V

The Congress, whenever two thirds of both Houses shall deem it necessary, shall propose Amendments to this Constitution, or, on the Application of the Legislatures of two thirds of the several States, shall call a Convention for proposing Amendments, which, in either Case, shall be valid to all Intents and Purposes, as part of this Constitution, when ratified by the Legislatures of three fourths of the several States, or by Conventions in three fourths thereof, as the one or the other Mode of Ratification may be proposed by the Congress; Provided that no Amendment which may be made prior to the Year One thousand eight hundred and eight shall in any Manner affect the first and fourth Clauses in the Ninth Section of the first Article; and that no State, without its Consent, shall be deprived of its equal Suffrage in the Senate.

## ARTICLE VI

[1] All Debts contracted and Engagements entered into, before the Adoption of this Constitution shall be as valid against the United States under this Constitution, as under the Confederation.

[2]   This Constitution, and the Laws of the United States which shall be made in Pursuance thereof; and all Treaties made, or which shall be made, under the Authority of the United States, shall be the supreme Law of the Land; and the Judges in every State shall be bound thereby, any Thing in the Constitution or Laws of any State to the Contrary notwithstanding.

[3]   The Senators and Representatives before mentioned, and the Members of the several State Legislatures, and all executive and judicial Officers, both of the United States and of the several States, shall be bound by Oath or Affirmation, to support this Constitution; but no religious Test shall ever be required as a Qualification to any Office or public Trust under the United States.

## ARTICLE VII

The Ratification of the Conventions of nine States shall be sufficient for the Establishment of this Constitution between the States so ratifying the Same.

## ARTICLES IN ADDITION TO, AND AMENDMENT OF, THE CONSTITUTION OF THE UNITED STATES OF AMERICA, PROPOSED BY CONGRESS, AND RATIFIED BY THE LEGISLATURES OF THE SEVERAL STATES PURSUANT TO THE FIFTH ARTICLE OF THE ORIGINAL CONSTITUTION.

### AMENDMENT I [1791]

Congress shall make no law respecting an establishment of religion, or prohibiting the free exercise thereof; or abridging the freedom of speech, or of the press; or the right of the people peaceably to assemble, and to petition the Government for a redress of grievances.

### AMENDMENT II [1791]

A well regulated Militia, being necessary to the security of a free State, the right of the people to keep and bear Arms, shall not be infringed.

### AMENDMENT III [1791]

No Soldier shall, in time of peace be quartered in any house, without the consent of the Owner, nor in time of war, but in a manner to be prescribed by law.

### AMENDMENT IV [1791]

The right of the people to be secure in their persons, houses, papers, and effects, against unreasonable searches and seizures, shall not be violated, and no Warrants shall issue, but upon probable cause, supported by Oath or affirmation, and particularly describing the place to be searched, and the persons or things to be seized.

## Amendment V [1791]

No person shall be held to answer for a capital, or otherwise infamous crime, unless on a presentment or indictment of a Grand Jury, except in cases arising in the land or naval forces, or in the Militia, when in actual service in time of War or public danger; nor shall any person be subject for the same offence to be twice put in jeopardy of life or limb; nor shall be compelled in any criminal case to be a witness against himself, nor be deprived of life, liberty, or property, without due process of law; nor shall private property be taken for public use, without just compensation.

## Amendment VI [1791]

In all criminal prosecutions, the accused shall enjoy the right to a speedy and public trial, by an impartial jury of the State and district wherein the crime shall have been committed, which district shall have been previously ascertained by law, and to be informed of the nature and cause of the accusation; to be confronted with the witnesses against him; to have compulsory process for obtaining witnesses in his favor, and to have the Assistance of Counsel for his defence.

## Amendment VII [1791]

In Suits at common law, where the value in controversy shall exceed twenty dollars, the right of trial by jury shall be preserved, and no fact tried by jury, shall be otherwise re-examined in any Court of the United States, than according to the rules of the common law.

## Amendment VIII [1791]

Excessive bail shall not be required, nor excessive fines imposed, nor cruel and unusual punishments inflicted.

## Amendment IX [1791]

The enumeration in the Constitution, of certain rights, shall not be construed to deny or disparage others retained by the people.

## Amendment X [1791]

The powers not delegated to the United States by the Constitution, nor prohibited by it to the States, are reserved to the States respectively, or to the people.

# CONSTITUTION OF THE UNITED STATES

## Amendment XI [1798]

The Judicial power of the United States shall not be construed to extend to any suit in law or equity, commenced or prosecuted against one of the United States by Citizens of another State, or by Citizens or Subjects of any Foreign State.

## Amendment XII [1804]

The Electors shall meet in their respective states and vote by ballot for President and Vice-President, one of whom, at least, shall not be an inhabitant of the same state with themselves; they shall name in their ballots the person voted for as President, and in distinct ballots the person voted for as Vice-President, and they shall make distinct lists of all persons voted for as President, and of all persons voted for as Vice-President, and of the number of votes for each, which lists they shall sign and certify, and transmit sealed to the seat of the government of the United States, directed to the President of the Senate;—The President of the Senate shall, in the presence of the Senate and House of Representatives, open all the certificates and the votes shall then be counted;—The person having the greatest number of votes for President, shall be the President, if such number be a majority of the whole number of Electors appointed; and if no person have such majority, then from the persons having the highest numbers not exceeding three on the list of those voted for as President, the House of Representatives shall choose immediately, by ballot, the President. But in choosing the President, the votes shall be taken by states, the representation from each state having one vote; a quorum for this purpose shall consist of a member or members from two-thirds of the states, and a majority of all the states shall be necessary to a choice. And if the House of Representatives shall not choose a President whenever the right of choice shall devolve upon them before the fourth day of March next following, then the Vice-President shall act as President, as in the case of the death or other constitutional disability of the President.— The person having the greatest number of votes as Vice-President, shall be the Vice-President, if such number be a majority of the whole number of Electors appointed, and if no person have a majority, then from the two highest numbers on the list, the Senate shall choose the Vice-President; a quorum for the purpose shall consist of two-thirds of the whole number of Senators, and a majority of the whole number shall be necessary to a choice. But no person constitutionally ineligible to the office of President shall be eligible to that of Vice-President of the United States.

## Amendment XIII [1865]

Section 1. Neither slavery nor involuntary servitude, except as a punishment for crime whereof the party shall have been duly convicted, shall exist within the United States, or any place subject to their jurisdiction.

# CONSTITUTION OF THE UNITED STATES

Section 2. Congress shall have power to enforce this article by appropriate legislation.

## AMENDMENT XIV [1868]

Section 1. All persons born or naturalized in the United States, and subject to the jurisdiction thereof, are citizens of the United States and of the State wherein they reside. No State shall make or enforce any law which shall abridge the privileges or immunities of citizens of the United States; nor shall any State deprive any person of life, liberty, or property, without due process of law; nor deny to any person within its jurisdiction the equal protection of the laws.

Section 2. Representatives shall be apportioned among the several States according to their respective numbers, counting the whole number of persons in each State, excluding Indians not taxed. But when the right to vote at any election for the choice of electors for President and Vice President of the United States, Representatives in Congress, the Executive and Judicial officers of a State, or the members of the Legislature thereof, is denied to any of the male inhabitants of such State, being twenty-one years of age, and citizens of the United States, or in any way abridged, except for participation in rebellion, or other crime, the basis of representation therein shall be reduced in the proportion which the number of such male citizens shall bear to the whole number of male citizens twenty-one years of age in such State.

Section 3. No person shall be a Senator or Representative in Congress, or elector of President and Vice President, or hold any office, civil or military, under the United States, or under any State, who having previously taken an oath, as a member of Congress, or as an officer of the United States, or as a member of any State legislature, or as an executive or judicial officer of any State, to support the Constitution of the United States, shall have engaged in insurrection or rebellion against the same, or given aid or comfort to the enemies thereof. But Congress may by a vote of two-thirds of each House, remove such disability.

Section 4. The validity of the public debt of the United States, authorized by law, including debts incurred for payment of pensions and bounties for services in suppressing insurrection or rebellion, shall not be questioned. But neither the United States nor any State shall assume or pay any debt or obligation incurred in aid of insurrection or rebellion against the United States, or any claim for the loss or emancipation of any slave; but all such debts, obligations and claims shall be held illegal and void.

Section 5. The Congress shall have power to enforce, by appropriate legislation, the provisions of this article.

## AMENDMENT XV [1870]

Section 1. The right of citizens of the United States to vote shall not be denied or abridged by the United States or by any State on account of race, color, or previous condition of servitude.

# CONSTITUTION OF THE UNITED STATES

Section 2. The Congress shall have power to enforce this article by appropriate legislation.

## AMENDMENT XVI [1913]

The Congress shall have power to lay and collect taxes on incomes, from
whatever source derived, without apportionment among the several States,
and without regard to any census or enumeration.

## AMENDMENT XVII [1913]

[1] The Senate of the United States shall be composed of two Senators
from each State, elected by the people thereof, for six years; and each Senator shall have one vote. The electors in each State shall have the qualifications requisite for electors of the most numerous branch of the State legislatures.

[2] When vacancies happen in the representation of any State in the
Senate, the executive authority of such State shall issue writs of election to
fill such vacancies: *Provided,* That the legislature of any State may empow-
er the executive thereof to make temporary appointments until the people fill
the vacancies by election as the legislature may direct.

[3] This amendment shall not be so construed as to affect the election
or term of any Senator chosen before it becomes valid as part of the Constitution.

## AMENDMENT XVIII [1919]

Section 1. After one year from the ratification of this article the man-
ufacture, sale, or transportation of intoxicating liquors within, the importation thereof into, or the exportation thereof from the United States and all
territory subject to the jurisdiction thereof for beverage purposes is hereby
prohibited.

Section 2. The Congress and the several States shall have concurrent
power to enforce this article by appropriate legislation.

Section 3. This article shall be inoperative unless it shall have been
ratified as an amendment to the Constitution by the legislatures of the several States, as provided in the Constitution, within seven years from the date
of the submission hereof to the States by the Congress.

## AMENDMENT XIX [1920]

[1] The right of citizens of the United States to vote shall not be denied or abridged by the United States or by any State on account of sex.

[2] Congress shall have power to enforce this article by appropriate
legislation.

# CONSTITUTION OF THE UNITED STATES

Section 1.  The terms of the President and Vice President shall end at noon on the 20th day of January, and the terms of Senators and Representatives at noon on the 3d day of January, of the years in which such terms would have ended if this article had not been ratified; and the terms of their successors shall then begin.

Section 2.  The Congress shall assemble at least once in every year, and such meeting shall begin at noon on the 3d day of January, unless they shall by law appoint a different day.

Section 3.  If, at the time fixed for the beginning of the term of the President, the President elect shall have died, the Vice President elect shall become President.  If the President shall not have been chosen before the time fixed for the beginning of his term, or if the President elect shall have failed to qualify, then the Vice President elect shall act as President until a President shall have qualified; and the Congress may by law provide for the case wherein neither a President elect nor a Vice President elect shall have qualified, declaring who shall then act as President, or the manner in which one who is to act shall be selected, and such person shall act accordingly until a President or Vice President shall have qualified.

Section 4.  The Congress may by law provide for the case of the death of any of the persons from whom the House of Representatives may choose a President whenever the right of choice shall have devolved upon them, and for the case of the death of any of the persons from whom the Senate may choose a Vice President whenever the right of choice shall have devolved upon them.

Section 5.  Sections 1 and 2 shall take effect on the 15th day of October following the ratification of this article.

Section 6.  This article shall be inoperative unless it shall have been ratified as an amendment to the Constitution by the legislatures of three-fourths of the several States within seven years from the date of its submission.

Section 1.  The eighteenth article of amendment to the Constitution of the United States is hereby repealed.

Section 2.  The transportation or importation into any State, Territory, or possession of the United States for delivery or use therein of intoxicating liquors, in violation of the laws thereof, is hereby prohibited.

Section 3.  This article shall be inoperative unless it shall have been ratified as an amendment to the Constitution by conventions in the several States, as provided in the Constitution, within seven years from the date of the submission hereof to the States by the Congress.

# CONSTITUTION OF THE UNITED STATES

## AMENDMENT XXII [1951]

Section 1. No person shall be elected to the office of the President more than twice, and no person who has held the office of President, or acted as President, for more than two years of a term to which some other person was elected President shall be elected to the office of President more than once. But this Article shall not apply to any person holding the office of President when this Article was proposed by the Congress, and shall not prevent any person who may be holding the office of President, or acting as President, during the term within which this Article becomes operative from holding the office of President or acting as President during the remainder of such term.

Section 2. This article shall be inoperative unless it shall have been ratified as an amendment to the Constitution by the legislatures of three-fourths of the several States within seven years from the date of its submission to the States by the Congress.

## AMENDMENT XXIII [1961]

Section 1. The District constituting the seat of Government of the United States shall appoint in such manner as the Congress may direct:

A number of electors of President and Vice President equal to the whole number of Senators and Representatives in Congress to which the District would be entitled if it were a State, but in no event more than the least populous state; they shall be in addition to those appointed by the states, but they shall be considered, for the purposes of the election of President and Vice President, to be electors appointed by a state; and they shall meet in the District and perform such duties as provided by the twelfth article of amendment.

Section 2. The Congress shall have power to enforce this article by appropriate legislation.

## AMENDMENT XXIV [1964]

Section 1. The right of citizens of the United States to vote in any primary or other election for President or Vice President, for electors for President or Vice President, or for Senator or Representative in Congress, shall not be denied or abridged by the United States or any State by reason of failure to pay any poll tax or other tax.

Section 2. The Congress shall have power to enforce this article by appropriate legislation.

## AMENDMENT XXV [1967]

Section 1. In case of the removal of the President from office or of his death or resignation, the Vice President shall become President.

Section 2. Whenever there is a vacancy in the office of the Vice President, the President shall nominate a Vice President who shall take office upon confirmation by a majority vote of both Houses of Congress.

# CONSTITUTION OF THE UNITED STATES

Section 3. Whenever the President transmits to the President pro tempore of the Senate and the Speaker of the House of Representatives his written declaration that he is unable to discharge the powers and duties of his office, and until he transmits to them a written declaration to the contrary, such powers and duties shall be discharged by the Vice President as Acting President.

Section 4. Whenever the Vice President and a majority of either the principal officers of the executive departments or of such other body as Congress may by law provide, transmit to the President pro tempore of the Senate and the Speaker of the House of Representatives their written declaration that the President is unable to discharge the powers and duties of his office, the Vice President shall immediately assume the powers and duties of the office as Acting President.

Thereafter, when the President transmits to the President pro tempore of the Senate and the Speaker of the House of Representatives his written declaration that no inability exists, he shall resume the powers and duties of his office unless the Vice President and a majority of either the principal officers of the executive department or of such other body as Congress may by law provide, transmit within four days to the President pro tempore of the Senate and the Speaker of the House of Representatives their written declaration and the President is unable to discharge the powers and duties of his office. Thereupon Congress shall decide the issue, assembling within forty-eight hours for that purpose if not in session. If the Congress, within twenty-one days after receipt of the latter written declaration, or, if Congress is not in session, within twenty-one days after Congress is required to assemble, determines by two-thirds vote of both Houses that the President is unable to discharge the powers and duties of his office, the Vice President shall continue to discharge the same as Acting President; otherwise, the President shall resume the powers and duties of his office.

## AMENDMENT XXVI [1971]

Section 1. The right of citizens of the United States, who are eighteen years of age or older, to vote shall not be denied or abridged by the United States or by any State on account of age.

Section 2. The Congress shall have power to enforce this article by appropriate legislation.

## AMENDMENT XXVII [Proposed]

Section 1. Equality of rights under the law shall not be denied or abridged by the United States or by any State on account of sex.

Section 2. The Congress shall have the power to enforce, by appropriate legislation, the provisions of this article.

Section 3. This amendment shall take effect two years after the date of ratification.

# CIVIL LIBERTIES
## AND
# CIVIL RIGHTS
# IN THE UNITED STATES

---

## Chapter I

### THE SUBSTRUCTURE OF THE AMERICAN LEGAL SYSTEM: HISTORY, PHILOSOPHY, TRADITION

". . . the object of government is not to change men from rational beings into beasts or puppets, but to enable them to develop their minds and bodies in security, and to employ their reason unshackled; . . . In fact, the true aim of government is liberty."

Baruch de Spinoza,

*Freedom of Thought and Speech*

"Liberty does not consist in mere declarations of the rights of man. It consists in the translation of those declarations into definite actions."

Woodrow Wilson, Address,
July 4, 1914.

The terms civil liberties and civil rights refer to more than a collection of personal freedoms. They refer to personal freedoms in a *governmental* setting. The word civil derives from the Latin *civis*, citizen. A citizen is not simply a resident of a community. He is a person with a legal relationship to a community that is politically organized. He owes allegiance to, and is entitled to protection from, a government. Thus, a discussion of civil liberties and civil rights must start with an understanding of what a government is.

If students are asked to define the term government, they will generally respond that it is an institution that makes laws for people in a given geographic area. The definition is correct but incomplete. Many institutions make rules for people in given areas. The Catholic Church makes rules for its members wherever they may reside; the United Auto Workers makes rules for the workers in Detroit's factories; Princeton University makes rules for its students, etc., but neither the Catholic Church, nor the United Auto Workers, nor Princeton University is a government in the usual sense of the word. The factor that differentiates a government from other rule making institutions is *force*: the ability to use physical coercion on recalcitrant individuals. The Catholic Church may expel or excommunicate, the United Auto Workers may bar the hiring in an automobile plant of a nonmember, Princeton University may refuse to grant a degree, but none of them may physically touch the individuals whom they wish to discipline. Only the government through its appointed agents: police, soldiers, prison guards, etc. may literally lay hands on another individual and physically force him to do what he would not otherwise do. The government can take property from an unwilling owner; the government may put a person in prison; the government may execute a person within its jurisdiction.

Not only does a government exercise awesome powers, but in the most effective, stable governments, such authority is considered legitimate: its citizens feel that it is *right* for the government to rule, even when some of its actions are punitive to part of the community. Physically coerced punitive action, moreover, is reserved to government—no other group may exercise such power. A robber may seize a citizen's purse, but his force is not *legitimate*. The tax collector, on the other hand, can legitimately seize private property in payment of taxes. A government, in short, is that institution which has a monopoly of legitimate force in the community.

Legitimacy is, however, a very troublesome problem, so difficult that it has been the central concern of most political philosophers. How can society be organized in such a way that unpleasant decisions—loss of property, loss of life or liberty, consignment to poverty or economic disadvantage—will be accepted, if not by the individuals affected, then at least by society at large? This is particularly difficult if the number of disaffected persons is large, as for example, in societies whose economies are based on slavery or serfdom. Very repressive regimes must expend large amounts of money and manpower to maintain themselves in power, e. g., Germany under Hitler, or Russia under Stalin, and they tend to be unstable. England and the United States, historically quite unrepressive governments, are among the oldest continuous governments in the world, whereas most authoritarian governments have been relatively short-lived. Every regime, thus, would prefer to be based on the consent of the governed rather than on force. Every regime would prefer its citizens to look upon it as legitimate, but how can this be done?

Historically, governmental legitimacy has assumed many forms. In simple tribal societies the strongest and most adept members took on the role of leadership and were deposed when their physical strength waned and younger and more vigorous members were able to challenge their authority successfully. More sophisticated primitive societies showed deference to the wisdom and experience of the elders of the tribe and considered them the legitimate rulers. Some societies have legitimatized government though a popularly accepted religion. In ancient Israel, Moses and other leaders were believed to have spoken directly to the Almighty and to have derived their authority directly from Him. In medieval Europe, the Pope was God's representative on earth, and feudal kings derived their legitimacy from their allegiance and obedience to him. Were a ruler to be excommunicated by the Pope, his subjects would be released from their obligation to obey him. Henry VIII's political problems stemmed precisely from the fact that if he defied the Pope by divorcing his first wife and was excommunicated, his legitimacy as king of England would be seriously threatened. Some societies, even in ancient times, attempted to base their legitimacy on the consent of the governed, i. e., on a form of majority rule. Athenian democracy was one such experiment. In most of those societies, however, participation in government was limited to certain categories of residents within the state, and others such as slaves, serfs, and aliens were excluded.

Since the seventeenth century, there has been a marked decline in attempts to legitimatize authority on the basis of religion. The divine right of kings and the influence of established churches increasingly have failed to persuade resident populations of the legitimacy of incumbent governments. Indeed, the eighteenth century was marked by the search for new theories of legitimacy which would serve to strengthen and stabilize the governments which appeared in the wake of the English Glorious Revolution and the French and the American revolutions. Hobbes, Locke, Montesquieu, Rousseau, Thomas Paine, Jefferson, were all political theorists in search of the same magic formula: how to establish a government that was both authoritative and acceptable to those whom it proposed to govern.

From the American point of view the most important of these theorists by far was John Locke, who legitimatized not only the Glorious Revolution of 1688, but whose writings served as the basis for Jefferson's justification of the American Revolution almost a century later.

In his *Second Treatise on Civil Government,* Locke theorized that, in the state of nature, men were created by God, free, equal, independent, and with inherent inalienable rights to life, liberty, and property. As a concomitant of these rights each individual had the right of self protection against those who would infringe on his personal liberties. While most men, in the Lockean view, were basically good, content to live and let live, some would be likely to prey on their fellows, who in turn would have to be constantly on guard against such wrongdoings. To avoid this brutish existence, men joined together to form governments to which they surrendered their rights of self protection; in return, they received governmental protection of their lives, liberty, and property. As in any proper contract there are benefits and considerations on both sides: men give up their right to protect themselves and receive protection in return. Governments give protection and receive loyalty and obedience in return. Government, in its control over men, cannot exceed the stated aims of the contract, however. Once it controls men more than is necessary for the protection of the mutual welfare it becomes illegitimate and no longer deserving of loyalty or obedience.

Locke, of course, had no notion of when or how the state of nature existed. Nor did he specify the mechanism by which the social contract was entered into. Like other Enlightenment thinkers, Locke derived this theory inductively, that is, by reasoning how it ought to have been. Although his theory reflected the desire of the rising mercantile middle class in England to have done with the absolutist divine right Stuart kings, it was enthusiastically, if perhaps unconsciously, adopted by the American colonists with whose experience and aspirations it fitted remarkably well. After all, could there have been anything closer to the state of nature than the New England shore that greeted the first Pilgrim settlers? To the men who carved a society out of a wilderness through their unaided individual efforts, the fruits of this society seemed surely to belong to themselves and not to a sovereign over whom they exercised no control. To a society that practiced, at least initially, equality of opportunity, it was only self-evident to preach that all men were created equal.

Thus, in 1776 when Jefferson was given the task of defending the rebellion of the colonies against the king, it is understandable that the most famous paragraph of the Declaration of Independence is virtually a summary of Lockean sentiments.

> We hold these truths to be self-evident, that all men are created equal, that they are endowed by their Creator with certain inalienable Rights, that among these are Life, Liberty and the pursuit of Happiness. That to secure these rights, Governments are instituted among Men, deriving their just powers from the consent of the governed, That whenever any Form of Government becomes destructive of these ends, it is the Right of the People to alter or abolish it.

The sentiments of the Declaration of Independence were more than a mere paraphrase of Locke, however. They were an accurate summary of widely held American political beliefs. Indeed, John Adams, stung by the acclaim his rival Jefferson received for writing the Declaration remarked resentfully that he did not understand why Jefferson was so widely praised since he simply repeated in the Declaration the things that everyone was saying anyway. Consciously or unconsciously, most Americans believed in Locke's theories so fervently that they could not accept the legitimacy of a government established on any other basis. Locke, from an American point of view, is the father of democratic theory.

A democratic government, thus, is one which is based on the consent of the governed, i. e., the majority, but a democratic government is far more than the political embodiment of the will of a simple majority. The will of the majority can be quite as tyrannical, and quite as illegitimate in Lockean terms, as the will of a single ruler. Democracy also requires not only awareness and respect for the rights of minorities, but a recognition that some aspects of private conduct are beyond the reach of government control. Democracy, therefore, is government in which the majority governs with respect for rights of the minority. Unfortunately, this definition while accurate, is also internally contradictory. To the extent that the majority, in governing, is carrying out its own wishes, the rights of the minority, if they conflict with the wishes of the majority, do not exist; conversely, to the extent that the rights of minorities are observed, the majority is not governing, at least in its own immediate interests. If a Jehovah's Witness wishes to proselytize in a hostile southern Baptist town, either the rights of the proselytizer to speak may be respected, or the right of the townspeople not to be affronted with (to them) offensive material will be maintained. The sensibilities of both cannot be preserved simultaneously; one side must give way to the other.

It can be argued, of course, that the Baptists in preserving the rights of the proselytizer are really preserving their own rights in the long run, should they ever be in a minority position, and that therefore the majority is really preserving its own long range interests. This, of course, is the ideal situation that a democratic society hopes to create, but most people do not live or think in the long run. Governments are constantly faced with short run conflicts which must be mediated immediately. Indeed, it is the effort to draw the line between the interests of majorities and minorities that is the most important work of the courts. Most constitutional litigation in the civil liberties and civil rights area is an attempt to balance the conflicting claims of the majority to govern in its own interest and the minority to protect its rights from the encroachment of government. Both groups justify their position by reference to Locke's theory of the social contract: that government must be based on the consent of the governed, but exists only for the purpose of protecting each individual's right to life, liberty and property. The balance the courts strike in handling civil liberties and civil rights cases is hopefully what we call justice, and it is never permanently struck. What was justice in 1865 is not necessarily justice in 1975. The whipping post may have been acceptable in colonial times; segregated schools may have been the order of the day in the nineteenth century. Today flogging and *de jure* segregation offend our notions of fairness. The social order changes and with it our notions of how things ought to be.

Civil liberties and civil rights thus, are personal freedoms set in the context of an authoritative government. These terms are frequently used interchangeably, but theoretically, at least, there is some difference between them. Civil liberties refer to private conduct that is beyond the scope of government control. Democratic government is, by definition, limited government, i. e., its functions are limited to preserving and protecting the rights of the individuals under its jurisdiction. Except in relation to this protective function, government has no legitimacy. A democratic government, for example, has a right to control a riot in which political dissidents take part. It has this right because other members of the community may be seriously disaffected by a riot: they may be injured, their property may be destroyed, etc. A democratic government, however, has no right to control the expression of political dissent that does not result in illegal action—riot or revolution. Such control is beyond the power of government because political dissenters, like all persons in a democracy, have a prior existing right to freedom of thought and freedom of conscience, and may be restrained only to the extent necessary to protect other members of the community. When no such protection is necessary, then no governmental action is permissible.

Civil rights, on the other hand, refer to the requirement that a democratic government afford all those within its jurisdiction equality before the law. This does not mean, of course, that everyone must be treated equally. It simply means that the basis for unequal treatment must be rational. It is rational to require rich people to pay income tax at a higher rate than poor people because it is less burdensome for the rich to pay taxes than the poor. It is rational to require large property holders to pay higher sewer and water fees than small property holders because they use more of the services provided. It is not rational, however, to tax individuals with blue eyes more than those with brown eyes because their eye color has no rational relationship to the problem of raising tax funds.

Civil rights problems arise in connection with governmental activities which are legitimate in scope but whose impact may be inequitable. It is not an infringement of civil liberty for a government to set up a school system, but the regulation of who may use the schools and under what conditions are problems in civil rights. A government has the right, indeed the duty, to make provision for the election of public officials, but the determination of who may vote and the procedures which prospective voters must follow are problems in civil rights.

The attempt to define precisely the parameters of civil liberties and civil rights is the attempt to spell out the specifics of the social contract. What rights must individuals give up in order for the government to function for the common good? What activities must the government forego because they limit unreasonably the inherent freedom of individual citizens? Though legislatures and administrators make the rules by which we live, it is the courts which make the final determination of whether the rules are in keeping with our basic notions of fairness. Tocqueville recognized this when he commented that in America most political questions tend to become legal issues. It is the courts which oversee the elected branches in mediating conflict between the individual and the state, and the legal phrase which encompasses our notions of fairness is "due process of law." When individuals feel that they have been mistreated by their government their ultimate means of seeking redress is to sue in the courts claiming that they have been denied "due process of law." The Communist speaker to whom the sheriff has denied a permit, the black child seeking admission to an all-white school, the parent who objects to state prescribed prayers in the schools, the criminal defendant whose confession is being used against him—all of these individuals have the same complaint: that the state is acting unfairly toward them, or, in legal terms, that some governmental agency or official has taken liberty or property from them without "due process of law."

There are two ways in which due process can be denied: procedurally or substantively. If one is denied procedural due process it is because some procedure employed by the state is faulty. Did the policeman have adequate grounds for arrest? Was the defendant's confession improperly obtained? Did the parolee have a right to a hearing before his parole was revoked? Was the State Department employee suspected of homosexuality given an opportunity to respond to charges against him before being fired? Most procedural due process cases that come to the United States Supreme Court relate to criminal procedure, but many relate to other areas such as voting procedures, hiring and firing practices for public employees, and school disciplinary procedures. In all of these cases, the question before the court is not whether the government had a right to do whatever it did, but whether having had this right, the procedures employed by the officials involved were fair. The government may have the right to arrest criminals, discipline students and fire employees, but it must do so in accordance with specific rules which are prescribed in advance and in keeping with contemporary community standards of fairness.

Questions of substantive due process are more basic than those relating to procedural due process because they challenge the government's right to regulate the conduct in question at all, under any kinds of procedures. Can a public employee be fired for being a homosexual, even if he is granted a hearing? Can a student be expelled for participating in a political demonstration, even if his parents are properly notified? Can the government make smoking marihuana a crime? Can the government force an employer to pay a minimum wage even if he could obtain workers willing to work for less? Substantive due process challenges stem directly from the concept of limited government: that individual rights may be curtailed only to the extent necessary to prevent harm to others, and that there are areas in which government may not legislate at all.

Today, the claim of denial of substantive due process is used primarily to protect personal rights such as free speech and freedom of religion, but in the nineteenth century denial of substantive due process was the basis for challenging state and federal regulation of the economy. Manufacturers and other business-men successfully fought workmen's compensation laws, factory health and safety regulations, etc. on the ground that their property was being taken without due process of law, i. e., unreasonably. They challenged maximum hours and minimum wage laws because they interfered with the liberty of contract—the freedom of workers to work more than 70 hours a week or for less than 25¢ per hour. For more than 50 years, the courts considered it reasonable to elevate private property rights over the right of the government to regulate the economy for the public good. Indeed, it is only since the constitutional triumph of the New Deal in the 1937–1941 period that such economic cases have not formed the bulk of substantive due process challenges.

Standards for due process are not immutable or fixed, but change as social values and practices change. Capital punishment in 1800 was certainly acceptable; today we are not so sure. Segregated public toilets, compulsory prayer in the public schools, trial of defendants without benefit of counsel, censorship of books and plays of mild erotic content—all were legally permissible in the recent past, but are impermissible today. Laws forbidding consensual sodomy, possession of marihuana and other morals offenses are constitutional today but may not be ten years from now. Similarly, certain kinds of manufacturing and advertising practices which are acceptable today may soon be declared illegal as our knowledge of environmental hazards increases. As the problems which a society faces and the resources with which it handles those problems change, so do notions of permissible and impermissible conduct, as well as fairness and unfairness, in relation to law. This does not mean to say that the courts may freely substitute the prejudices of the sitting judges for precedent in due process cases. It simply means that the law is a dynamic instrument of a living society, and not the sterile heritage of a dead past.

## THE AMERICAN COURTS

When the founding fathers met in Philadelphia in 1787, they created a form of government which was, at the time, structurally unique. The importance they attached to the legislative branch is reflected by the fact that fully one-half of the text of the Constitution is taken by Article I which deals with the structure and powers of Congress. Article II, on the presidency, was perhaps the most difficult to draft since no one seemed to have a clear idea what role an executive who was neither a hereditary monarch nor a popularly elected governor ought to play, or indeed, how he was to be chosen. However, it was in Article III, establishing a Supreme Court, that the founding fathers created a really new institution: a court that could sit in judgment on the actions of both legislature and executive. This power, judicial review, is nowhere spelled out in the text of the Constitution, which simply gives the Court the power to hear all cases in law and equity arising under the laws, treaties, and Constitution of the United States; but it was assumed for the Court by Chief Justice John Marshall in the famous case of *Marbury v. Madison*:

> If an act of the legislature, repugnant to the Constitution is void, does it, notwithstanding its validity, bind the courts and oblige them to give it effect? . . . This . . . would seem, at first view, an absurdity too gross to be insisted on. . . .

> It is emphatically the province and duty of the judicial department to say what the law is. . . .

> So if a law be in opposition to the Constitution; if both the law and the Constitution apply to a particular case, so that the court must either decide that case conformably to the law, disregarding the Constitution; or conformably to the Constitution, disregarding the law; the court must determine which of these conflicting

rules governs the case. This is the very essence of judicial duty.[1]

Scholars have long argued the question of whether the founding fathers intended for the Supreme Court to have the power to sit in judgment on its co-equal legislative and executive branches. Neither the Constitution, nor the Federalist Papers, nor any official documents of the times indicate unequivocally that it was intended for the Supreme Court to have this power. On the other hand, that part of the *Marbury v. Madison* decision which enunciated judicial review excited very little opposition even among Jeffersonians. Contemporary evidence seems to indicate that the notion of judicial review was well understood and expected of the Supreme Court. By 1803, state high courts had on previous occasions, sat in judgment on the actions of their state legislatures, and, during colonial times, disputes over whether actions of a colonial legislature violated the colony's charter had been referred to the Privy Council in England for resolution. On balance, the preponderance of historical evidence tends to favor Marshall's interpretation of the powers of the Court, and the argument today has become almost totally irrelevant in view of the firm establishment of judicial review as an accepted practice.

However, there is still an ongoing debate as to how activist the Court ought to be. Those who favor judicial self-restraint, perhaps influenced by lingering doubts as to the legitimacy of judicial review, argue that the Court is essentially an anti-democratic institution inasmuch as it is elitist (drawn from the upper socioeconomic groups), unrepresentative (not elected), and not responsible to the public (justices appointed for life). For all these reasons, they conclude the Court ought to confine its activities to the bare minimum required for it to act as umpire of the federal system. The Court should avoid, wherever possible, involvement in disputes that can be handled by the popularly elected branches of government.

1.  *Marbury v. Madison*, 5 U.S. (1 Cranch) 137 at 177–178, 2 L.Ed. 60 (1803).

The judicial activists, on the other hand, claim that an uninhibited, fully active Court is necessary to maintain a balance within the system between the right of the majority to govern, and the right of minorities to preserve their inalienable rights from infringement by the governing majority. Democracy, the activists reason, is not simply majority rule. Individual rights are an important part of the governmental scheme, and in a government where both the legislature and the executive are essentially instruments of the majority, it is essential that one branch respond to the needs of those who cannot succeed in influencing either president or congress. Were the Court to be unduly modest the democratic balance would be upset.

Like the argument over the historical validity of the Court's assumption of the power of judicial review, the argument over whether the justices should be restrained or activist cannot be resolved. It is clear, however, that whichever course of action the Supreme Court chooses in a particular controversy, it of necessity, influences the outcome of that controversy. Whether it chooses to intervene or modestly declines to participate, the outcome of the dispute will be affected. For the Court there is no neutral middle ground. Once it is agreed that the Court could, if it would, intervene, failure to do so is as much a decision as direct intervention. Most partisans in the judicial activism-judicial restraint controversy choose sides according to their preference for certain substantive results in a current dispute. While it is perfectly proper to advocate that the Court not intervene in a given situation because one hopes to preserve the ruling of the lower court, there is no moral superiority in the non-intervention position. It is, in a negative way, as activist as a more aggressive stance on the part of opponents of the *status quo*. The ongoing argument over whether the Supreme Court ought to be more or less active generally resolves itself into a question of whose ox is being gored.

### State and Federal Judicial Systems

The United States has fifty-one court systems: fifty state and one federal. Typically, most court systems operate on three levels: courts of original jurisdiction (trial courts); intermediate appellate courts; and final appellate courts. Unfortunately for students and laymen, there is no uniform terminology for the designation of these courts. In most states, and in the federal system, the highest appellate court is called the Supreme Court, and the intermediate court is called the Court of Appeals. In New York State however, the lowest state-wide court of general jurisdiction is the Supreme Court, and the final appellate court is called the Court of Appeals. Despite the lack of uniformity in terminology, however, there are widespread uniformities of practice in both state and federal systems.

Most state courts of general jurisdiction are called superior or county courts. It is in these courts that important civil and criminal actions are initially heard, that is, suits involving large sums of money and felonies. They also hear, on appeal, minor cases which originated in local magistrates' courts or with justices of the peace. The intermediate courts of appeal hear cases appealed from the county, superior, or other courts of original jurisdiction. Above this level appeal may be had to the highest court of the state, although such appeal may be of right (not at the discretion of the court) only if certain procedural or other requirements are met. State judges are generally elected rather than appointed, usually for seven to fourteen years.

The federal court system parallels that of the states. The lowest federal court of general jurisdiction is the District Court, of which there were ninety-four in 1977, handling all criminal cases arising under federal law and civil suits in excess of $10,000. Cases from the District Courts are appealed to the federal Courts of Appeals of which there were eleven in 1977, ten for the states and one for the District of Columbia. An exception to this appellate jurisdiction is that the decisions of certain specially constituted federal district courts, known as three-judge courts, are appealed directly to the Supreme Court, by-passing the Courts of Appeals. These three-judge district courts are convened on an *ad hoc* basis to consider important cases usually involving constitutional principles, and are comprised of two district judges and one judge from the Court of Appeals. All federal judges are appointed for life.[2]

The highest court in the federal hierarchy is the United States Supreme Court, whose docket encompasses a small number of cases arising under a constitutionally prescribed original jurisdiction which must be heard, and a very much larger number of cases on appeal which may be heard. The great bulk of the Court's agenda comes to it on appeal from the lower state and federal courts. Technically, there are two methods by which cases may be appealed to the United States Supreme Court: by appeal or by writ of *certiorari*. Cases come on appeal generally when they involve: federal courts which have declared state laws unconstitutional; state courts which have declared federal laws unconstitutional; or two Federal Courts of Appeals which have made conflicting decisions on the points of law. All other cases come on writ of *certiorari,* that is, a petition from the appellant to the Supreme Court for an order from the high court that the lower court, which had previous jurisdiction over the case, send up the records of the case for review. Although technically the Supreme Court is required to hear all cases which come up on writ of appeal, in practice it dismisses those cases it does not wish to consider with the brief notation, "Dismissed for want of a substantial federal question." Petitions for *certiorari* are granted at the option of the Supreme Court. The net effect, thus, is to make the appellate caseload of the Court almost entirely that of the Court's own choosing. The Court tends to select for review those cases which present questions of national importance. All cases in the federal courts must arise under the laws, treaties, or Constitution of the United States; must allege the infringement of a federal right; or must present problems of diversity of citizenships between litigants, that is, must involve actions between citizens of different states, or between citizens and foreigners.

2.  An exception are those judges appointed to legislative courts such as the United States Court of Claims, the United States Customs Court, and the United States Court of Customs and Patent Appeals.

The state and federal systems overlap. It is possible for a given civil or criminal case to be handled by either system or both. The overlap affects the actions of both public officials and litigants. On the whole, the relationship between state and federal law enforcement officials is one of somewhat distant politeness. Most cases are handled exclusively by one jurisdiction or the other. In those cases which are handled simultaneously at both levels, problems arise on occasion either because of over-competitiveness or, even worse, over-cooperativeness.

The Weinberger kidnapping case was an example of a case which created hostility between the local police and the FBI. The Weinberger infant was kidnapped from his carriage in front of his parents' Long Island home in July 1956. Seven days later (in accordance with the traditional presumption that the victim might, after one week, have been transported across state lines in violation of federal law) the FBI entered the case.[3] From an analysis of handwriting samples taken from the ransom note, it was determined that one Angelo LaMarca was the likely kidnapper. Federal agents, accompanied by Nassau County detectives, thereupon arrested LaMarca. The baby was found dead and subsequent investigation disclosed that the child had never left New York State. Since no federal law had been violated, the suspect was turned over to county officials who succeeded in convicting LaMarca of the crime. He was electrocuted two years later. Despite the successful outcome of the case in terms of apprehending and punishing the criminal, strained relations developed between Nassau County officials and the FBI because the local authorities felt that the federal agents had unfairly taken all the credit for the results.

Not all such parallel handling arouses federal-local antagonism, of course. In November 1962, Roberto Santiesban, a Cuban, and two of his compatriots residing in the United States were arrested in New York City by the FBI and charged with conspiring to blow up department stores, utilities and other in-

3. *New York Times*, July 5, 1956, p. 27; July 12, 1956, p. 12.

stallations around New York Harbor.[4]  Because the attempted bombing involved delicate questions of international relations, the FBI had not called in the New York City police (who had concurrent jurisdiction) during the original investigation, but asked their help only later, in the disposal of the explosives. Conspiracy charges were dropped against the three Cubans who, along with a fourth Cuban arrested on a separate charge, were exchanged for twenty-three Americans held in Cuba on political charges.  In this case the New York City authorities made no objection to the FBI's actions, because it was patent that important national interests were involved rather than the handling of local criminals.

Sometimes over-cooperativeness, rather than over competitiveness, becomes a problem, and relations between the state and federal agents become too close for legality.  Until quite recently, it was a fairly common practice for state police to illegally seize evidence of a federal crime and turn it over to the federal authorities, who were then permitted to use it against the accused.  While the rules of procedure in federal court did not permit the introduction of evidence illegally obtained by *federal* agents, under the terms of the notorious "silver platter" doctrine, such evidence could be used if obtained by non-federal agents.  State officials working on a state case that was also of interest to federal agents were thus permitted to commit illegal acts in the name of "law enforcement."  In 1960, however, the United States Supreme Court put an end to this practice by excluding from federal court *all* illegally seized evidence.[5]

---

4.  *New York Times*, November 18, 1962, p. 1; November 22, 1962, p. 9.

5.  *Elkins v. United States*, 364 U.S. 206, 80 S.Ct. 1437, 4 L.Ed.2d 1669 (1960).  It should be noted that the Fourth Amendment prohibition against illegal search and seizure applies only to government officials, both state and federal.  In

1921, in *Burdeau v. McDowell*, 256 U.S. 465, 41 S.Ct. 574, 65 L.Ed. 1048, the United States Supreme Court (Holmes and Brandeis dissenting) ruled that stolen, incriminating evidence might be used in federal courts if the evidence had been seized by private parties and government officials had played no part in the theft.  No further Supreme Court review of this ques-

Private litigants, too, are affected by the bifurcated state-federal structure. It is, for example, a common practice among attorneys handling civil suits which procedurally could be heard in either state or federal court, to shop for the court that will provide the most favorable forum for the client's interests. In the criminal field, defense attorneys, by use of the appropriate writ, will sometimes shift a case from the state court system, where appeals have been decided unfavorably to the client, to the federal system in the hope that a federal judge will be more sympathetic to the client's cause. When Dr. Samuel Sheppard contended vainly in the Ohio courts that he had been unable to receive a fair trial because of prejudicial pre-trial publicity engendered by a Cleveland newspaper, his attorneys were able to appeal to the federal courts on the ground that Sheppard's due process rights had been infringed. Sheppard's appeal went up the federal judicial ladder, and ultimately succeeded when the Supreme Court ordered that he be released from custody unless the State of Ohio retried him within a reasonable time.[6]  On retrial in 1966, he was acquitted, twelve years after the murder.

The NAACP Legal and Education Fund in 1968 used a petition for a writ of *habeas corpus* to the United States District Court for the Eastern District of New York as a means of terminating a New York State addiction program that had been severely criticized, but upheld as constitutionally permissible by the New York State appellate courts. Under the program, criminal addicts were confined to a state institution, ostensibly for rehabilitation, for periods longer than the maximum penal sentence for the crime for which they were convicted. It was the contention of the Legal Defense Fund, on behalf of one Edward Johnson, that the addiction treatment program on Riker's Island, New York City, was almost entirely punitive and not rehabilitative, and therefore the lengthened sentence was a violation of the defendant's due process rights. Since the New York State

tion has occurred since 1921. State and lower federal courts have reaffirmed the *Burdeau* doctrine over the years.

6. *Sheppard v. Maxwell*, 384 U.S. 333, 86 S.Ct. 1507, 16 L.Ed.2d 600 (1966).

Court of Appeals had recently held in regard to Rudolph Blunt, a similarly situated appellant, that the program, although inadequate, was not a violation of due process rights, the Federal District Court agreed to consider Johnson's case on the merits. When the New York State Narcotics Addiction Control Commission officials were informed of the federal court's intention, they sent word that the program was being terminated, and that they had no objection to Johnson's release from custody.[7] In both the *Sheppard* and *Johnson* cases, federal court action released defendants who had been denied relief in the state courts.

The dual state-federal judicial structure of the United States can also, on occasion, act like twin millstones grinding a hapless defendant between them. As of the present writing, a man tried and convicted in federal court for an offense such as robbery of a federally insured bank (a violation of both state and federal law) can be retried and reconvicted in the state court for the same offense.[8] It is only since 1964, moreover, that the Supreme Court has ruled that testimony compelled under a grant of immunity by one jurisdiction may not be used by the other to try and convict a defendant;[9] and only in the last 25 years has the Court ruled that evidence illegally seized by law enforcement officers of a state cannot be used for prosecuting purposes in the federal court, and *vice versa*.[10]

7. See *New York Times*, October 15, 1968, p. 94, for details on *People ex rel. Rudolph Blunt v. Narcotics Addiction Control Commission*. For *Edward Johnson v. Warden, Riker's Island Prison*, see Michael Meltsner, "The Future of Correction: A Defense Attorney's View," *Crime and Delinquency* 17, No. 3 (July 1971): 266–270.

8. *Bartkus v. Illinois*, 359 U.S. 121, 79 S.Ct. 676, 3 L.Ed.2d 684 (1959);

*Abbate v. United States*, 359 U.S. 187, 79 S.Ct. 666, 3 L.Ed.2d 729 (1959).

9. *Murphy v. Waterfront Comm.*, 378 U.S. 52, 84 S.Ct. 1594, 12 L.Ed. 2d 678 (1964).

10. *Elkins v. United States*, 364 U.S. 206, 80 S.Ct. 1437, 4 L.Ed.2d 1669 (1960); *Rea v. United States*, 350 U.S. 214, 76 S.Ct. 292, 100 L.Ed. 233 (1956).

## DUE PROCESS AND THE NATIONALIZATION OF PERSONAL RIGHTS

Another consequence of the federal structure of American government is ambiguity and controversy concerning the scope of constitutional guarantees of personal rights. Both the Fifth and Fourteenth Amendments provide, in identical terms, that no person shall be denied life, liberty or property without due process of law. Do these constitutional provisions mean that an action forbidden to the federal government is *ipso facto* denied to the states and vice versa? Are individual rights protected to precisely the same extent in either jurisdiction? The identical wording of the two due process clauses would suggest that both should be equal in scope, but the difference in the historical origins of the Fifth and Fourteenth Amendments, as well as the almost eighty year gap between their enactments, preclude such a conclusion.

The Fifth Amendment was adopted at a time when the locus of virtually all governmental power was in the hands of the individual states. The intent of the Bill of Rights was unquestionably to prevent the movement of the new federal government into areas which many Americans wished to reserve for state action, or to be beyond the reach of any governmental action at all. Thus, while the First Amendment provides that "Congress shall make no laws respecting an establishment of religion," this prohibition applied only to Congress and not to the states. Indeed, in some of the New England states the Congregational Church remained the established church, supported by tax revenues for 40 years after the adoption of the Bill of Rights. In a similar manner, it is *Congress* which is forbidden to infringe the right of the people to keep and bear arms; to be secure in their persons, houses, papers, and effects; to be free from cruel and unusual punishment, etc. Whether a state had the right to curtail such personal liberties, depended in every instance on the scope of the state constitution, and was unrelated to either the federal Constitution or the Bill of Rights.

The landmark case on this question was *Barron for use of Tiernan v. Mayor and the City Council of Baltimore*,[11] in which Barron's property was taken without compensation by the city of Baltimore to be used for a public purpose. Barron sued, claiming that he had been denied due process in that the Fifth Amendment prohibited the taking of private property for public use without compensation. The United States Supreme Court ruled, however, that the prohibition applied only to the federal government and not to the state of Maryland or its political subdivisions. Thus, originally, due process protections for the individual existed only against the federal government. There were no comparable protections against state action until the adoption of the Fourteenth Amendment after the Civil War.

The Fourteenth Amendment was adopted in 1868 largely for the purpose of protecting freed slaves against state action adverse to their newly won rights. The first part of the amendment declares that all native born and naturalized persons are citizens not only of the United States, but of the state in which they reside. The Amendment then goes on to forbid the states to abridge the privileges and immunities of citizens; to deprive any persons of life, liberty or property without due process of law; or to deny any person within its jurisdiction the equal protection of the laws. While the initial purpose of the Amendment was clearly to defend the rights of blacks, in the century since its adoption, many other groups, from industrialists to political dissidents have claimed its protection, and inevitably, the question has arisen of whether individuals have identical rights under the Fifth and Fourteenth Amendments. The United States Supreme Court has considered this question dozens, if not hundreds of times, in a great variety of contexts: manufacturers seeking to strike down regulatory state laws; Communists defending themselves from state criminal syndicalist charges; birth control advocates trying to run a clinic in defiance of state law; and most numerously and importantly perhaps, a host of

11.  32 U.S. (7 Pet.) 243, 8 L.Ed. 672 (1883).

defendants in criminal cases challenging the fairness of state criminal procedures. The Court has given no final, clear cut answer to the question of the relationship between the due process clauses of the Fifth and Fourteenth Amendments, but it is possible to discern three basic positions that have been assumed by various justices.

The traditional position of the Court, and the one adhered to by a majority of justices who have considered the question, is that the due process clause of the Fourteenth Amendment bears no direct relationship to either the due process clause of the Fifth Amendment or the Bill of Rights. This position is illustrated by the decisions in cases such as *Twining v. New Jersey*,[12] *Palko v. Connecticut*,[13] and *Adamson v. California*.[14] In *Palko,* which raised the question of whether the double jeopardy clause of the Fifth Amendment protected a defendant against retrial by the state for an offense of which he had already been convicted, Justice Cardozo commented,

> . . . [Appellant's] thesis is even broader. Whatever would be a violation of the original Bill of Rights (Amendments 1 to 8) if done by the federal government is now equally unlawful by force of the Fourteenth Amendment if done by a state. There is no such general rule.
>
> . . . If the Fourteenth Amendment has absorbed [the provisions of the Bill of Rights], the process of absorption has had its source in the belief that neither liberty nor justice would exist if they were sacrificed.
> . . . [15]

Justice Reed repeated this theme in *Adamson* where the defendant sought to have his conviction set aside because the prosecutor's comments on his failure to testify in his own behalf

12.  211 U.S. 78, 29 S.Ct. 14, 53 L.Ed. 97 (1908).

13.  302 U.S. 319, 58 S.Ct. 149, 82 L. Ed. 288 (1937).

14.  332 U.S. 46, 67 S.Ct. 1672, 91 L. Ed. 1903 (1947).

15.  *Palko v. Connecticut*, at 323 and 326.

were considered to have denied him due process under the Fourteenth Amendment by violating the Fifth Amendment's ban on self-incrimination.

> We shall assume  .  .  .  that permission by law to the court, counsel and jury to comment upon and consider the failure of defendant "to explain or to deny by his testimony any evidence or facts in the case against him" would infringe defendant's privilege against self-incrimination under the Fifth Amendment if this were a trial in a court of the United States under a similar law.  Such an assumption does not determine the appellant's rights under the Fourteenth Amendment.  It is settled law that the clause of the Fifth Amendment, protecting a person against being compelled to be a witness against himself, is not made effective by the Fourteenth Amendment as a protection against state action on the ground that freedom from testimonial compulsion is a right of national citizenship, or because it is a personal privilege or immunity secured by the Federal Constitution as one of the rights of man that are listed in the Bill of Rights.  .  .  .

> .  .  .  The due process clause of the Fourteenth Amendment  .  .  .  does not draw all the rights of the federal Bill of Rights under its protection.  That contention was made and rejected in *Palko*  .  .  .  [which] held that such provisions of the Bill of Rights as were "implicit in the concept of ordered liberty," became secure from state interference by the clause.  But it held nothing more.[16]

Justice Frankfurter, in a concurring opinion vigorously denounced "incorporators," who argued that the due process of the Fourteenth Amendment incorporated all of the provisions of the Bill of Rights.

---

16.  *Adamson v. California*, 332 U.S. 46, at 50–51 and 53–54, 67 S.Ct.    1672, 1674–1677, 91 L.Ed. 1903 (1947).

Between the incorporation of the Fourteenth Amendment into the Constitution and the beginning of the present membership of the Court—a period of seventy years—the scope of that Amendment was passed upon by forty-three judges. Of all these judges, only one, who may respectfully be called an eccentric exception, ever indicated the belief that the Fourteenth Amendment was a shorthand summary of the first eight Amendments theretofore limiting only the Federal Government, and that due process incorporated those eight Amendments as restrictions upon the powers of the States.  .   .   .

.   .   . The [Fourteenth] Amendment neither comprehends the specific provisions by which the founders deemed it appropriate to restrict the federal government nor is it confined to them. The Due Process Clause of the Fourteenth Amendment has an independent potency, precisely as does the Due Process Clause of the Fifth Amendment in relation to the Federal Government.   .   .   . [17]

Undeterred by Frankfurter's thunder, Justice Black "the eccentric exception" to whom Frankfurter referred, took quite a different view of the question.

.   .   . In my judgment that history [the Fourteenth Amendment's] conclusively demonstrates that the language of the first section of the Fourteenth Amendment, taken as a whole, was thought by those responsible for its submission to the people, and by those who opposed its submission, sufficiently explicit to guarantee that thereafter no state could deprive its citizens of the privileges and protections of the Bill of Rights.   .   .   . And I further contend   .   .   . the "natural law" formula   .   .   . to be itself a violation of our Constitution, in that it subtly conveys to courts,

17.   Ibid., at 62 and 66.

at the expense of legislatures, ultimate power over public policies in fields where no specific provision of the Constitution limits legislative power. And my belief seems to be in accord with the views expressed by this Court, at least for the first two decades after the Fourteenth Amendment was adopted.

.   .   .

.   .   . I would follow what I believe was the original purpose of the Fourteenth Amendment—to extend to all the people of the nation the complete protection of the Bill of Rights. To hold that this Court can determine what, if any, provisions of the Bill of Rights will be enforced, and if so to what degree, is to frustrate the great design of a written Constitution.[18]

To Black, thus, the due process clause of the Fourteenth Amendment (and of the Fifth Amendment) equalled the Bill of Rights, and conversely, the Bill of Rights equalled the due process clause of the Fourteenth Amendment. When the Founding Fathers inserted the phrase due process into the Fifth Amendment they meant to encompass the specific guarantees enumerated in Amendments 1 through 8; and when the post-Civil War Congress passed the bill which later became the Fourteenth Amendment, they too used the words "due process" in precisely the same sense: a short hand for the fundamental rights made explicit in the Bill of Rights. To Black, the meaning of due process was very clear cut: it meant the specific guarantees of the Bill of Rights, no more and no less. The framework of our personal liberties had been set down in permanent, unchangeable form by the Founding Fathers in 1789 in the Constitution, and in 1791, in the Bill of Rights. He rejected scathingly the "natural law" theory of Constitutional rights as an "accordion" theory of justice, the limits of which were determined by individual justices who expanded and contracted the meaning of due process according to their own moods and whims. For him, such

18.   Ibid., at 74–75 and 89.

wide ranging judicial decision making was illegitimate and subversive of the whole purpose of a written constitution.

Though for many of his years on the United States Supreme
Court Black was part of a liberal majority, and rarely lacked
for a colleague sympathetic to his point of view, no other justice
ever espoused his particular position.  His conservative brethren
generally agreed on the desirability of limiting judicial discretion; his liberal brethren agreed even more fervently that the
protections of the Bill of Rights ought to be made applicable to
the states;  but no one agreed with him that the due process
clause of either the Fifth or Fourteenth Amendments could not,
under certain circumstances, *mean more than the specific rights
enumerated in the Bill of Rights*.  The difficulties of Black's position are perhaps best illustrated by *Griswold v. Connecticut,*
a case challenging the constitutionality of Connecticut's birth
control law.[19]

In 1879, Connecticut enacted a statute prohibiting the use of
contraceptives (a law which Justice Stewart later called "an un-
commonly silly law").  This statute remained in effect, virtually
unchanged, for 80 years despite extraordinarily vigorous efforts
to get rid of it.  For 50 years attempts at repeal were made in
almost every session of the state legislature, all of which were
unsuccessful due largely to the organized opposition of the Catholic Church.  In 1943 and 1961 the law was challenged unsuccessfully in the United States Supreme Court.  Finally, in 1965,
in the *Griswold* case, in a 7–2 ruling, the law was declared unconstitutional.

Mrs. Estelle Griswold and Dr. Lee Buxton were directors of a
birth control clinic in New Haven, Connecticut.  They were arrested under a general accessory statute for their activities in
making contraceptives available to patients of the clinic.  (Since
the use of contraceptives was a crime in Connecticut, Mrs. Griswold and Dr. Buxton became accessories to the crime.)  They
were convicted after a trial in New Haven and ultimately ap-

19.    381 U.S. 479, 85 S.Ct. 1678, 14
L.Ed.2d 510 (1965).

pealed their convictions to the United States Supreme Court. The United States Supreme Court had rejected two earlier appeals from the Connecticut statutes largely on technical grounds. Many observers at the time, felt that these rejections were the Court's way of evading a political issue that it felt could not be resolved satisfactorily. By 1965, however, the political climate had changed markedly and it was clear that the time was ripe for the law to be struck down on its merits. The Catholic Church had all but given up its intransigent opposition to repealing birth control statutes, and the use of contraception was so widespread that failure to strike down such a law was subversive of respect for the law in general. There was from the beginning, strong consensus on the Court that the law was a bad one, and indeed all nine justices agreed that it was morally wrong for Connecticut to forbid people to use contraceptives. What the justices could not agree upon, however, was whether the law was *unconstitutional,* and if so why? Where, after all, does it say in the Constitution that individuals have the right to use contraceptives? What part of the Bill of Rights, or any other section of the Constitution for that matter, forbids any government, state or federal, from making a law prohibiting the use of birth control devices?

The Court ultimately decided that the law was indeed unconstitutional, and the majority opinion written by Justice Douglas could well be described as a search for a constitutional peg on which to hang the judicial hat. Since the Bill of Rights certainly had no provision which related to the specific issue raised by the Connecticut law, Douglas pointed out that some liberties exist and are protected by the Constitution even though they are unspecified. He cited as examples of such liberties the right of association, and the right to educate children in the school of the parents' choice. He then went on to assert that the Bill of Rights was more than a collection of specific prohibitions on government. It radiated a spirit of protection which should be generously construed.

The foregoing cases suggest that specific guarantees in the Bill of Rights have penumbras, formed by emanations from those guarantees that help give them life and substance. . . . Various guarantees create zones of privacy. The right of association contained in the penumbra of the First Amendment is one . . . . The Third Amendment in its prohibition against the quartering of soldiers "in any house" in time of peace without the consent of the owner is another facet of that privacy. The Fourth Amendment explicitly affirms the "right of the people to be secure in their persons, houses, papers, and effects, against unreasonable searches and seizures." The Fifth Amendment in its Self-Incrimination Clause enables the citizen to create a zone of privacy which government may not force him to surrender to his detriment. The Ninth Amendment provides: "The enumeration in the Constitution, of certain rights, shall not be construed to deny or disparage others retained by the people." . . .

We have had many controversies over these penumbral rights of "privacy and repose." . . .

The present case . . . concerns a relationship lying within the zone of privacy created by several fundamental constitutional guarantees. . . . Would we allow the police to search the sacred precincts of marital bedrooms for telltale signs of the use of contraceptives? The very idea is repulsive to the notions of privacy surrounding the marriage relationship.

We deal with a right of privacy older than the Bill of Rights—older than our political parties, older than our school system. . . .[20]

From the facts of the Griswold case, thus, Douglas was able to deduce a right of privacy supported by the meaning of the Bill of Rights taken as a whole rather than by a specific portion

20.  Ibid., at 484–486.

thereof. This was precisely the type of interpretation that Black found offensive.

The Court talks about a constitutional "right of privacy" as though there is some constitutional provision or provisions forbidding any law ever to be passed which might abridge the "privacy" of individuals.

Black said, adding, "but there is not." [21]

If Black's position was correct however, and the due process clause of the Fourteenth Amendment meant no more and no less than the Bill of Rights, how could a law like the Connecticut birth control statute have been struck down? Only two solutions to the dilemma were apparent; either the traditional rationale—that the Fourteenth Amendment due process clause simply meant basic fairness and had no necessary relationship to the Bill of Rights (the position that Justice Harlan did in fact take, in concurring in *Griswold*); or the Douglas Bill of Rights plus rationale—that due process meant the specific provisions of the Bill of Rights *plus* such other rights as seemed appropriate to the occasion in the opinion of the sitting judges. Both the Douglas and Harlan rationales were vague and ambiguous in contrast to the neatness and certainty of the Black position. Unfortunately however, the real world is frequently untidy, and clear-cut formulae have a way of becoming Procrustean beds if not applied with discretion. *Griswold* illustrates the limits and dangers of Black's position; he was trapped by his logic into voting to uphold a law which he declared to be every bit as offensive to him as to his brethren in the majority.

One may argue of course, as Justice Frankfurter did in the *Dennis* [22] case, that much legislation that is undesirable may well not be unconstitutional. Even if true, however, it would merely follow that the Court should be modest in its aspirations and circumspect in its jurisdiction. It should hesitate to foist the yoke

21.  Ibid., at 508.

22.  *Dennis v. United States*, 341 U. S. 494, 71 S.Ct. 857, 95 L.Ed. 636 (1951).

of national standards on local governmental entities (or to assume policy making best left to the legislative or executive branches). Perhaps Connecticut should have had the right to forbid the use of contraceptives, even if her sister forty-nine states allowed contraceptives to be sold in every corner candy store. This was not the issue that struck in the craws of the dissenters, however. All the justices agreed that the Connecticut law was extraordinarily offensive, and had there been a specific provision of the Bill of Rights bearing on the particular liberty threatened, the Court would have unanimously struck down the statute in question. The issue for the dissenters was not one of local option, or deference to a coordinate branch of government, but of adherence to a formula relying on textual exegesis of the Bill of Rights, designed, not so much to curb the activism of the Court as a whole, as to restrain the unbridled discretion of the sitting judges.

To recapitulate: there are three distinct positions relating to the meaning of the due process clause of the Fourteenth Amendment which have been enunciated by members of the United States Supreme Court: (1) that due process means basic fairness and bears no direct relationship to the Bill of Rights; (2) that due process is shorthand for the Bill of Rights and means the liberties specified therein and no more and no less; and (3) that due process means the Bill of Rights plus other basic unspecified rights. The first position, closely associated with such justices as Cardozo, Frankfurter and Harlan is the traditional "official" position of the Court and the only one that to which a majority of the justices who have considered the question have been willing to subscribe. The second position has had only one adherent—Black—an adherent so monumental, of such intellectual stature, that his position came to be one to reckon with seriously. The third position, closely associated with Justice Douglas, has been most often espoused by the liberals on the Court, and was especially characteristic of the liberal majority on the Warren Court. As a theory, this position has not been able to muster the support of a majority of the justices, but it has been, in a real sense, the *de facto* position of the Court for at least the last decade. In the cases which have come to the Court, claiming the protection against state action of some clause of the Bill of Rights as subsumed in the due process clause of the Fourteenth Amendment, the Court in recent times, has nearly always agreed with the claimant, if not in theory, then in fact.

Thus, the First Amendment was held to be applicable to the states in a series of cases ranging from *Gitlow v. New York* [23] in 1925 through *Everson v. Board of Education* [24] in 1947. Most of the Fourth, Fifth, Sixth, and Eighth Amendments encompassing the bulk of criminal procedural protections were nationalized from 1961 through 1969, during the period of the Warren Court's greatest influence. *Mapp v. Ohio,* [25] *Gideon v. Wainwright,* [26] and *Malloy v. Hogan,* [27] were landmark decisions in which the Fourth Amendment protection against unreasonable search and seizure, the Sixth Amendment right to counsel, and the Fifth Amendment protection against self-incrimination, were all held applicable to the states. Nor has there been any inclination on the part of the more conservative Burger Court to withdraw from this nationalist stance, although in individual instances, the Burger Court has been more inclined to allow the states to follow procedures which are not identical to federal procedures, and the more conservative justices, moreover, frequently reiterate the Harlan position that the Fourteenth Amendment due process clause does not automatically incorporate the Bill of Rights. Yet, there has been no general retreat from the fact that in practice, if not in theory, the provisions of the Bill of Rights do apply to the states. The Burger Court has, moreover, in such cases as *Roe v. Wade,* [28] relating to the right

23.   268 U.S. 652, 45 S.Ct. 625, 69 L. Ed. 1138 (1925).

24.   330 U.S. 1, 67 S.Ct. 504, 91 L.Ed. 711 (1947).

25.   367 U.S. 643, 81 S.Ct. 1684, 6 L. Ed.2d 1081 (1961).

26.   372 U.S. 335, 83 S.Ct. 792, 9 L. Ed.2d 799 (1963).

27.   378 U.S. 1, 84 S.Ct. 1489, 12 L. Ed.2d 653 (1964).

28.   410 U.S. 113, 93 S.Ct. 705, 35 L. Ed.2d 147 (1973).

to have an abortion, accepted Douglas' reasoning in *Griswold,* including his theory that a right to privacy exists though unspecified in the Constitution.

Thus, as the United States enters its third century of nationhood, the United States Supreme Court has developed as the peculiarly American way of balancing the rights of minorities against the claims of majorities. Where Congress and the President speak for those groups which have strength at the polls, the Court is the forum for those whose claims may not be as popular in the short run, but which have important implications for society as a whole. The specifics of the way in which the Court has attempted to strike an acceptable balance among competing claims will be the subject of the remainder of this book.

## Chapter II

## THE FIRST AMENDMENT: FREEDOM OF SPEECH, PRESS, AND ASSEMBLY

"What has been the effect of coercion [of opinion]? To make one half the world fools, and the other half hypocrites. To support roguery and error all over the earth."

Thomas Jefferson, *Notes on Virginia*

American democracy has English roots. Until 1776, the colonists were, and thought of themselves as, Englishmen; the rights they defended were English rights, rights which, even in 1776, had shaped English government very differently from other European governments. While hardly democratic in the modern sense of the word, the unique quality of British and later, American government, was already apparent: not so much the right of the majority to govern, as the right of individuals to be free from arbitrary government repression. Britain may be the mother of parliaments, but it is instructive to remember that universal male suffrage did not come to Great Britain until the end of the nineteenth century, and universal suffrage, for both men and women until 1928. In the United States, despite an early withering away of property and religious requirements for voting, women did not vote until 1920, and it is only within the last decade that serious efforts have been made to enable black voters to exercise their rights.

By way of contrast, the protection of individual (minority) rights dates back at least as far as 1215 to Magna Carta, which declared that, "no freeman shall be arrested, or imprisoned, or disseized, or outlawed, or exiled, or in any way molested; nor will we proceed against him, unless by the lawful judgment of his peers or by the law of the land." Similarly, the Petition of Right in 1628 asked that "freemen be imprisoned or detained only by the law of the land, or by due process of law, and not by the King's special command without any charge." These astonishingly modern and sophisticated protections of personal freedom were enunciated at a time when representative government as we conceive it either did not exist or was in very rudimentary form. Indeed, the early history of English government was of attempts to contain the authority of the monarch, in contrast to the continental countries where the effort was to create a central authority able to dominate the warring factions of a feudal society.

The hallmark of British and American democracy has been personal freedom rather than representative government. In Britain, these freedoms are guaranteed largely by the strength of tradition. In the United States the Constitution and its amendments—in particular the Bill of Rights and the Civil War Amendments—are the legal guarantors of personal freedom. Three kinds of personal rights are protected: (1) freedom of the intellect and of conscience (First Amendment); (2) freedom from arbitrary arrest or punishment (Fourth, Fifth, Sixth, and Eighth Amendments); and (3) freedom from discrimination by virtue of status (Thirteenth, Fourteenth, and Fifteenth Amendments).

This chapter will deal with what many see as the *sine qua non* of a free society, the freedom of speech, press, and assembly protected by the First Amendment.

*Freedom of Speech: General Considerations*

> Congress shall make no law respecting an establishment of religion, or prohibiting the free exercise thereof; or abridging the freedom of speech, or of the press; or the right of the people peaceably to assemble, and to petition the Government for a redress of grievances.

The wording of the First Amendment to the United States Constitution is deceptively simple, so simple that the reader is lured into ready acceptance of what seem to be commonplace and unremarkable ideas. On closer examination, however, the

First Amendment contains ideas that are quite revolutionary, and in all probability, unacceptable to many people even in this country. The basic notion underlying the First Amendment is that it is not the business of the government to tell anyone how to think or what to believe. Put another way, it means that the elite of society—as David Halberstam put it "the best and the brightest"—are legally no more in possession of truth than the *lumpen proletariat*. Well born, well educated, well meaning, affluent pillars of the community have no more right, as a matter of law, to impose their opinions on society as a whole than do illiterate migrant workers in the lettuce fields of California, or the newly arrived immigrant seamstresses in the sweatshops of New York City; nor is it more permissible for the government to stifle the opinions of the lowly, than of the well born. The First Amendment means that no one, by law, can be ordained as the possessor of truth.

Perhaps the best single explanation of the rationale underlying the First Amendment is that written by John Stuart Mill:

> Let us suppose, therefore, that the government is entirely at one with the people, and never thinks of exerting any power of coercion unless in agreement with what it conceives to be their voice. But I deny the right of the people to exercise such coercion, either by themselves or by their government. The power itself is illegitimate. The best government has no more title to it than the worst. It is as noxious, or more noxious, when exerted in accordance with public opinion, than when in opposition to it. If all mankind minus one, were of one opinion, and only one person were of the contrary opinion, mankind would be no more justified in silencing that one person, than he, if he had the power, would be justified in silencing mankind. Were an opinion a personal possession of no value except to the owner; if to be obstructed in the enjoyment of it were simply a private injury, it would make some difference whether the injury was inflicted only on a few persons

or on many.  But the peculiar evil of silencing the expression of an opinion is, that it is robbing the human race;  posterity as well as the existing generation; those who dissent from the opinion, still more than those who hold it.  If the opinion is right, they are deprived of the opportunity of exchanging error for truth;  if wrong, they lose, what is almost as great a benefit, the clearer perception and livelier impression of truth, produced by its collision with error.

It is necessary to consider separately these two hypotheses, each of which has a distinct branch of the argument corresponding to it.  We can never be sure that the opinion we are endeavoring to stifle is a false opinion;  and if we were sure, stifling it would be an evil still.[1]

The point of Mill's exposition is that the government, even when it represents the will of the people, has no right to stifle the expression of ideas, even false ideas, because the free expression of ideas is a value to society in general rather than to the speaker himself.  It is from the free exchange of ideas that the truth will emerge;  the role of falsehood is to serve as the background against which truth may be perceived.

However acceptable the First Amendment may be in theory, in practice most people want ideas that are distasteful to them repressed and speakers that they hate arrested.*  Despite the current search for *detente* with the Soviet Union, many Americans believe that Communist speakers are dangerous and should be

1. John Stuart Mill, *On Liberty*, New York: Appleton-Century Crofts, 1947, pp. 16–17.

* In 1940, the Gallup Poll asked a cross-section of the national population "Do you believe in freedom of speech?"  97% said "Yes."  Those 97% were then asked "Should a Fascist or a Communist be allowed to hold meetings and express their views in this community?"  Only 22% answered "Yes."  70% answered "No."  Fred I. Greenstein, *The American Party System and the American People*. 2nd ed. (Englewood Cliffs: Prentice-Hall, Inc., 1970), p. 7.

punished for preaching revolution; most blacks are eager to
have the remnants of the Ku Klux Klan imprisoned for advocating white supremacy; and many Jews who pride themselves as
civil libertarians, would gladly see members of the American
Nazi Party sent to jail.   Anti-communists, blacks, and Jews
*know* that they possess truth and that what their enemies are
saying is false and evil.   Freedom of speech, of course, is desirable, but not for "such miserable merchants of unwanted ideas."
It is these very "merchants," however, that Mill's theory and the
First Amendment are designed to protect.   Speakers who express popular ideas, after all, do not need a constitution to protect them.   It is only those who say things that people don't
want to hear that need the support of the law to protect them
from the community.   The speech guarantees of the First
Amendment have frequently been a source of bitter controversy,
centering largely around two kinds of speech: radical political
speech (mainly of the left, but sometimes of the right); and
speech relating to sex and erotica.   Communism and obscenity
have provided most of the free speech grist for the mill of the
United States Supreme Court.

*Communism and the First Amendment*

Except for the ill-starred and short lived Alien and Sedition
Acts of 1798, there was no federal regulation of speech in the
United States until 1917.   Historically, radical movements of the
left seem to have provided the impetus for regulation of speech
in this country.   The excesses of the French Revolution are
thought to have been the underlying factor in the passage of the
Alien and Sedition Acts, and the growth of militant trade union-
ism and socialist and anarchist groups at the end of the nineteenth century led to the passage of state laws against criminal
syndicalism.   No federal law regulating speech was enacted,
however, until 1917 when the entry of the United States into
World War I coincided with the Russian Revolution and the seizure of power by Lenin and the Bolsheviks.   The Espionage Act
of 1917 and the Sedition Act of 1918 were modeled loosely on

the Alien and Sedition Acts of 1798 and were designed to curb criticism of the government which might interfere with the war effort. Charges brought under these laws provided the occasion for the first test of the free speech guarantees of the First Amendment.

In 1917 Charles T. Schenck, an official of the Socialist Party, sent through the mails some 15,000 leaflets urging eligible young men to resist the draft on the grounds that a conscription law was an unconstitutional invasion of individual freedom. As described by the United States Supreme Court, Schenck's document

> . . . recited the first section of the Thirteenth Amendment, said that the idea embodied in it was violated by the Conscription Act and that a conscript is little better than a convict. In impassioned language it intimated that conscription was despotism in its worst form and a monstrous wrong against humanity in the interest of Wall Street's chosen few. It said, "Do not submit to intimidation," but in form at least confined itself to peaceful measures such as a petition for the repeal of the act. . . . It stated reasons for alleging that any one violated the Constitution when he refused to recognize "your right to assert your opposition to the draft," and went on, "If you do not assert and support your rights, you are helping to deny or disparage rights which it is the solemn duty of all citizens and residents of the United States to retain." . . . It denied the power to send our citizens away to foreign shores to shoot up the people of other lands, and added that words could not express the condemnation such cold-blooded ruthlessness deserves, . . .[2]

Schenck and other officials of the Socialist Party were charged with conspiracy to violate the 1917 Espionage Act by

2. *Schenck v. United States*, 249 U. S. 47, at 50–51, 39 S.Ct. 247, 248–249, 63 L.Ed. 470 (1919).

causing and attempting to cause insubordination in the armed forces of the United States, and obstruction of the recruiting and enlistment service of the United States, when at war with Germany, by printing and circulating to men accepted for military service the document described in the opinion. They were tried and convicted and appealed their convictions to the United States Supreme Court which, in an opinion by Justice Oliver Wendell Holmes, unanimously upheld the judgment of the trial court.

The question presented to the Court was whether Schenck's leaflet had violated the provisions of the Espionage Act, particularly that section which made it a crime to "willfully obstruct the recruiting or enlistment service of the United States." Could a communication obstruct a governmental process? Further, if Schenck's communication was in and of itself illegal under the terms of the Espionage Act, what then became of the sweeping prohibition of the First Amendment "Congress shall make no law . . . abridging the freedom of speech?" Holmes responded to these questions in perhaps his most famous opinion:

> . . . We admit that in many places and in ordinary times the defendants in saying all that was said in the circular would have been within their constitutional rights. But the character of every act depends upon the circumstances in which it is done. The most stringent protection of free speech would not protect a man in falsely shouting fire in a theatre and causing a panic. It does not even protect a man from an injunction against uttering words that may have all the effect of force. The question in every case is whether the words used are used in such circumstances and are of such a nature as to create a clear and present danger that they will bring about the substantive evils that Congress has a right to prevent. It is a question of proximity and degree. When a nation is at war many things that might be said in time of peace are such a

hindrance to its effort that their utterance will not be endured so long as men fight and that no Court could regard them as protected by any constitutional right. It seems to be admitted that if an actual obstruction of the recruiting service were proved, liability for words that produce that effect might be enforced. The statute of 1917 punishes conspiracies to obstruct as well as actual obstruction. If the act, (speaking, or circulating a paper,) its tendency and the intent with which it is done are the same, we perceive no ground for saying that success alone warrants making the act a crime. . . .[3]

Holmes said, in effect, that while the First Amendment was ordinarily a comprehensive and sweeping protection of free speech, under certain conditions the government had a right to prohibit speech: when the speech in question created a danger, a *clear and present danger,* of bringing about evils that Congress had a right to prevent. Since Congress clearly had the right to prevent obstruction of the draft, the question thus became, did Schenck's leaflet present such a clear and present danger? Holmes obviously thought so, but the historical data do not support his conclusions. Contemporary accounts indicate Schenck's chances of success were probably remote. Indeed, Holmes' opinion, by implication, suggests that obstruction of the draft, in fact, was not likely to occur. If success were unlikely, however, then how could the danger involved be said to be either clear or imminent?

Whether Holmes was ever struck by the difficulties inherent in his *Schenck* opinion or regretted his part in affirming Schenck's conviction is not known, but within a few months he assumed quite a different stance in another speech case considered by the Court.[4] Jacob Abrams and five associates were indicted in 1918 for violation of the Sedition Act of 1918. The de-

3.  Ibid., at 52.

4.  *Abrams v. United States,* 250 U.S. 616, 40 S.Ct. 17, 63 L.Ed. 1173 (1919).

fendants were Russian Jewish immigrants who distributed leaflets critical of United States' foreign policy by throwing them from the window of a New York City factory located in a tenement district. The leaflets protested American involvement on the side of the White armies in the Russian Revolution. Written in English and Yiddish, they accused President Wilson of hypocrisy, labelled him a tool of Wall Street imperialists, and called on workers to participate in a general strike intended to interfere with the production of munitions designed "to murder not only the Germans, but also your dearest, best, who are in Russia and are fighting for freedom." The defendants were indicted on four counts for conspiracy to violate the Sedition Act in that they published disloyal, scurrilous and abusive language about the government; used language to bring the government into contempt and disrepute; used language intended to incite and encourage resistance to the United States in the war against Germany; and wilfully incited or advocated curtailment of the production of commodities necessary to the prosecution of said war. The overt acts alleged were simply the printing and distribution of the leaflets. No evidence of the success of the plot was introduced. There was neither a general strike nor a curtailment of war production. Four of the defendants ranging in age from 21 to 29 years, were convicted in Federal District Court and sentenced to 20 years in prison.

While the underlying question in *Abrams,* as in *Schenck,* was the limits of political dissent, the immediate issue was whether the defendants intended by their actions to cripple or hinder the United States prosecution of the war against *Germany.* Their stated purpose was to hinder American intervention in Russia, and in their leaflet they had reaffirmed their opposition to Imperial Germany, declaring that they hated Germany more than did "the coward of the White House." Did their advocacy of a general strike to prevent munitions being delivered to Russia constitute the crime of conspiring to hinder the war effort with Germany, an act forbidden by the Sedition Act? The defendants argued that American policy towards Russia could readily have been changed without hindrance to the German war effort and therefore, intent to hinder the war against Germany could not be deduced from their appeal to stop the war against Russia.[5] Justice Clark, speaking for a majority of the Supreme Court, however, disagreed arguing that "the obvious effect of this appeal, if it should become effective  . . . would be to persuade persons  . . . not to aid government loans and not to work in ammunition factories." [6] Using the *Schenck* formula, the Court majority saw a clear and present danger that a substantive evil—interference with the war effort against Germany—was about to occur. Holmes and Brandeis disagreed, in a dissent as memorable for the quality of its language as for its substance:

> . . . when men have realized that time has upset many fighting faiths, they may come to believe even more than they believe the very foundations of their own conduct that the ultimate good desired is better reached by free trade in ideas—that the best test of truth is the power of the thought to get itself accepted in the competition of the market, and that truth is the only ground upon which their wishes safely can be carried out. That at any rate is the theory of our Constitution. It is an experiment, as all life is an experiment. Every year if not every day we have to wager our salvation upon some prophecy based upon imperfect knowledge. While that experiment is part of our system I think that we should be eternally vigilant against attempts to check the expression of opinions that we loathe and believe to be fraught with death, unless they so imminently threaten immediate interference with the lawful and pressing purposes of the law that an immediate check is required to save the country. . . . [7]

5. Zechariah Chaffee, Jr., *Free Speech in the United States*, Cambridge: Harvard University Press, 1964, Chap. 3.

6. *Abrams v. United States*, 250 U.S. 616, at 621, 40 S.Ct. 17–19, 63 L.Ed. 1173 (1919).

7. Ibid., at 630.

The dissenters addressed themselves to the central issue of the *Abrams* case: At what point did criticism of governmental action and advocacy of alternate plans of action become dangerous to the government and the implementation of legitimate programs? If every criticism and every call for militant action against the government was impermissible, then of course, the baby had been thrown out with the bath water. A democracy could not preserve itself by destroying the hallmark of a democracy, freedom of speech and conscience. On the other hand, speech could at times be dangerous. The way to draw the line between permissible and impermissible speech, for Holmes, was to permit all speech provided that there would be sufficient time for counter arguments, for refutation of the ideas set forth by the original speaker. Did this pose a certain amount of danger to the community? Of course, but democracy was "an experiment, as all life is an experiment"—an experiment to determine whether the public had the capacity to distinguish truth from falsehood; whether having distinguished them, the people would choose truth; and whether, when chosen, the truth would, as the Bible promises, set us free.

The dissent expresses an almost religious faith in the good sense and basic decency of the masses, and a belief in a basic order in the universe, which if perceived and followed, will lead to a good society. It exposes both the weaknesses and the strengths of democracy. (Winston Churchill is said to have characterized democracy as the worst of all possible forms of government until one considered the alternatives. A cynic with doubts about the capacity of the general public for self government, may, on reviewing the historical record have even graver doubts about the wisdom and probity of self appointed, self perpetuating elites.)

The majority and minority positions in the *Abrams* case have formed the parameters of the discussion of free speech in the United States by the Supreme Court for the last half century. The Court has ranged between two polar positions: the "dangerous or bad tendency" standard adopted by Clark for the majority of the Court, i. e., that if speech has a tendency at some time in the future to produce bad actions, such as riot or revolution, it is impermissible; and, the "clear and present danger" standard of the Holmes-Brandeis dissent: that only speech which may produce illegal actions before there is time for refutation of the ideas expressed, may be suppressed. The semantics of the Court's decisions have varied. What was labelled "bad tendency" in the *Gitlow* case [8] became "the gravity of the evil as discounted by the improbability" in the *Dennis* case.[9] The precise meaning of the "clear and present danger" formula was a matter of dispute in several of the opinions in the Pentagon Papers case.[10] Nevertheless, the polar positions of the Court have remained very similar to those enunciated in *Abrams,* with each position dominating the Court by turn, as the social and political contexts in which cases arose changed.

Following *Abrams,* the Court upheld, in 1925, the conviction of Benjamin Gitlow, the leader of the radical wing of the Socialist Party, for violation of the New York State criminal anarchy act of 1902 which forbade advocating or teaching the necessity or propriety of overthrowing the government by force or violence. The principal evidence against Mr. Gitlow was his *Left Wing Manifesto,* a theoretical defense of Marxist theory. No evidence as to the probable success of Gitlow's preaching was introduced. The majority of the Court, basing its decision on *Abrams,* affirmed the conviction, conceding however, in a rather casual aside that Gitlow had rights under the First Amendment, i. e., that the due process clause of the Fourteenth Amendment encompassed the free speech protection of the First Amendment. Again Holmes and Brandeis protested vigorously. There was no reasonable likelihood of substantive evil resulting from Gitlow's

8.  *Gitlow v. New York,* 268 U.S. 652, 45 S.Ct. 625, 69 L.Ed. 1138 (1925).

9.  *Dennis v. United States,* 341 U.S. 494, 71 S.Ct. 857, 95 L.Ed. 1137 (1951).

10.  *New York Times v. United States,* 403 U.S. 713, 91 S.Ct. 2140, 29 L.Ed.2d 822 (1971).

preachings.  Admittedly he advocated revolution, an idea which the majority held to be an incitement but

> .  .  . *Every idea is an incitement.*  It offers itself for belief and if believed it is acted on unless some other belief outweighs it or some failure of energy stifles the movement at its birth.  The only difference between the expression of an opinion and an incitement .  .  . is the speaker's enthusiasm for the result. .  .  . If in the long run the beliefs expressed in proletarian dictatorship are destined to be accepted by the dominant forces of the community, the only meaning of free speech is that they should be given their chance and have their way.[11]

The majority was unmoved.  Two years after *Gitlow*, in 1927, it affirmed the conviction of Charlotte Anita Whitney, convicted under the California Criminal Syndicalism Act for her role in the convention which set up the Communist Labor Party of California.[12]  Again, Holmes and Brandeis disagreed, pointing out that Whitney was convicted under a statute aimed, not at those who would overthrow the government, or even at those who preached such overthrow, but at those who associated with those who preached revolution.

*Gitlow* and *Whitney* were, as it turned out, the high watermark of repression of speech in the United States Supreme Court.  During the 1930's the Court decided three cases in which the rights of Communists to believe in and express the basic notions of theoretical Communism, or to be associated with the Communist Party, were upheld.  In *Stromberg v. California*,[13] Miss Stromberg, a Communist, raised a red flag at

---

11.  *Gitlow v. New York*, 268 U.S. 652, at 673, 45 S.Ct. 625–632, 69 L. Ed. 1138 (1925).

12.  *Whitney v. California*, 274 U.S. 357, 47 S.Ct. 641, 71 L.Ed. 1095 (1927).

13.  283 U.S. 359, 51 S.Ct. 532, 75 L. Ed. 1117 (1931).

a children's summer camp.  In *DeJonge v. Oregon*,[14] DeJonge addressed a Communist sponsored meeting to protest police violence against strikers.  In *Herndon v. Lowry*,[15] Herndon, a Communist organizer, was convicted in Georgia of possessing inflammatory literature addressed to blacks.  In all three cases the prosecution argued that the defendants' ideas might at some future time produce substantive criminal acts which the government had a right to prevent.  In fact, however, these cases involved the expression of ideas, rather than plans for action.  The Hughes Court recognized that the suppression of theoretical ideas was indistinguishable from the suppression of legitimate political dissent.  No advocacy of controversial views would be safe from interference by the police if the defendants' convictions were permitted to stand.  The law would amount to "a dragnet which may enmesh anyone who agitates for a change of government if a jury can be persuaded that he ought to have foreseen his words would have some effect on the future conduct of others." [16]  The Court also held that the guilt of a speaker or writer must be personal—he himself must have desired the illegal consequence.  The fact that he associated with others who may have had illegal aims was insufficient ground for conviction.

By the beginning of World War II the Court had arrived at a position much closer to the Holmes-Brandeis clear and present danger formula than to the old Gitlow bad tendency test.  In 1940 however, Congress passed the Smith Act which made it a crime knowingly to advocate or teach the overthrow of any government of the United States by force or violence, or to organize or knowingly become a member of a group which so advocates; or, to conspire to accomplish any of these ends.  The Smith Act, based, like the 1917–1918 Espionage Acts, loosely on the Alien and Sedition Acts of 1798, dealt with speech offenses only, not

14.  299 U.S. 353, 57 S.Ct. 255, 81 L. Ed. 278 (1937).

16.  Ibid., at 263–264.

15.  301 U.S. 242, 57 S.Ct. 732, 81 L. Ed. 1066 (1937).

overt acts. It was not concerned with attempts to overthrow the government; but only with those who taught the desirability of such overthrow, or who conspired to teach such desirability, or who conspired to organize a political party which would teach such overthrow. Although the Communist Party was not mentioned by name in the act, it is clear that it was the target of Congressional supporters of the legislation. Ironically, the first prosecution of the Smith Act was brought in 1943 against the Socialist Workers Party, a small Trotskyite group bitterly at odds with the Communists. They were convicted in Federal Court. On appeal, the United States Supreme Court refused certiorari. Their conviction was little noted and less protested at the time, least of all by the leaders of the Communist Party, soon to become the Smith Act's chief victims.

Following the end of World War II, the disenchantment of the United States with her erstwhile ally, the USSR, took the form of a wave of anti-communist sentiment, which quickly became reminiscent of the repressive anti-radicalism of the Schenck-Abrams period. In 1948, eleven leaders of the American Communist Party were indicted by the federal government for violation of the Smith Act in that they, (1) willfully and knowingly conspired to organize, as the United States Communist Party, a society of persons who taught and advocated the overthrow of the United States government by force and violence; and (2) knowingly and willfully advocated and taught the duty and necessity of overthrowing and destroying the government by force and violence. No overt actions were charged, and at the trial the chief evidence against the defendants was four theoretical works of Communist literature whose doctrines the defendants were alleged to have preached: *Foundations of Leninism,* by Stalin (1924), *The Communist Manifesto,* by Marx and Engels (1848), *The State and Revolution,* by Lenin (1917), and *History of the Communist Party of the Soviet Union* (1939). Eugene Dennis and ten other Communist leaders were convicted in Federal District Court in New York City at a trial presided over by Judge Harold Medina which lasted nine months and compiled a record of 16,000 pages.  Medina instructed the jury, as a matter of law, that the acts charged did in fact constitute the conduct prohibited by the Smith Act.  The jury then was left to determine whether the defendants had committed the alleged acts, i. e., advocating the ideas expressed in the literature introduced as evidence.  Since the defendants admitted the advocacy, conviction was inevitable.  On appeal, the United States Supreme Court granted certiorari limited to the question of whether the Smith Act, inherently or as applied to the defendants, was unconstitutional as an abridgment of the First Amendment.

The *Dennis* case was, in many respects, a replay of *Gitlow*. Justice Vinson, purporting to be reworking the Holmes-Brandeis clear and present danger formula arrived at a position very close to the Gitlow bad tendency test.  Although he indicated that some likelihood of success was necessary for the law to be constitutional, the danger presented by the defendants' speech had to be neither imminent, nor even likely.  Vinson adopted as his formula the words of Learned Hand who had presided over the appeal in the Federal Court of Appeals for the Second Circuit. "In each case [courts] must ask whether the gravity of the 'evil,' discounted by its improbability, justifies such invasion of free speech as is necessary to avoid the danger." [17]  Perhaps reacting to the wave of *coup d'etats* and *putschs* which had overtaken Europe during the 1930's, Vinson went on to explain his reasoning:

> Obviously, the words cannot mean that before the Government may act, it must wait until the *putsch* is about to be executed, the plans have been laid and the signal is awaited.  If Government is aware that a group aiming at its overthrow is attempting to indoctrinate its members and to commit them to a course whereby they will strike when the leaders feel the circumstances permit, action by the Government is required.  The argument that there is no need for Government to con-

17. *Dennis v. United States*, 183 F.
2d 201 at 212 (2d Cir. 1950).

cern itself, for Government is strong, it possesses ample powers to put down a rebellion, it may defeat the revolution with ease needs no answer. For that is not the question. Certainly an attempt to overthrow the Government by force, even though doomed from the outset because of inadequate numbers or power of the revolutionists, is a sufficient evil for Congress to prevent. The damage which such attempts create both physically and politically to a nation makes it impossible to measure the validity in terms of the probability of success, or the immediacy of a successful attempt. In the instant case the trial judge charged the jury that they could not convict unless they found that petitioners intended to overthrow the Government "as speedily as circumstances would permit." This does not mean, and could not properly mean, that they would not strike until there was certainty of success. What was meant was that the revolutionists would strike when they thought the time was ripe. We must therefore reject the contention that success or probability of success is the criterion.[18]

Clearly, for Vinson the question of whether the defendants contemplated illegal action in the foreseeable future was irrelevant. It was enough that they hoped and desired that such action would take place "as speedily as circumstances would permit." How the revolution was to occur, when the overthrow would take place, and even who would be instrumental in bringing it about was unclear but immaterial. It was enough that the defendants were true believers in a revolutionary faith.

Justice Douglas responded bitterly,

If this were a case where those who claimed protection under the First Amendment were teaching the

18. *Dennis v. United States*, 341 U. S. 494 at 509–510, 71 S.Ct. 857, 867–868, 95 L.Ed. 1137 (1951).

techniques of sabotage, the assassination of the President, the filching of documents from public files, the planting of bombs, the art of street warfare, and the like, I would have no doubts.  The freedom to speak is not absolute; the teaching of methods of terror and other seditious conduct should be beyond the pale along with obscenity and immorality.  This case was argued as if those were the facts.  The argument imported much seditious conduct into the record.  That is easy and it has popular appeal, for the activities of Communists in plotting and scheming against the free world are common knowledge.  But the fact is that no such evidence was introduced at the trial.  There is a statute which makes a seditious conspiracy unlawful.  Petitioners, however, were not charged with a "conspiracy to overthrow" the Government.  They were charged with a conspiracy to form a party and groups and assemblies of people who teach and advocate the overthrow of our Government by force or violence and with a conspiracy to advocate and teach its overthrow by force and violence.  It may well be that indoctrination in the techniques of terror to destroy the Government would be indictable under either statute.  But the teaching, which is condemned here is of a different character.

So far as the present record is concerned, what petitioners did was to organize people to teach and themselves teach the Marxist-Leninist doctrine contained chiefly in four books: .   .   .

The opinion of the Court does not outlaw those texts nor condemn them to the fire, as the Communists do literature offensive to their creed.  But if the books themselves are not outlawed, if they can lawfully remain on library shelves, by what reasoning does their use in a classroom become a crime?  It would not be a crime under the Act to introduce these books to a class, though that would be teaching what the creed of violent overthrow of the Government is. The Act, as construed, requires the element of intent—that those who teach the creed believe in it. The crime then depends not on what is taught but on who the teacher is. That is to make freedom of speech turn not on *what is said,* but on the *intent* with which it is said. Once we start down that road we enter territory dangerous to the liberties of every citizen.

. . . never until today has anyone seriously thought that the ancient law of conspiracy could constitutionally be used to turn speech into seditious conduct. Yet that is precisely what is suggested. I repeat that we deal here with speech alone, not with speech *plus* acts of sabotage or unlawful conduct. Not a single seditious act is charged in the indictment. To make a lawful speech unlawful because two men conceive it is to raise the law of conspiracy to appalling proportions. . . .[19]

After protesting the failure of the Court to distinguish between political dissent and seditious conduct, Douglas went on to restate the substance of the old Holmes and Brandeis clear and present danger test.

There comes a time when even speech loses its constitutional immunity. Speech innocuous one year may at another time fan such destructive flames that it must be halted in the interests of the safety of the Republic. That is the meaning of the clear and present danger test. When conditions are so critical that there will be no time to avoid the evil that the speech threatens, it is time to call a halt. . . .

Yet free speech is the rule, not the exception. The restraint to be constitutional must be based on more

19. Ibid., at 581–583, 584.

than fear, on more than passionate opposition against the speech, on more than a revolted dislike for its contents. There must be some immediate injury to society that is likely if speech is allowed. . . . [20]

Justice Black, in a separate dissent, agreed with Douglas and added,

. . . I cannot agree that the First Amendment permits us to sustain laws suppressing freedom of speech and press on the basis Congress' or our own notions of mere "reasonableness." Such a doctrine waters down the First Amendment so that it amounts to little more than an admonition to Congress. The Amendment as so construed is not likely to protect any but those "safe" or orthodox views which rarely need its protection. . . . [21]

Black pointed out the obvious: that speakers who are for the home and mother and against sin rarely need governmental protection. It is those who say things that the public does not want to hear that the First Amendment was designed to protect, and when the Court denies such protection to unpopular speakers, the Constitution becomes an exercise in futility.

Six years later the Court had another opportunity to interpret the Smith Act, and did so, this time with very different results. The defendants, in *Yates v. United States* [22], were fourteen California Communists, "second string" leaders of the Communist Party of the United States, charged with violation of the Smith Act in that they (1) advocated and taught the duty and necessity of overthrowing the federal government by force and violence, and (2) organized as the Communist Party of the United States, a group which did so advocate and teach, with the intent of causing such overthrow as speedily as circumstances would permit. They were convicted in the lower federal courts. The

20. Ibid., at 585.

21. Ibid., at 580.

22. 354 U.S. 298, 77 S.Ct. 1064, 1 L. Ed.2d 1356 (1957).

Supreme Court granted complete certiorari: a review of the entire case as well as the constitutionality of the Smith Act itself.

By a 6–1 vote, the Court reversed the convictions of five of the defendants and remanded the remaining nine for new trials based on new standards of evidence enunciated by the Court. The Smith Act, said Justice Harlan for the majority, was constitutional, but only if one recognized the distinction between advocacy of abstract doctrine and advocacy of action. While the former was permissible under the First Amendment, the latter was not and it was only the latter the Smith Act was intended by Congress to prohibit. In the *Yates* case, both the petitioners and the government had submitted proposed instructions "which would have required the jury to find that the proscribed advocacy was not of a mere abstract doctrine of forcible overthrow, but of action to that end. . . . "[23] The trial judge rejected this request and instead instructed the jury that "the kind of advocacy and teaching which is charged and upon which your verdict must be reached is not merely a desirability but a necessity that the government of the United States be overthrown and destroyed by force and violence . . ."[24] Harlan indicated that the judge had erred in so instructing the jury and found the trial record barren of evidence that the defendants—or at least the five whose convictions were set aside—did in fact advocate any kind of specific future illegal activity.

> We recognize that distinctions between advocacy and teaching of abstract doctrines, with evil intent, and that which is directed to stirring people to action, are often subtle and difficult to grasp, for in a broad sense, as Mr. Justice Holmes said in his dissenting opinion in *Gitlow,* "Every idea is an incitement." . . . The need for precise and understandable instructions . . . is further emphasized by the equivocal character of the evidence in this record, . . . Instances of speech that could be considered to amount to

23.  Ibid., at 315–316.          24.  Ibid., at 313.

"advocacy of action" are so few and far between as to be almost completely overshadowed by the hundreds of instances in the record in which overthrow, if mentioned at all, occurs in the course of doctrinal disputation so remote from action as to be almost wholly lacking in probative value. . . .[25]

In short, it was not enough for Communists to have preached about revolution the way evangelistic Christian ministers preach about heaven—in the sweet by and by; they must have advocated specific illegal actions in which they would engage as speedily as circumstances would permit.*

The net result of *Yates* was an affirmation of the constitutionality of the Smith Act through a reinterpretation of its meaning so extensive as to virtually repeal it. The quality of evidence needed for conviction under the act was such that not only were the nine defendants remanded for new trials never retried but no further prosecutions for advocacy of political doctrine were undertaken under the Smith Act. In *Dennis* the Court had opted for the "bad tendency" test; in *Yates,* they had returned to the "clear and present danger" standard.

Following *Yates,* prosecutions for simple speech offenses virtually disappeared, and prosecutions of Communists on other grounds became increasingly infrequent and unsuccessful. Since 1957 the Court has not deviated appreciably from the "clear and present danger" standard for political speech, which is the more remarkable when one considers that since *Yates* the United

25.  Ibid., at 326–327.

* Professor Walter Gelhorn stated the distinction nicely, "[O]ne can recognize a qualitative distinction between a speaker who expresses the opinion before a student audience that all law professors are scoundrels whose students should band together to beat them within an inch of their lives, and a second speaker who, taking up that theme, urges the audience to obtain baseball bats, meet behind the law faculty building at three o'clock next Thursday afternoon, and join him in attacking any professor who can then be found. The first speaker, in [the *Yates* court's] view, should not be prosecuted; the second has stepped over the line between advocating a belief and advocating an illegal action."

States has passed through a tumultuous period of civil rights agitation and an even more tumultuous period of opposition to the war in Viet Nam.  The level of inflammatory rhetoric and criticism and derogation of the government has seldom been exceeded, yet there have been no parallels to the *Abrams, Gitlow* or *Dennis* prosecutions.  Even the agony of Viet Nam produced at most a handful of relatively minor cases relating to "symbolic speech," e. g., draft card burning, flag desecration, the wearing of black armbands and the like.  The only noteworthy case involving free speech for political dissenters was the Pentagon Papers case which arose in a context entirely different from the earlier Communist cases, and which related to the freedom of newspapers to publish rather than of speakers to speak.  Nevertheless, it once again raised the issue of the bad tendency versus clear and present danger standards.

In June of 1971, the *New York Times* and the *Washington Post* published classified papers relating to the origin and conduct of the Viet Nam War up to 1968.  These papers, known as the "Pentagon Papers" were a multivolume study prepared for the Defense Department, one of the authors of which was Daniel Ellsberg.  At the conclusion of the study, Ellsberg returned to his original employer, the Rand Corporation, taking with him his personal copy of the papers.  These papers were classified by the Defense Department as top secret, although much of the material in them had already been published in various government publications and privately published periodicals.  Early in 1971, Ellsberg, who by this time was convinced that the war in Viet Nam was a disaster for both the United States and the Vietnamese, gave copies of the papers to the *New York Times* and the *Washington Post,* in the hope that publication of the history of the blunders, deceptions and misjudgments of the Defense Department and the President in relation to the war would precipitate a tidal wave of hostile public opinion which would force the Nixon administration to withdraw from Viet Nam.

The *New York Times* and the *Washington Post* proceeded to publish the documents serially, much to the horror of the Administration.  After several installments had been published, the Justice Department obtained temporary restraining orders from the federal district courts in New York City and Washington, D.C., and injunctions against further publication by the *New York Times* and the *Washington Post*.  The orders were upheld by the Court of Appeals for the Second Circuit and struck down by the Court of Appeals for the District of Columbia.  The case was accepted for review by the United States Supreme Court which rendered its decision in a *per curiam* opinion accompanied by no less than nine separate statements by the individual justices.  Astonishingly, the litigation ran its entire course in two weeks, from June 15th, 1971 when the government obtained its first injunction in a federal district court to June 30th, 1971 when the Supreme Court handed down its opinion.

The government's contention was that the President had inherent power to restrain the publication of any document that would cause grave and irreparable injury to the United States. The two newspapers in question responded that the First Amendment protected their right to publish these papers.  The *per curiam* decision of the Court was that the injunction against publication could not stand because "any system of prior restraints  .   .   .   comes to this Court bearing a heavy presumption against its constitutional validity." [26]  The burden of proof was on the government to justify such a restraint, and it did not meet that burden.  This opinion, apparently supported by six members of the Court was, in effect, a statement of the preferred position of the First Amendment, and by implication, of the clear and present danger formula.  The Court decided that at least as far as prior restraint of publication was concerned, the action of the government had to be more than reasonable; it had to be essential to the well being of the country, or to state the matter differently, it had to be necessary in order

**26**.  *New York Times Co. v. United States*, 403 U.S. 713, 91 S.Ct. 2140, 29 L.Ed.2d 822 (1971).  *United*     *States v. Washington Post Co.*, 403 U.S. 713 at 714, 91 S.Ct. 2140–2141, 29 L.Ed.2d 822 (1971).

to forestall an immediate and inevitable danger to the country. This theme was repeated by Justice Brennan who declared

> . . . Unless and until the Government has clearly made out its case [that untoward consequences would result], the First Amendment commands that no injunction may issue.[27]

This theme was repeated in Stewart's opinion in which he stated that while he believed the executive had plenary power over foreign affairs, nevertheless, he, Stewart, could not

> . . . say that disclosure of any of them [the Pentagon Papers] will surely result in direct, immediate, and irreparable damage to our Nation or its people. That being so, there can under the First Amendment be but one judicial resolution of the issues before us. I join the judgments of the Court.[28]

White also agreed that,

> . . . the United States has not satisfied the very heavy burden that it must meet to warrant an injunction against publication in these cases, at least in the absence of express and appropriately limited congressional authorization for prior restraints in circumstances such as these.[29]

The most sweeping criticism of the government's position, however, was made by Justice Black:

> . . . for the first time in the 182 years since the founding of the Republic, the federal courts are asked to hold that the First Amendment does not mean what it says, but rather means that the Government can halt the publication of current news of vital importance to the people of this country.

27. Ibid., at 727.    29. Ibid., at 731.

28. Ibid., at 730.

. . . Both the history and language of the First Amendment support the view that the press must be left free to publish news, whatever the source, without censorship, injunctions, or prior restraints.

In the First Amendment the Founding Fathers gave the free press the protection it must have to fulfill its essential role in our democracy. The press was to serve the governed, not the governors. The Government's power to censor the press was abolished so that the press would remain forever free to censure the Government. The press was protected so that it could bare the secrets of government and inform the people. Only a free and unrestrained press can effectively expose deception in government. . . .

. . . To find that the President has "inherent power" to halt the publication of news by resort to the courts would wipe out the First Amendment and destroy the fundamental liberty and security of the very people the Government hopes to make "secure." . . . [30]

The arguments raised by the dissenters were chiefly that the cases had been heard with too much haste, with insufficient time to consider the issues carefully; and that the courts could not second guess the executive in his determination that this publication might cause grave and irreparable injury to this country. Chief Justice Burger, protested that if the *New York Times* had taken three or four months preparing the material for publication, there was no reason why the courts should not take an equal amount of time to consider the legal issues involved.* Harlan raised more thoughtful substantive objections

---

30. Ibid., at 715, 717, and 719.

* Burger's opinion seems lacking in logic. The roles of the *New York Times* and the United States Government are hardly comparable: The *New York Times* is under no obligation to publish anything it does not choose to; the United States Government is under a strong Constitutional obligation to refrain from interfering with the *Times*. Every day that the *Times* is enjoined wrongfully from publi-

listing the questions which the Court had not had time to consider. Reluctantly he came to the conclusion that the government's position should be upheld on the merits since the Court did not have the expertise to second guess the President, who after all, had full Constitutional authority over the conduct of foreign affairs. Justice Blackmun scolded the *New York Times* and the *Washington Post* for risking national security in the interests of sensationalism. Presumably, the prosecution had offered to the Court evidence of the danger to the country that would ensue from publication of the papers which Blackmun found persuasive. The nature of this evidence has never been completely revealed but a columnist for the *New York Times* in 1976 mentioned in passing, some of the items involved.

> Just this summer, . . . a Freedom of Information suit exposed the Government's pitifully weak attempt to justify, in 1971, its claim that publication of the Pentagon Papers endangered national security. In a secret hearing before Federal Judge Gerhard Gesell, officials offered the following "evidence."

> "One contact that I personally had in Hanoi . . . dried up," said a deputy assistant secretary of defense dealing with American prisoners in North Vietnam; no further details were given.

> Canadian officials "expressed concern" about what the Canadian people would think about Canadian efforts to help the United States reach a peace settlement in Vietnam.

cation is a day of invasion of constitutional rights. Delay in speech cases is defeat for the speaker, *de facto* if not *de jure*. Cf. *Carroll v. President and Comm'rs of Princess Anne County*, 393 U.S. 175, 89 S.Ct. 347, 21 L.Ed.2d 325 (1968), in which right wing speakers ultimately were upheld in their claim of a right to speak, but where the right to speak had been effectively vitiated by the two year hiatus resulting from the litigation.

The Prime Minister of Australia found publication of the Pentagon Papers "appalling." [31]

Certainly, if these items are indicative of the government's case, the importance of the clear and present danger rationale becomes obvious.  Any speech, any communication, any publication that is less than laudatory may, at some time in the future, have an adverse effect on the government in power.  The question is how adverse, what kind of danger, and when will it occur?  The experience of the Nixon years demonstrates clearly how easily the bad tendency test which seemed so reasonable to Justices Vinson, Frankfurter, and Jackson in the *Dennis* case could be subverted through the magic phrase "national security," into a shield for heinous crimes and malfeasance of high public officials.  The clear and present danger test, if it does nothing else, insists that prosecutors remain in the real world, that they present real evidence rather than conjure up bogeymen who can be used to divert the attention of the public from embarrassing facts the government may wish to conceal.

*Freedom of Assembly*

Theories as to the constitutionality of speech relate to pure speech, i. e., speech unmixed with action, only.  Speech, in the constitutional sense, means communication, and as such refers not only to the spoken word, but to the written word—books, pamphlets, newspapers, etc.—and to movies, the theater, television, pictures, and the graphic arts as well.  Communication, however, can also take the form of action: picketing, demonstrating, marching, draft card burning, to mention a few possibilities.  The act of communication, moreover, while it implies at least one speaker and one listener, can occur in a wide variety of social settings.  One may read a book or newspaper alone in the privacy of one's home, or one may be part of a march of 250,000 persons protesting the war against Viet Nam.  One may discuss political theory at a tea party in a neighbor's home, or

31. Tom Wicker, "A Far Greater Danger," *New York Times*, September 14, 1976, p. 39.

one may lead a chanting picket line outside a factory. As speech becomes more and more mixed with physical action or the potential for physical action, the degree of protection afforded by the First Amendment diminishes. The United States Supreme Court, for example, has hinted strongly that a person may possess in the privacy of his own home speech materials which might be of dubious legality in a more public setting; [32] but even a relatively innocuous message, such as a plea for housing integration, may be forbidden if communicated under circumstances so inflammatory as to pose an immediate risk of riot or disorder. The control of speech that is mixed with action presents not only theoretical but practical problems. The police must maintain peace in the community, and they must be given guidelines as to how to do so without, at the same time, unnecessarily restricting speech.

Clearly, a speaker who waves an ideological red flag before the enraged bull of a hostile audience will provoke disorder. The problem presented to the criminal justice system under these circumstances is: who is to be restrained—the speaker or the audience?

As in the case of pure speech, the guidelines handed down by the Supreme Court have been ambiguous. In 1948, one Terminiello addressed eight hundred members of the Christian Veterans of America in a Chicago auditorium. In his address he referred to "Queen Eleanor Roosevelt, Queen of America's Communists," and referred to Jews and Negroes as "slimy scum," "snakes," and "bedbugs." Outside the hall two thousand opponents of Terminiello's fascist supporters staged a riot, throwing bricks and bottles, and breaking into the hall. Terminiello was arrested and convicted of disorderly conduct.[33] During the 1948 presidental campaign, one Feiner, a student at Syracuse University, addressed a crowd of seventy-five to eighty people on a street corner in a Negro residential section of Syracuse, New

32.  *Stanley v. Georgia*, 394 U.S. 557, 89 S.Ct. 1243, 22 L.Ed.2d 542 (1969).

33.  *Terminiello v. Chicago*, 337 U.S. 1, 69 S.Ct. 894, 93 L.Ed. 1131 (1949).

York.  He urged his audience to attend a meeting supporting the candidacy of Henry Wallace, and referred to President Truman as a "bum" and to the American Legion as a "Nazi Gestapo."  He also made some remarks urging blacks and whites to join in and fight for their rights.  His statements stirred up a little excitement and some muttering and pushing.  A bystander with an infant in his arms approached one of the two policemen in the audience and said that if the police did not get that "s.o. b." off the stand he would do so himself.  The policemen thereupon arrested Feiner who was ultimately convicted of disorderly conduct.[34]

Both cases were appealed to the United States Supreme Court. The Court held that, in the *Terminiello* case, where an actual riot was in progress, the conviction should be reversed because it was the duty of the police to have restrained the crowd and protected the rights of the speaker.  In the *Feiner* case, on the other hand, the court upheld the defendant's conviction on the ground that the police had the right to arrest a speaker who was threatening the peace, even though the imminence of the disorder was by no means clear.

These two cases, although both involved speakers and hostile audiences, are not identical.  Terminiello was speaking inside a closed auditorium, rented and paid for by his supporters;  Feiner was speaking on the street, where problems of traffic obstruction, noise, and crowd movement presented themselves.  Terminiello was speaking to an invited sympathetic audience.  Feiner was speaking to an uninvited, somewhat unsympathetic, audience.  Nevertheless, the two Supreme Court decisions taken together are somewhat contradictory and present grave problems. If the Feiner rationale is followed, there is freedom of speech only for those speakers who do not displease their audiences. That is, in effect, to limit street meetings to those who love little children, apple pie, and the flag.  On the other hand, while the

34.  *Feiner v. New York*, 340 U.S. 315, 71 S.Ct. 303, 95 L.Ed. 295 (1951).

two thousand people who howled for Terminiello's blood might have been controlled by a police force the size of Chicago's, what if that size crowd had gathered in a small town with an inadequate police force, or for that matter, what if the Chicago crowd had numbered twenty thousand or two hundred thousand instead of two thousand?

Another problem related to freedom of assembly is how much discretion local authorities have to forbid demonstrations which they think may provoke civil disorder. An interesting case, originating in the Chicago, Illinois area is currently moving through the appellate courts, possibly towards United States Supreme Court review. On May 1, 1977 and again on July 4, 1977 the National Socialist Party of America, a group of Chicago based Nazis, planned to march in Skokie, Illinois, a town on the northern border of Chicago. On May 3, 1977, Skokie adopted a group of ordinances requiring that no parade or assembly involving more than 50 persons could be held without giving 30 days notice in advance and putting up a $35,000 bond to cover public liability and property damage. While Nazis were not mentioned by name, prohibited under any circumstances were any demonstrations that would "incite violence, hatred, abuse, or hostility toward a person or group of persons by reason or reference to racial, ethnic, national, or religious affiliation." An escape clause permitted the governing body of Skokie to waive any of the ordinances for a particular demonstration.

Of Skokie's 70,000 residents, 40,000 are Jews, and among the latter group are 7,000 survivors of the World War II Nazi holocaust. Responding to the anger of the townspeople, an injunction was obtained from an Illinois Circuit Court prohibiting the demonstration. The Nazis, represented by the Illinois division of the American Civil Liberties Union (ACLU), on free speech grounds appealed to the United States Supreme Court. On June 14, 1977, the Court in a 5–4 decision ordered the Illinois Appellate Court to rule immediately by either lifting the injunction or by reviewing the case.

Accordingly, on July 12, 1977, the Illinois Appellate Court ruled that the Nazis could march in Skokie but would be barred from wearing or displaying the swastika. Apparently, the reasoning behind the Illinois Appellate court decision was that the swastika is unprotected speech because it could provoke violent reaction among many of the Skokie Jews. (In *Chaplinsky v. New Hampshire*,[35] a 1942 case, the United States Supreme Court ruled that epithets, curses and similar "fighting words" were not protected under the First Amendment.) The ACLU on behalf of the Illinois Nazis maintained that the swastika is symbolic speech, and under the First Amendment must be protected. Observers predict that should the case reach the United States Supreme Court the vote will be close.

The probabilities are that no court can draw *a priori* hard-and-fast rules for the guidance of police, prosecutors, and judges in such situations. Each case must be judged in terms of the realities of the situation: the actual ability of the existing law force to handle a realistically perceived threat to the public peace. On the other hand, the feeling on the part of many police officers, that a speaker who is inflammatory is *ipso facto* liable to arrest for disorderly conduct or disturbing the peace, does not square with the need of an open society for gadflies and critics. If the First Amendment is to be something more than a pious platitude, speakers who express the sentiments we loathe must have protection comparable to that afforded speakers who preach the gospel of love, peace, and patriotism.

It is worth noting that even at the Supreme Court level there appears to be differential handling of political offenders of the Right and of the Left. There is no conviction of a right-wing speaker that has been upheld by the United States Supreme Court. On the other hand, left-wing speakers such as Schenck, Abrams, Gitlow, and Dennis have been convicted of abstract advocacy of ideas, and on review these convictions have been affirmed by the high court. Similarly, left-wing agitators are normally treated with more hostility than their right-wing counterparts by the police. Why this is true is not entirely clear, but

35.   315 U.S. 568, 62 S.Ct. 766, 86 L.
Ed. 1031 (1942).

two reasons suggest themselves. Many policemen conceive it their duty to maintain the *status quo*. The radical who threatens the *status quo* by advocacy of armed revolution is therefore more dangerous than the radical who threatens to protect the *status quo* from social change, albeit in an equally violent manner. A new Left student group advocating Maoism is more dangerous than a Minuteman group, even though the Minuteman group may advocate the arming of private citizens. That the forcible slowing down of the normal process of social change can be as subversive of stability as the forced acceleration of such change is perhaps not obvious to many police officials. At the Supreme Court level, the dearth of right-wing convictions may stem from the fact that liberals will oppose such convictions on civil libertarian grounds, and conservatives do not perceive right-wing ideology as sufficiently dangerous to warrant restraint.

Problems posed by public meetings aside, a technique which gained increasing popularity during the civil rights movement of the 1960's and the Viet Nam War protests of the 1970's presents the criminal justice system with new problems. The use of civil disobedience, that is, the deliberate public violation of a law to dramatize profound disapproval of the existing state of affairs, has been utilized increasingly by reformers of many political hues. Martin Luther King's leadership of the Montgomery bus boycott, the march to Selma, Alabama, the sit-ins at Selective Service headquarters, the demonstrations in Grant Park in Chicago at the Democratic National Convention in 1968, all involved conduct at least partially illegal in terms of existing local law. All were designed to bring to public attention conditions perceived as unjust and inexcusable by the demonstrators. The chief result of police attempts to break up such demonstrations was frequently the spread of social unrest. To justify their actions, demonstrators claimed that there was a law higher than the statutes on the books, higher even than the Constitution. Such law was "natural law," "justice," "the principles of morality." The police, on the other hand, were paid by the public to enforce the very law the demonstrators claimed was not binding on them. Inevitably, confrontation and conflict resulted from these two opposing positions.

Civil disobedience takes two forms. In one, the demonstrators disobey a law which they hold to be basically unjust or even unconstitutional, for example, civil rights demonstrators' violation of southern segregation statutes. When the demonstrators were arrested for such violations they appealed their cases to higher courts in the hope of obtaining a declaration of unconstitutionality. This technique was very successful in eliminating legalized segregation throughout the United States.

The second type of civil disobedience is the deliberate breaking of a law to which one has no objection in order to demonstrate one's disapproval of some unrelated social policy. Students who seized college buildings were not protesting the criminal trespass laws. They seized buildings in order to make it impossible for the Establishment to ignore their objections to the Viet Nam War, research sponsored by the military, or racist admission policies.

Should such demonstrators be punished? And if so, to what extent? It must be appreciated at the outset that the Judeo-Christian morality on which this country claims to be based clearly holds that there *is* a law higher than the stated law of the political sovereign, and that therefore, each individual has a moral right to resist injustice where he finds it. Demonstrators thus have a strong moral basis for their actions. The problem, however, in terms of the criminal justice system, is whether they have a legal basis for their actions, that is, whether they can pursue their chosen course of conduct without the imposition of legal sanctions.

If, like Martin Luther King, they challenge laws they feel are unconstitutional, and win favorable verdicts in the appellate courts, they are clearly entitled to be free from legal punishment. The situation however, with regard to the second type of demonstrator, the one who breaks a "legitimate" law, is far more complex. The great writers who developed theories of civil disobedience, Thoreau and Ghandi, held that such violators should offer themselves to the civil authorities for punishment in much the same way that Jesus offered to be crucified for the sins of mankind.  Hopefully the sympathies of the uncommitted will thereupon be stirred to rectify the underlying social injustice and to prevent further punishment of the demonstrators.  In the real world however, not too many people are capable of Christ-like conduct, and many demonstrators seek to avoid punishment.*  The uncommitted public, moreover, is seldom effectively stirred from its apathy.  The problem thus usually takes forms such as:  should students be punished for disrupting universities, though their cause is admittedly just, if the disruption is clearly illegal and produces great hardship to innocent people?  Or, should anti-war protestors have been permitted to disrupt the military operations of the government if they truly believed that we were engaged in an unjust war?

Once again, there are no clear guidelines for the police.  Certainly, to exempt automatically all sincere protestors from punishment for their law-breaking is an invitation to anarchy.  No society can realistically aid in the process of its own dissolution.

* Protestors who violate the law but seek to avoid punishment sometimes provoke responses both unintended and horrifying.  Consider the following statement by Jeb Stuart Magruder, an official of the Committee to Reelect the President, made to the Senate Watergate Committee:

".  .  .  I tried to point out the frustrations we in the White House had felt in trying to cope by legal means with antiwar people who resorted to illegal acts—the draft-card burning, the leak of the Pentagon Papers, the May Day attempt to shut down Washington, the bombing of the Capitol and so on.

"I believed as firmly as they did that the President was correct in this issue.  So, consequently .  .  .  we have become somewhat inured to using some activities that would help us in accomplishing what we thought was a cause, a legitimate cause.

"Now, that is absolutely incorrect; two wrongs do not make a right.  .  .  .  But that is basically, I think, the reason why that decision was made, because of that atmosphere that had occurred and to all of us who had worked in the White House, there was that feeling of resentment and of frustration at being unable to deal with issues on a legal basis."  Jeb Stuart Magruder, *An American Life: One Man's Road To Watergate*, New York: Atheneum, 1974, p. 306.

Chaos would reign if each individual were free to exempt himself at will from the laws governing social conduct. On the other hand, to treat sincere moral protest in the same manner as the unprincipled violation of law for private gain is counterproductive in terms of achieving a just society. Probably some balance between the social costs of forgiving violations and the social benefit of the reform proposed is in order. The mothers who obstruct traffic in order to force the installation of a traffic light at a dangerous school crossing must be forgiven, because the social cost of their protest is small and the social gain proposed is great. The forcible kidnapping of school officials in order to change university policy with regard to military recruiting is probably indefensible because of the enormity of the social wrong involved in kidnapping and the marginal utility of the act in rectifying the alleged social wrong.

Thus, in civil disobedience situations the police become the men in the middle. They are the visible agents of a society which must decide on its proper course of action. It is those who make social policy who must determine the extent to which the civilly disobedient must be punished. The greater the extent of society's recognition and approbation of the protestors' cause, and the more defensible the techniques employed, the more lenient must be the instructions given the criminal justice system for the handling of demonstrators. If there is no public identification with the cause in question, harsh treatment may be meted out without risk of causing widespread social disorder. In any case, policy in regard to the treatment of the civilly disobedient cannot be made by the police, local prosecutors, or the courts. It must be made at far more politically responsive and responsible levels such as the presidency, Congress, and the state legislature. Police cannot function intelligently in this area unless they accept the fact that they are only agents of a policy that must be determined elsewhere.

*Obscenity: When is Speech not Speech?*

In recent years, obscenity cases, like proverbial bad pennies, keep turning up before the United States Supreme Court. With each decision, the Court makes a mighty effort to find some formula, hit on some rationale, that will settle the question once and for all, but to no avail.  No matter how each set of nine justices tries, some book, some movie, some magazine inevitably is declared obscene by local authorities;  its publisher or exhibitor, raising a constitutional issue, appeals his conviction to the United States Supreme Court;  and the problem is before the Court once again.  The obscenity issue continues to recur because the Court has not been able to deal with the basic problem: should obscenity be censored at all?  Is there really such a thing as obscenity?  Or is obscenity simply speech protected by the First Amendment?

One Supreme Court justice, Hugo Black, consistently took a clear-cut position that all regulations of obscenity were invalid because the First Amendment forbids *all* regulation of speech. Indeed, Justice Black went so far as to refuse to examine the allegedly obscene exhibits that constituted the evidence in the cases brought before him, on the ground that the content of the material was irrelevant since no regulation of speech (in the larger sense, books, periodicals, films, live entertainment—all communication, written and oral, verbal and nonverbal) was permissible.  His fellow justices were not so fortunate or unfortunate.  Their view of the problem led them to read, look, listen, or otherwise to examine all the titillating tidbits brought before them.

Historically, the struggle between the state and individuals who wish to say things the ruling authorities consider impermissible has been a long one.  Originally, most regulation of speech occurred in the political or religious arena.  In Tudor England, for example, censorship was concerned mostly with speech that attacked either the monarch or the church—treason or heresy. As the British political system matured, political criticism became more legitimate;  and as religious authority became further separated from secular authority, criticism of religion and the church was likewise less subject to regulation.  In the eighteenth and ninteenth centuries, however, British censors became increasingly concerned over antireligious material with a *sexual* theme. The first successful obscenity prosecution of a publisher was of Edmund Curll in 1727 for a book entitled, *Venus in the Cloister,* or *The Nun in Her Smock;* and the landmark case of *Regina v. Hicklin* [36] dealt with an antireligious tract entitled *The Confessional Unmasked.* This pamphlet, published by a militant Protestant society, purported to publicize the improper questions put to women in the confessional, and also described actual seductions of women during confessions.

The *Hicklin* case was important because it was the first test of an 1857 act that provided a mechanism for police seizure of obscene material; but its greater significance lies in the fact that for the first time the presiding judge attempted to define obscenity. The so-called Hicklin Rule states that

> . . . [T]he test of obscenity is this, whether the tendency of the matter charged as obscenity is to deprave and corrupt those whose minds are open to such immoral influences, and into whose hands a publication of this sort may fall.[37]

The Hicklin Rule became the standard for American obscenity prosecutions for almost a century. It was applied to all disputed materials with a sexual theme regardless of their religious content. And it was interpreted to mean that parts of books, as opposed to a work as a whole, could be taken out of context and declared obscene if they were likely adversely to affect the most susceptible and easily influenced groups in the potential audience as opposed to that audience as a whole. Thus, purple passages in any work, no matter how respectable, might be the basis for legal suppression of that work if somebody, anybody, were shown to be unhealthfully stimulated by such passages. Indeed, a photograph of the ceiling of the Sistine Chapel in the Vatican was seized as obscene by customs officials in New York City. The great anti-vice crusader Anthony Comstock was characterized by one of his critics as a man who tried to make the world

36.  L.R. 3 Q.B. 360 (1868).          37.  Ibid., p. 369.

safe for a fourteen-year-old school girl with pronounced erotic tendencies. This, in effect, is what the Hicklin Rule attempted to do in relation to materials with a sexual theme for British and American society.

In the United States, rebellion against such censorship took the legal form of challenges to official suppression under the First Amendment, the argument being that suppression of communication is forbidden by the very definite statement that "Congress shall make no law . . . abridging the freedom of speech or of the press." * These challenges did not take the form of a head-on attack on all obscenity regulation. They took, instead, the more customary route of chipping away at a particular suppression based on a particularly undesirable standard. In 1934, in a case involving the suppression of James Joyce's *Ulysses*, Morris Ernst, on behalf of Random House, the publisher who attempted to import the book, argued that books as a whole, rather than particular passages, should be considered in a determination of obscenity. Judges Learned and Augustus Hand, sitting in the United States Court of Appeals for the Second Circuit, agreed that "the proper test of whether a given book is obscene is its dominant effect," and that the

> . . . relevancy of the objectionable parts to the theme, the established reputation of the work in the estimation of approved critics, if the book is modern, and the verdict of the past, if it is ancient, are persuasive evidence; . . . [38]

The net effect of the *Ulysses* decision was to base future obscenity verdicts on a work in its entirety rather than on titillating passages.

---

* Although the First Amendment refers only to Congress, in *Gitlow v. New York*, 268 U.S. 652, 45 S.Ct. 625, 69 L.Ed. 1138 (1925) the United States Supreme Court held the speech provisions of the First Amendment to be binding on the states.

38. *United States v. One Book Called "Ulysses", by James Joyce*, 72 F.2d 705 (2d Cir. 1934).

A further modification of the Hicklin Rule came with the *Roth* decision in 1957.[39] Samuel Roth, a New York publisher convicted for mailing obscene advertising and an obscene book in violation of the federal obscenity statutes, challenged the conviction on the ground that these statutes "on their faces and in a vacuum, violated the freedom of expression guarantees . . . of the Constitution." The U. S. Supreme Court unfortunately for Mr. Roth, affirmed his conviction but agreed with a good many of his philosophical arguments by specifically rejecting the Hicklin test.

> . . . The *Hicklin* test, judging obscenity by the effect of isolated passages upon the most susceptible persons, . . . must be rejected as unconstitutionally restrictive of the freedoms of speech and press. . . .[40]

The Court went on to cite with approval the standard of the trial court that had convicted Roth:

> ". . . The test is not whether it would arouse sexual desires or sexual impure thoughts in those comprising a particular segment of the community, the young, the immature or the highly prudish or would leave another segment, the scientific or highly educated or the so-called worldly-wise and sophisticated indifferent and unmoved.
>
> The test in each case is the effect of the book, picture or publication considered as a whole, not upon any particular class, but upon all those whom it is likely to reach. . . . you determine its impact upon the average person in the community. . . ."[41]

*Roth* thus dealt the *coup de grace* to Hicklin by requiring not only that a work be considered in its entirety but that its impact on the average, normal person constitute the relevant standard.

39. *Roth v. United States*, 354 U.S. 476, 77 S.Ct. 1304, 1 L.Ed.2d 1498 (1957).

40. Ibid., at 489.

41. Ibid., at 490.

The problem with *Roth,* however, was that the unresolved issue of whether there should be regulation of obscenity at all became increasingly more insistent as the lower courts attempted to apply the liberalized standard in an increasingly libertarian era. It became apparent quite soon that contemporary community standards of what was desirable and what had "redeeming social value" were impossible to apply from the standpoint of police and prosecutors since fewer and fewer works seemed to fit the definition of what was obscene. In cosmopolitan areas like New York and San Francisco, relatively few prosecutions for obscenity resulted in convictions since there was insufficient consensus as to what was offensive to the community and what was totally worthless from a social or literary point of view. Subtly, the burden of proof became increasingly difficult for police and prosecutors to sustain. At the same time there was no general agreement to eliminate all obscenity prosecutions, and so the courts were faced with the problem of finding yet another rationale for limiting the distribution of obscene materials.

That rationale appeared with the case of *Ginzburg v. United States.*[42] In 1962 Ralph Ginzburg, an independent publisher who previously had been highly successful in promoting and circulating popular periodicals such as *Look* and *Esquire,* undertook to merchandise three obscure, erotic publications: *Eros,* an expensive, artfully contrived magazine on sex directed toward an upper-middle-class audience ($25.00 annual subscription, $10.00 per single issue); *The Housewife's Handbook on Selective Promiscuity,* which purported to be a sexual autobiography detailing with complete candor the author's sexual experiences from age three to age thirty-six; and *Liaison,* a rather trivial biweekly newsletter. These three publications, while highly erotic in content, were hardly pornography, and might indeed have circulated unmolested by the United States government had not Ginzburg chosen to publicize his publications in a manner that was not only somewhat lewd, but that hinted slyly that it was permis-

42. 383 U.S. 463, 86 S.Ct. 942, 16 L.
Ed.2d 31 (1966).

siveness in relation to sexual materials on the part of the United States Supreme Court that permitted their publication and circulation. Like a bad boy who has learned words he knows he shouldn't use, Ginzburg applied for mailing privileges from both Blue Balls and Intercourse, Pennsylvania. When those facilities refused his application because of their inability to handle a large volume of mail, he applied to Middlesex, New Jersey. Worse yet, in the advertisements he subsequently sent out, he boldly proclaimed that

> *Eros* is the result of recent court decisions that have realistically interpreted America's obscenity laws and have given this country a new breath of freedom of expression.[43]

Ginzburg ran into trouble when a number of complaints were made to the post office by recipients of his advertisements who were highly offended both by the description of the advertised publications and by his statement that he planned to go as far as recent Supreme Court decisions allowed. He was indicted in 1963 for violation of postal regulations forbidding the mailing of obscene material. He was convicted in the Federal District Court for the Eastern District of Pennsylvania and sentenced to five years in prison and personally fined $28,000. On appeal to the United States Supreme Court, Ginzburg argued that by the standards of *Roth* none of his publications was obscene because all had at least some redeeming social value if taken as a whole. The prosecution, however, had argued that the offense, i. e., the merchandising of these materials, had to be considered in the context of the circumstances of the production, sale or publicity, even if the publications themselves, standing alone, might not have been obscene. The Court agreed, holding in effect that what Ginzburg said about his materials was as relevant as the materi-

43. Merle Miller, "Ralph Ginzburg, Middlesex, New Jersey, and the First Amendment." *New York* *Times Magazine*, April 30, 1972, p. 67.

als themselves. Justice Brennan, writing for the majority, told Ginzburg "thou sayest it":

> This evidence, . . . was relevant in determining the ultimate question of obscenity . . . . The deliberate representation of petitioners' publications as erotically arousing . . . stimulated the reader to accept them as prurient; he looks for titillation, not for saving intellectual content. . . . the circumstances of presentation and dissemination of material are equally relevant to determining whether social importance claimed for material in the courtroom was, in the circumstances, pretense or reality . . . . Where the purveyor's sole emphasis is on the sexually provocative aspects of his publications, that fact may be decisive in the determination of obscenity. . . .[44]

The Court had a new rationale. Obscenity had become a question not only of erotic materials themselves, but of the way they were merchandised. If the material was of borderline permissibility, and if the purveyor chose, in his advertising copy, to describe it in terms which, if true, might render it impermissible, the advertiser's description, rather than the material itself would form the basis for the determination of obscenity.

Poor Ginzburg! Even admirers of the Warren Court must admit that Ginzburg got less than justice from that body. Until the decision was rendered there had been no suggestion outside a concurring opinion by Chief Justice Warren alone in *Roth* that merchandising might enter into a determination of obscenity. Ginzburg was, in fact, convicted on the basis of an *ex post facto* standard. Furthermore, it is hard to escape the impression that Ginzburg was convicted not for being a purveyor of lewd materials, but for being a smart aleck. The Court seemed far less offended by the "artiness" of *Eros* than by the slip inserted in

44. *Ginzburg v. United States*, 383 U.S. 463 at 470, 86 S.Ct. 942–947, 16 L.Ed.2d 31 (1966).

each advertisement labeled "GUARANTEE" and reading "Documentary Books, Inc. [the publisher] unconditionally guarantees full refund on the price if the book fails to reach you because of United States Post Office censorship and interference."

Nevertheless, the Court had bumbled its way into a new guideline for the permissible, legitimate suppression of communication: that such suppression was justified when offensive material is inflicted on an unwilling audience through unsolicited advertising. The Court, in effect, was justifying the infringement of the publisher's civil liberties by the protection of the public's civil liberties. It was putting restrictions on those who would speak in the name of the general public's right not to have to listen. Certainly, if any restriction of the First Amendment could be made palatable to its civil libertarian defenders, this one, based on the protection of a competing civil liberty, might succeed. In fact, while the injustice to Ginzburg himself created a furor, the notion that the general public had a right not to be exposed to the "leer of the sensualist" proved quite palatable, and for a time it seemed as if the matter of obscenity regulation might be handled on the basis of tight controls on pandering and advertising, with few if any controls on private consumption. The decision in *Stanley v. Georgia*,[45] where the Supreme Court affirmed the right of an individual to show an obscene film in his own home, conformed to this principle.

The problem, however, once again lay in the application of the principle to the real world. It was easy enough for police and prosecutors to handle panderers, offensive bookstore and movie theater displays, and mailed advertising. This left, however, virtually no restriction on discreetly advertised pornography: films such as *Deep Throat,* stag movies sold in "sex boutiques," hard-core pornographic novels in plain, unadorned covers, etc. Unadvertised obscenity, in short, had ceased to be regulated, and many people objected. The result of these objections was a June 1973 Supreme Court decision relating to a group of obscenity

45.  394 U.S. 557, 89 S.Ct. 1243, 22 L.Ed.2d 542 (1969).

cases of which *Miller v. California* and *Paris Adult Theater v. Slaton,* are the best known.[46] These cases involved various situations: the mailing of unsolicited sexually explicit material in violation of state law; the showing of an allegedly obscene film to a consenting adult audience in a commercial movie theater; the importation of obscene material (8 mm. film) for the private use of the importer in violation of federal law; the knowing transportation of obscene material by common carrier in interstate commerce in violation of federal law; and the sale in an adult bookstore of a plain-covered, unillustrated book containing repetitively descriptive materials of an explicitly sexual nature.

In five lengthy, rather turgid, majority opinions written by Chief Justice Burger for the majority (over the vigorous dissents of Justices Douglas, Brennan, Stewart, and Marshall), the Court held that there was something called obscenity which is not protected by the First Amendment. The guidelines for recognizing such obscenity were essentially a stricter version of the guidelines enunciated in *Roth* and *Memoirs v. Massachusetts.**

To be considered obscene, a work taken as a whole must appeal to the prurient interest in sex; portray in a patently offensive way sexual conduct specifically defined by law; and, taken as a whole, may not have "serious" literary, artistic, political, or scientific value. Such "obscene" works may be prohibited by localities on the basis of local standards, either on general principles,

**46.** *Miller v. California,* 413 U.S. 15, 93 S.Ct. 2607, 37 L.Ed.2d 419 (1973); *Paris Adult Theatre I v. Slaton,* 413 U.S. 49, 93 S.Ct. 2628, 37 L.Ed. 2d 446 (1973); *United States v. 12 200-Ft. Reels of Super 8 MM Film,* 413 U.S. 123, 93 S.Ct. 2665, 37 L. Ed.2d 500 (1973); *United States v. Orito,* 413 U.S. 139, 93 S.Ct. 2674, 37 L.Ed.2d 513 (1973); *Kaplan v. California,* 413 U.S. 115, 93 S.Ct. 2680, 37 L.Ed.2d 492 (1973). (All decided June 21, 1973).

\* *A Book named "John Cleland's Memoirs of a Woman of Pleasure"*

*v. Massachusetts,* 383 U.S. 413, 86 S.Ct. 975, 16 L.Ed.2d 1 (1966) was the case in which the United States Supreme Court held the novel popularly known as *Fanny Hill* to be not obscene. The standards for the determination were essentially that of the *Roth* case with increased emphasis on the requirement that to be found obscene, the material in question must be found to be utterly without redeeming social value.

or because of local fear that antisocial conduct might result from the dissemination of such works. Expert testimony need not be introduced in the determination of whether the work is, in fact, obscene, nor is the burden of proof on the community to show that antisocial conduct may result from such works. If communities have widely divergent standards as to the same work, such divergence is not in and of itself a basis for a claim of First Amendment infringement.

The net result of these decisions was to revert to the *status quo ante* Ginzburg, i. e., the standards prevailing at the time of *Roth* and *Memoirs* with the added complication of varying local standards rather than one national standard. Unfortunately the problem with the *Roth-Memoirs* standard is that it runs squarely into the First Amendment. Despite the Court's semantic gymnastics, obscenity is speech.* Wishing won't make it so, and no matter how many times the Court says that pornography is nonspeech, in the real world it is speech, and its relationship to the First Amendment must be handled in as rational a manner as possible. Restrictions on other forms of speech have been legitimatized at the United States Supreme Court level in recent years by variants of the clear and present danger formula: that the speech in question will lead imminently and probably to antisocial action, usually riot or revolution. The effort of the Burger court to suggest that the states have a legitimate interest in preventing the antisocial action that might result from obscenity would, of course, be consistent with this rationale. The problem here, however, is one of proof. There is virtually no widely acceptable evidence that crime, sexual or otherwise, is a result of the "consumption" of obscene materials. The Burger opinion seeks to avoid this dilemma by suggesting that the burden of proof is on the distributor of the questioned material to show that it is *not* socially harmful. To shift the burden of proof in this manner, however, undercuts substantially the impact of the

---

* If you call a tail a leg, how many
legs has a dog? Five? No, calling
tail a leg don't *make* it a leg.
Abraham Lincoln

First Amendment.   The absolute prohibition in the wording: "Congress shall make no law   .   .   .   abridging   .   .   . freedom of speech," suggests strongly that the burden of proof must be on the government when it violates this express prohibition, and this indeed has been the interpretation of the court, *de facto* if not necessarily in theory, for at least the last two decades.

Not only have the 1973 obscenity decisions run squarely into the theoretical First Amendment problem, but the reluctance of the Court to establish a national standard, and its reversion to the specious comfort of local standards has already had a chilling effect on publication and communication in this area, and given rise to a host of practical problems as well.   In a nation where publishing and film making are nationally based commercial enterprises rather than small local businesses, such enterprises cannot be carried on when publishers and exhibitors have no way of knowing in what communities their output is legal and in what communities it is not.

The difficulty is illustrated by the prosecution in 1977 of Larry C. Flynt, the publisher of *Hustler* magazine.   *Hustler* was a "girlie" magazine, third ranking in the United States, behind *Playboy* and *Penthouse*.   Its contents were such that it could be defended virtually only on general principles: that the First Amendment protects *all* speech even the vulgar, crude, and disgusting.   It had, nevertheless, a circulation in millions.   Flynt was indicted and convicted in Hamilton County, Ohio (Cincinnati) court of pandering obscenity and engaging in organized crime.   (The latter charge was based on a routine contract between Flynt and local distributors for the distribution of the magazine.)

The case bore the earmarks of a zealous prosecutor and judge out to make an example of a particularly unlikeable publication. Flynt did not live or work in Hamilton County, nor was the magazine printed, published or distributed from there.   The organized crime charge was based on a strained interpretation of the Ohio statute which defines organized crime as "the combina-

tion of five or more participants in illegal activity for profit."
(The distributors were not brought to trial.)    The trial judge
would not allow similar magazines to be introduced as evidence
of contemporary community standards.    Flynt was sentenced to
7 to 25 years in prison and fined $10,000 on the organized crime
charge and $1,000 fine and 6 months in jail on the obscenity
charge.    He was denied bail pending appeal.[47]

If Flynt's conviction is upheld on appeal, Hamilton County,
Ohio will have dictated to the residents of New York City and
San Francisco what they may or may not read.    The net effect
will have been to force every community to the lowest common
denominator of the least tolerant and accepting community, because only at that level could a national market be assured.
This, of course, would no doubt be precisely what those who
view the dissemination of obscenity with alarm would prefer.
But the conflict with the First Amendment and the implications
for American society as a whole cannot be shrugged off lightly.
Critics have suggested that although the United States Supreme
Court sanctioned restrictions on speech relate only to explicitly
sexual materials, the rationale may well be extended to other
controversial and offensive communications.    A minor, though
perhaps, significant example of this tendency occurred in New
York City in connection with a controversy over a speaker
whose ideas were profoundly repugnant to a large section of the
metropolitan community.    Dr. William B. Shockley, a professor
of physics at Stanford University, and a Nobel Prize winner,
with very unorthodox views on genetics, was invited to speak at
Staten Island Community College in New York.    Dr. Shockley
believes that intelligence is largely inherited and that the disadvantaged place of blacks in our society is due more to heredity
than environment.    Such views understandably are highly controversial and abrasive, the more so since Dr. Shockley's expertise and professional credentials lie in the field of physics rather
than genetics.    When the invitation was announced, a sizeable

47.  *New York Times*, January 30,
1977.

group of students at the college protested vigorously, denouncing Shockley for his racist views, calling him a charlatan, his views unscientific, etc. They urged the president of the college to withdraw the invitation. One student went so far as to justify this request, which clearly was an infringement of academic freedom, by saying that since the Supreme Court had turned over the setting of moral standards to local communities in its obscenity decisions, there was no reason why localities should not set standards for local speakers.*

Perhaps it is unfair to take seriously a comment which extended a decision that the Supreme Court very specifically applied to the obscenity area only, to the area of political speech. Yet the pressure to do so is very great. If a community can determine what kind of sexually oriented communications it wish-

---

* Tom Wicker, "The Shockley Case," *New York Times*, November 16, 1973, p. 41. The invitation was not withdrawn despite student protests. When Shockley appeared, however, hecklers in the audience made it impossible for him to speak, and he withdrew without having addressed the audience.

Another spin-off of the 1973 Supreme Court obscenity rulings is a comment expressed in a letter to the editor of the *New York Times* regarding the "book-burning" in Drake, North Dakota. The Drake local school board made a determination that Kurt Vonnegut's *Slaughterhouse Five*, which had been assigned reading in the local high school, was pornographic. They removed the books from the school bodily and apparently for want of better disposal methods, burned them. This incident gave rise to considerable criticism in view of the fact that the book, which is a work of serious literary reputation, was generally not regarded as pornographic, and the burning led to some unpleasant memories of fascist performances in Nazi Germany. The letter writer took exception to the criticism of the actions of the school board by saying "I have noted your editorial comment about the so-called book burning at Drake, N. D., and while the rights of man and freedom of the press are precious, *so are the rights of a community, according to the Supreme Court, to determine what is and what is not pornographic.*" (emphasis added, December 7, 1973, p. 40.) The point is, however, that while a school board assuredly has the right to select appropriate materials for its students, the words of the First Amendment say that the *community per se has no rights in the matter of determining what any individual may or may not say.*

es to receive, why indeed should it not determine what kind of politically oriented communications it wishes to receive? The 1973 Supreme Court obscenity decisions have started us down a very dangerous path because they have ignored the central meaning of the First Amendment: *that what is to be communicated in a democratic society is not a decision for majorities to make.* The First Amendment protects minorities, meaning precisely that unpleasant, abrasive, stupid, and provocative individuals can say what they wish without the approval of the communities of which they are a part. Though the Court would like, through semantic sleight of hand, to say that obscenity is not communication and therefore the rules don't apply, in the real world and in the public mind, the transition between obscene communications and other undesirable types of speech is logical and easy. The price of suppressing *Deep Throat* or *Hustler* very possibly is the suppression of Dr. Shockley, and after Dr. Shockley, George Wallace, George McGovern, and eventually anyone else who does not please the ruling establishment.

The regulation of obscenity has a certain superficial attractiveness to those who see such regulation as a way of elevating the moral tone of society at very little social cost. The social cost is greater than appears at first blush, and the effects of such regulation are complex and far-reaching. Obscene communications—books, films, pictures, plays, or whatever—are highly distasteful to many, perhaps to most people of the United States. Many others overtly or covertly enjoy such communications. Certainly, those who find such material offensive can and should be protected against having those materials inflicted upon them. The attempts to limit "pandering" are a proper and legitimate way of protecting those who don't want to see or hear erotic presentations. In addition, if the consumption of the obscene or pornographic does indeed lead to antisocial action—crime or sexual deviance—then it should be regulated to the extent necessary to prevent such social deviance. Before this can be done, however, respectable, honest research must be done to ascertain the impact on the public at large, or special publics, such as juveniles, of such materials. If such undesirable impact can be shown, then reasonable regulation will be relatively easy to frame. The gravamen of this approach should be not to define what many people consider poor taste, but to determine that which is demonstrably and measurably socially harmful in the sense of causing aberrant behavior. The burden of proof of demonstrating that such impact exists, however, must be on the regulating authority.

Freedom for obscene speech (to willing listeners) does not mean, however, that sexually-oriented *conduct* is protected by the First Amendment. Certainly, solicitation on the street by prostitutes of unwilling persons could be forbidden on the same basis as the pandering of sexual literature to the public at large. Adult bookstores, peep-shows, sex "boutiques" and topless and bottomless bars, however, present more complex problems. While offensive advertising can be forbidden, does the First Amendment protect the establishments themselves? Civil libertarians argue that "adult" bookstores and topless bars are simply the vulgar equivalent of libraries and the ballet. Outraged citizens point to the deterioration of those urban areas where sex establishments proliferate, and to the connection between crime and commercialized sex.

Probably both views are correct. A recent approach to the problem of controlling neighborhood decay without restricting freedom of expression has been attempts to use municipal zoning laws to control sex establishments. Boston, in a variant of the "red light" district prevalent in European cities, zoned all its "adult" businesses into one downtown area. Detroit, on the other hand, zoned such establishments so as to disperse them widely throughout the city, preventing their concentration in one area, much as liquor stores are zoned in many cities. The Boston plan, whose constitutionality has not been tested, seems to have led to a marked upsurge in crime. The Detroit plan, however, was upheld by the United States Supreme Court, and so far appears to be moderately successful.[48] New York City currently is considering a variant of the Detroit plan to aid in the rehabilita-

48. *New York Times*, January 30, 1977, Section 4, p. 7.

tion of the Times Square area and prevent the spread of "adult" entertainment into residential areas of Manhattan.

Certainly municipalities have the power to use zoning to limit and regulate offensive industries, and much of the public would so define sex establishments. Yet there are important First Amendment considerations which zoning cannot be permitted to subvert. The experience of the Scandinavian countries where pornography has been legalized successfully, suggests that emphasis should be placed on making sexual establishments both legal and discreet—to permit adults to express themselves sexually as long as such expressions is private, confined to adults, and does not involve third parties as unwilling spectators.

Chapter III

## THE FIRST AMENDMENT: FREEDOM OF RELIGION

"If there were one religion in England, its depotism would be terrible; if there were only two, they would destroy each other; but there are thirty, and therefore they live in peace and happiness."

Voltaire

"As to religion, I hold it to be the indispensible duty of government to protect all conscientious professors thereof, and I know of no other business which government hath to do therewith."

Thomas Paine, *Common Sense*

"I cannot give up my guidance to the magistrate, because he knows no more of the way to heaven than I do, and is less concerned to direct me right than I am to go right."

Thomas Jefferson,
*Notes on Religion*

In the matter of church-state relations, the United States has been singularly fortunate. From the beginning of its national existence there has been general agreement by Americans that church and state be separated—that religion remain in that realm which government may not enter. Compared to Europe's history of religious wars and persecution, American religious problems have been relatively minor and few in number.

It may seem remarkable that religious zealots such as the Puritans, having staked their claim to a perilous new Zion, should have come to tolerate other sects and even nonbelievers in their midst. In the early days, dissenters like Roger Williams and

86

Anne Hutchinson were forced to leave the Massachusetts Bay Colony. Yet the fact remains that while the colonial period saw the existence of established churches and legally mandated religious observance, by the time of the adoption of the Constitution, there was little disagreement on the principle of separation of church and state (for the national government at least). The very first words of the Bill of Rights were "Congress shall make no law respecting the establishment of religion or prohibiting the free exercise thereof."

This remarkable development occurred for a whole complex of reasons.[1] Probably the most obvious and the most important of these is that the existing multiplicity of sects, as a practical matter, led to mutual toleration. Although there were few Catholics (outside of Maryland) and even fewer Jews in colonial America, there were literally dozens of Protestant groups: Quakers, Mennonites, Moravians, Lutherans, Presbyterians, Baptists, Anglicans, to mention just a few. Not only, moreover, were there a great number of religious groups, but the importance of formal church affiliation declined steadily and was astonishingly low at the time of the Revolution. Leo Pfeffer, probably the leading American scholar on church-state relations, suggests that the best estimate of church affiliation in 1776 was about 4 percent as compared to over 60 percent in the mid-1960's.[2] The growing importance of commerce in the colonies also tended to divert attention from religious matters to more secular concerns. Concern about religious practice was detrimental to establishing trade or business relationships, and the practical minded colonists opted for enhancement of commerce rather than propagation of a true faith.

The American Revolution, moreover, coincided with the mid-eighteenth century religious phenomenon known as the Great

1. For an excellent discussion of the history of church-state relations in the United States, see Leo Pfeffer, *Church, State and Freedom*, revised edition, Boston: Beacon Press, 1967.

2. Pfeffer, *Church, State, and Freedom*, p. 95.

Awakening.  This was a movement which saw the growth and
increasing popularity of evangelical proselytizing sects which
laid emphasis on personal religious participation.  These movements were frequently antagonistic to the older established
church hierarchies, and members of such sects resented government support for the church groups from which they had recently branched off.  Many members of these newer sects lived on
the frontier and were outraged by laws compelling them to pay
taxes for the support of churches and ministers that were not
only unpalatable to them, but inaccessible as well.  For such individuals the solution was obvious: separation of church and
state.  If the state neither protected nor supported any religious
sect, all would be free to grow in proportion to their acceptability to the public.

In addition to strong sentiment at the time of the Constitutional Convention for mutual toleration by the various sects,
there was also considerable support for a much more radical notion: freedom for non-religion.  Not only should Americans be
free to choose among the veritable smorgasbord of religious dog-
mas that were available, but they ought to be free to choose no
religion at all, to be non-believers.  This remarkably modern
concept was related directly to the Lockean ideas which were so
popular in the colonies: that the purpose of government was the
protection of private natural rights—life, liberty and property.
Beyond the protection of those rights, government had no authority.  Religion fell in the area that was prohibited to government.  Thus, the Baptists memorialized the Continental Congress in 1774:

> The care of souls cannot belong to the civil magistrate,
> because his power consists only in outward force; but
> pure and saving religion consists in the inward persua-
> sion of the mind without which nothing can be accepta-
> ble to God.[3]

3.  As quoted in Pfeffer, p. 102.

Atheism and renunciation of a belief in God were probably socially unacceptable doctrines at the time of the American Revolution. Yet, the desire for limited government was so strong that freedom for non-belief was a price many were willing to pay.

The consensus as to the need for separation of church and state applied initially only to the new national government brought into being by the Constitution. At the time of the Revolution, church and state were not separated in any of the individual colonies. However, within a relatively short time, a strong movement developed toward the disestablishment of dominant churches, and the removal of religious restrictions on office holding and voting. In Virginia, for example, as late as 1776 laws provided for compulsory attendance at Anglican services, tax assessments for the support of Anglican ministers, punishment of dissenting preachers and believers, etc. By 1786, however, all of these privileges and penalties had been removed, the last of them by Jefferson's Bill for Establishing Religious Freedom, part of which read:

> Be it therefore enacted   .   .   .   that no man shall be compelled to frequent or support any religious worship, place or ministry whatsoever, nor shall be enforced, restrained, molested or burdened in his body or goods, nor shall otherwise suffer on account of his religious opinions or beliefs, but that all men shall be free to profess, and by argument to maintain, their opinions in matters of religion, and that the same shall in no wise diminish, enlarge or affect their civil capacities.[4]

Virginia was the most liberal of the states; only she and Rhode Island granted full freedom of religion at the time of the Revolution. All the other states to some extent demanded public support for religion and imposed civil penalties for religious reasons. Yet, many of the demands were minimal compared to the total intertwining of church and state prevalent a century

---

4.  As quoted in Pfeffer, p. 114.

earlier.  Seven of the states, for example, excluded ministers from certain types of public offices;  eight of them required assent to belief in Christianity or heaven or hell or the divine inspiration of the Bible.  Ultimately all of these statutory supports for religion were to wither away, though not before the Jacksonian period.

Although the Constitution did not require it,* new states which came into the union after the Revolution invariably came in with either constitutional or statutory mandatory separation of church and state, despite the fact that according to Pfeffer many of these states were homogeneous in religion and were settled by deeply religious people.  The separation of church and state stemmed from the strong underlying agreement that religion should be beyond the reach of civil government as an unregulated area of private conduct.  This belief, still strongly dominant in the United States, historically has led to great reluctance on the part of the courts to become involved in controversies which present religious questions.  Consider, for example, the intriguing case of *United States v. Ballard*.[5]

Early in the 1940's, Guy W., Edna W. and Donald Ballard organized the "I Am" religion.  The Ballards maintained that they had supernatural powers to heal the sick, and that they had in fact cured hundreds of persons.  Guy Ballard also claimed that he had been selected as a divine messenger, and was a kind of reincarnation of St. Germain, Jesus, and George Washington, all of whom had dictated messages to him to be propagated by the I Am movement.  The Ballards claimed finally, that Jesus had appeared before them and had shaken hands with them.  When the Ballards used the United States mail to solicit money for their I Am religion, the federal government, in a sadly skeptical mood, indicted the Ballards for using the mails to defraud.

---

* The Bill of Rights, including the First Amendment, applied only to the national government.  Only after the adoption of the Fourteenth Amendment were some provisions of the Bill of Rights held to be applicable to the states.

5.  322 U.S. 78, 64 S.Ct. 882, 88 L. Ed.2d 1148 (1944).

At the trial, the presiding judge instructed the jury that they should decide, not whether the statements that the Ballards had made in regard to their religion were true, but whether the Ballards believed them to be true. The Ballards were convicted and appealed to the Federal Court of Appeals which held the judge's instructions to have been erroneous: the jury should have considered the truth or falsity of the claims. The case was then appealed to the United States Supreme Court which affirmed the convictions.

The case itself is interesting, not so much for the fertility of the Ballards' imagination, as for the diversity of views expressed in the justices' opinions on the proper relationship between religious belief and secular authority. Justice Douglas, writing for the majority, agreed with the instructions of the trial judge. The jury, he said, was incompetent to decide the truth of a religious belief. Certainly, no jury could pass on the authenticity of the miracle at Lourdes or the divine origins of the Torah.

> .　.　. Men may believe what they cannot prove.
> .　.　. The miracles of the New Testament, the Divinity of Christ, life after death, the power of prayer are deep in the religious convictions of many. If one could be sent to jail because a jury in a hostile environment found those teachings false, little indeed would be left of religious freedom. .　.　. [6]

Chief Justice Stone disagreed with Douglas' views. He felt that a jury should not be precluded from determining the truth or falsity of Ballard's statements. After all, he reasoned, if Ballard claimed that he had, in fact, shaken hands with St. Germain in San Francisco, and the government could prove that Ballard had never been in San Francisco, why should not the jury be permitted to take cognizance of those facts in determining whether Ballard's money raising constituted fraud?

Justice Jackson also disagreed with Douglas. In a powerful and provocative dissent, he argued that the entire case should

6.　Ibid., at 86–87.

have been dismissed;  that the government had no right to challenge either Ballard's beliefs or the sincerity with which those beliefs were held.  Not only was no jury competent to pass on another person's spiritual experiences, but the principle of separation of church and state—the notion that government had no right to intrude itself into what is quintessentially a private matter—should not be sacrificed even in the interest of preventing fraud.

> The chief wrong which false prophets do to their following is not financial.  The collections aggregate a tempting total, but individual payments are not ruinous.  I doubt if the vigilance of the law is equal to making money stick by over-credulous people.  But the real harm is on the mental or spiritual plane  .  .  . .  The wrong of these things, as I see it, is not in the money the victims part with half so much as in the mental and spiritual poison they get.  But that is precisely the thing the Constitution put beyond the reach of the prosecutor, for the *price of freedom of religion or of speech or of the press is that we must put up with, and even pay for, a good deal of rubbish.*  (emphasis added) [7]

Justice Jackson's view was a minority one, and the Ballard case is perhaps *sui generis*.  Nevertheless, the overriding principle of American political life has been one of government non-interference with religion.  This principle, however, has been challenged at times during the past two hundred years.  Despite the firmness of consensus on the separation of church and state, there have been constitutional problems in this area primarily of two kinds:  (1) where religious practices have been in some way inimical to important needs or values of the dominant secular society, as for example, the conflict with the Mormons over polygamy, or the claim of conscientious objectors to exemption from military duty;  and (2) where particular religious groups

---

7.  Ibid., at 94–95.

have attempted to utilize the power of the state to further their own religious purposes, as for example, requests for aid to parochial schools or released time from the public schools for religious instruction.

Both these kinds of conflicts have been endemic throughout American history although church-state issues generally have not been as important or as bitterly contested as issues in other areas such as free speech, or economic regulation, or criminal procedure. They wax and wane with the militancy of religious groups and the social and political context in which these groups find themselves. The end of the Viet Nam war and the concomitant decline of the conscientious objector issue, the public tolerance of unorthodox religious preaching, and the ecumenical movement among the dominant religions have all contributed to the current decline in church-state controversy. Outside of an ongoing effort to obtain public support for the parochial schools, and intermittent grumbling over the prohibition of prayers in the public schools, there are virtually no religious issues in the public forum today. There is, of course, strong feeling over the United States Supreme Court decision legalizing abortion, and the leadership of the "pro-life forces" has been drawn largely from the Catholic Church. Nevertheless, the abortion controversy is not, strictly speaking, a church-state issue. Opponents of the Supreme Court ruling have made their objections as Americans, not as Catholics, and their objections are based not on Catholic teachings but on what they see as universal moral law applicable to all. Abortion, and other moral issues such as gambling, birth control, obscenity and pornography, divorce and homosexuality have drawn opponents and defenders disproportionately from one religious group or another. These morals controversies, however, are not based on the claims of a particular church for protection or preference, nor do they involve religious observance such as prayer. They, therefore, do not fit into the context of a discussion of First Amendment religious rights, though in fact the public perceives them, sometimes quite realistically, as religious controversies.

*Freedom of Religion: The Free Exercise Clause*

In the United States, when church and state clash because individuals wish to do something in the name of religion that is questionable under secular law, the ensuing litigation frequently calls into question the "Free Exercise Clause" of the First Amendment. "Congress shall make no law respecting an establishment of religion, or prohibiting the free exercise thereof; . . . ." The phraseology of the First Amendment suggests that the authors intended that the government should neither compel nor prohibit religious observance, neither promote nor forbid religious practice or institutions. What is not clear, however, is the extent to which the state may prohibit acts which are religiously motivated. Can conduct which is required by one's religion be constitutionally prohibited under the First Amendment?

The courts have quite definitely taken the position that the government can indeed prohibit actions taken in the name of religion that violate statutory law. Perhaps the best known case of this type is *Reynolds v. United States* [8] in which Reynolds, a Mormon, having been convicted of bigamy for having knowingly married a second time while his first marriage was in force, appealed his conviction to the United States Supreme Court, contending that polygamy was required by his religion, and that to punish him would be to deny him the free exercise of his religion. The Court had little difficulty in disposing of Reynolds' claim. The First Amendment, declared the Court, guaranteed freedom of conscience and freedom of thought, but did not extend to the whole range of actions which individuals might undertake in the name of religion.

> . . . Laws are made for the government of actions, and while they cannot interfere with mere religious belief and opinions, they may with practices. Suppose one believed that human sacrifice were a necessary part of religious worship, would it be seriously

8. 98 U.S. 145, 25 L.Ed. 244 (1879).

contended that the civil government under which he lived could not interfere to prevent a sacrifice? Or if a wife religiously believed it was her duty to burn herself upon the funeral pile of her dead husband, would it be beyond the power of the civil government to prevent her carrying her belief into practice?

So here, as a law  .   .   . it is provided that plural marriages shall not be allowed. Can a man excuse his practices to the contrary because of his religious belief? To permit this would be to make the professed doctrines of religious belief superior to the law of the land, and in effect to permit every citizen to become a law unto himself. Government could exist only in name under such circumstances.[9]

While most people would find quite acceptable the notion that Mormons should not be permitted to practice polygamy in the name of religion, the Court's confident declaration that the professed doctrines of religion cannot be superior to the law of the land raises several problems. For one thing, while the distinction between freedom of thought and freedom of action is useful and essential, it is ambiguous. Religions command one not only to think and believe, but also to do. All religions require certain actions on the part of their adherents as well as certain beliefs. While most of these beliefs do not fall afoul of secular law, some do, and to simply state grandly as the Court did in *Reynolds* that the criminal law is always superior to religious practice is, to some extent, to ignore the mandate of the First Amendment. Clearly, some differentiation must take place. Sometimes religious practice must give way to civil law, and sometimes the law must dominate religious practice. The problem, as always, is where to draw the line.

Some issues have been disposed of with relatively little political controversy. The polygamy decision was eminently satisfactory to everyone except the Mormons, a group too small in num-

9.   Ibid., at 166–167.

bers and too lacking in allies to dispute the decision in the public forum. In similar fashion the Court has forbidden the handling of dangerous snakes as part of religious observance. Regulations involving health and welfare generally have been upheld when they conflict with religious practice, especially when the health and welfare of a child is involved: * laws requiring vaccination of school children have been sustained over the religious objections of parents, and blood transfusions have been ordered for the children of Jehovah's Witnesses who object on principle to such transfusions. (There has been no United States Supreme Court review of the permissibility of compelling an *adult* Jehovah's Witness to receive a life saving blood transfusion, and the lower courts have been divided in their opinions.)

Other free exercise claims have caused the Court considerable anguish, however. Consider the case of the children of Walter Gobitis, a Jehovah's Witness, who refused to salute the flag in their public school as required by law, because their religion viewed the flag salute as a forbidden form of idol worship. When his children were expelled for their recalcitrance, Gobitis applied to the Federal District Court for an injunction against the enforcement of the expulsion order claiming that their ac-

---

* An exception to this rule was *Wisconsin v. Yoder*, 406 U.S. 205, 92 S.Ct. 1526, 32 L.Ed.2d 15 (1972), in which members of the Amish Church won the right to refuse to comply with the Wisconsin State Education Law which compelled children to attend school through age 16. The Amish contended that education past the eighth grade (age 14) was undesirable because it exposed their children to worldly values and otherwise interfered with their socialization into the parochial agricultural world of the Amish. To force Amish children into the high schools thus was an interference with the free exercise of the parents' religion. Wisconsin, however, claimed that a secular law regulating the welfare of all children in the state could not be held to violate the First Amendment. The Court agreed with the Amish, reasoning that the Amish community had been successful in providing a peaceful orderly way of life for its members, and the State had failed to show how the extra two years of schooling demanded was of more benefit to the children involved than the informal vocational education they would receive during the same time period on their family farms.

tion was based on religious practice, and could not be challenged by a public official. The District Court judge granted the injunction, and on appeal the Court of Appeals affirmed the ruling of the lower court. When the case arrived at the United States Supreme Court, much to the dismay of civil libertarian groups and many segments of the legal community, the high court held, in an 8–1 decision, that it was not unreasonable for the school board to require students to salute the flag and that the Court, therefore, could not set aside a valid local regulation:

> . . . The religious liberty which the Constitution protects has never excluded legislation of general scope not directed against doctrinal loyalties of particular sects. . . . [10]

Justice Frankfurter, for the majority, recognized the importance of the protections of the First Amendment but felt that the appropriate role of the judiciary was to defer to the will of popular majorities as expressed by the elected branches of government. Only Justice Stone dissented, pointing out that to force a patriotic observance on an unwilling child was hardly conducive to promoting feelings of love or loyalty for the government.

The reaction of the legal community to the *Gobitis* decision was uniformly unfavorable, and civil libertarians joined with religious leaders of other faiths in condemning it. Worse yet, the decision was followed by a wave of violence against the Witnesses in which local mobs beat, kidnapped, tortured and maimed members of the sect. The flag salute issue was apparently the precipitating factor in the violence. In any case, three years later the Court accepted for review another case raising precisely the same issue. Walter Barnette applied to the Federal District Court in West Virginia for an injunction to prevent the West Virginia Board of Education from expelling his children following their refusal to salute the flag. This time, in a 6–3 de-

10. *Minersville School Dist. v. Gobitis*, 310 U.S. 586 at 594, 60 S.Ct. 1010, 84 L.Ed. 1375 (1940).

cision written by Justice Jackson, the Court upheld the claims previously denied in *Gobitis*.[11]  To Justice Frankfurter's argument that the Court ought to defer to the judgment of the elected branches of government, Justice Jackson responded:

> The very purpose of a Bill of Rights was to withdraw certain subjects from the vicissitudes of political controversy, to place them beyond the reach of majorities and officials and to establish them as legal principles to be applied by the courts.  One's right to life, liberty, and property, to free speech, a free press, freedom of worship and assembly, and other fundamental rights may not be submitted to vote; they depend on the outcome of no elections.[12]

The Barnette children had a right to refuse to utter sentiments which they did not share, and this right was theirs even if religion were not the motive for their refusal to participate in the school exercises.

> .  .  .  To sustain the compulsory flag salute we are required to say that a Bill of Rights which guards the individual's right to speak his own mind, left it open to public authorities to compel him to utter what is not in his mind.
>
> Nor does the issue as we see it turn on one's possession of particular religious views  .  .  .  many citizens who do not share these religious views hold such a compulsory rite to infringe constitutional liberty of the individual.  .  .  .[13]

Jackson went on to deliver a spirited defense of civil liberties in a free society: a nation's security and its unity must be achieved by faith that comes from within each citizen rather than from conformity that is imposed externally.  The attempt

---

11. *West Virginia State Bd. of Educ. v. Barnette*, 319 U.S. 624, 63 S.Ct. 1178, 87 L.Ed. 1628 (1943).

12. Ibid., at 638.

13. Ibid., at 634–635.

to coerce loyalty may be motivated by a sincere and honest effort to preserve a government that those in power perceive as beneficent. It must end, however, in violence and tyranny.

.   .   . Those who begin coercive elimination of dissent soon find themselves exterminating dissenters. Compulsory unification of opinion achieves only the unanimity of the graveyard.

.   .   . the First Amendment to our Constitution was designed to avoid these ends by avoiding these beginnings.   .   .   .[14]

It is not a denigration of the importance of the Barnette decision to say that, in a nation which endured the bitterness, alienation and violent criticism of the government engendered first by American participation in the war in Viet Nam, and later by Watergate, it seems almost quaint that only thirty years ago, the refusal of a handful of children to salute the flag should have caused such concern. This is especially true, since the Free Exercise claim that emerged during the Viet Nam period was a much more serious one: the right of an individual to refuse, on grounds of conscience, to participate in a war he regarded as immoral.

The problem of conscientious objectors came to national attention during World War I with the passage of the Selective Service Law of 1917. In passing this act, Congress made specific provision for the exemption of those whose religious scruples prevented their bearing arms. Such exemption was constitutionally necessary if such individuals were to be freed from the obligations of combatant service, since the United States Supreme Court has stated quite clearly that the First Amendment in and of itself does not forbid the drafting of men whose religion opposes warfare.

.   .   . The conscientious objector is relieved from obligation to bear arms in obedience to no constitution-

14.   Ibid., at 641.

al provision, express or implied; but because, and only because, it has accorded with the policy of Congress thus to relieve him. . . .[15]

Not only may the government draft men in wartime, it may draft them in peacetime as well, or require them to undergo compulsory training as part of the educational process. Thus, when Albert Hamilton refused on religious grounds to participate in the compulsory military drill required of all students at the University of California, the United States Supreme Court upheld the right of the state to expel him for his refusal.[16] The inadequacy of the Constitution to protect conscientious objectors has never been squarely tested, because Congress has always provided for their exemption in each selective service law. While these statutory exemptions worked reasonably well during World Wars I and II, some difficulties developed during the Viet Nam War, one of the most unpopular military actions in American history.

There have been basically two problems relating to exemptions: (1) whether conscientious objector exemptions can be granted constitutionally on religious grounds only, or whether they must also be extended to those whose principles derive from non-theistic beliefs or moral systems; and (2) how to distinguish between those whose claims of conscience are *bona fide,* and those who merely wish to avoid the unpleasantness of military service. Obviously, the second problem is closely related to the first. If conscientious objector status could be reserved for members in good standing of religious sects which espouse non-violence, then the problem of whose claim is *bona fide* is relatively simple to resolve. On the other hand, if the claim is to be permitted not only for religious groups that are non-pacifist in nature, but also for individuals who belong to no group at all but simply claim a general right of freedom of conscience, then the

15. *United States v. Macintosh,* 283 U.S. 605 at 623, 51 S.Ct. 570, 574–575, 75 L.Ed. 1302 (1931).

16. *Hamilton v. Regents of the Univ. of California,* 293 U.S. 245, 55 S.Ct. 197, 79 L.Ed. 343 (1934).

problem of distinguishing the sincere individual from the malingerer becomes overwhelming.

A further complication was introduced during the Viet Nam conflict by men who asserted objection not to all wars, but only to that war which they viewed as immoral. To have rejected such claims out of hand was difficult, at least theoretically, since the United States at Nuremberg had taken the position that the Nazi defendants had had an obligation to refuse to commit immoral acts even when commanded to do so by a legal order of the established government. This accorded with democratic theory, which, like most religions, assumes the existence of a moral law higher than the secular law of the state, and the right and duty of individuals to refuse to commit acts they perceive as morally wrong. The Courts recognized this assumption in convicting Lt. Calley of atrocities in Viet Nam—acts he claimed were performed pursuant to an order from his superiors. Since the Viet Nam action was extremely unpopular, especially after conscription began to affect large numbers of young middle-class men, to have permitted each individual to decide for himself whether he approved of the war would have been impossible. Further, democracy also presupposes that majorities make rules for the governing of the country and disaffected minorities must accept the will of the majority under normal circumstances. Were this not so, anarchy would result. The exception to this rule, of course, is in those areas of civil liberties and civil rights specified by the Constitution in the Bill of Rights. Thus, the question came full circle: under what circumstances did the First Amendment of the United States protect an individual who refused to bear arms in the service of his country?

The principal selective service acts of this century were the Selective Service Acts of 1917 and 1940, both of which made provision for conscientious objectors. The earlier act, however, extended exemption on the basis of membership in a recognized church with established pacifist beliefs; the later act extended the exemption to potential draftees who were not necessarily church members, but whose scruples were based on "religious

Ch. 3

training and belief." The 1940 statute, which was reenacted in
1948 and 1951, was the statute which governed the recruitment
of personnel for the armed forces during the Viet Nam War. In
1965 three young men applied for conscientious objector status
under the 1951 statute which granted such status to "persons
who by reason of religious training and belief are conscientiously opposed to any participation in war." The statute went on to
define "religious training and belief" as:

> Religious training and belief in this connection means
> an individual belief in a relation to a Supreme Being in-
> volving duties superior to those arising from any hu-
> man relation, but does not include essentially political,
> sociological or philosophical views, or a merely personal
> moral code.[17]

Daniel A. Seeger, Arno S. Jakobson, and Forrest B. Peter
claimed to be conscientious objectors but refused to acknowledge
an explicit belief in the existence of a Supreme Being. Seeger
said that he was conscientiously opposed to participation in war
because of his "religious" beliefs, but he refused to answer "yes"
or "no" to the question relating to his belief in a Supreme Being.
Jakobson indicated that he believed in a Supreme Being who
was the "Creator of Man" and the "Supreme Reality" of which
"the existence of man is the result." His "most important religious law" was that "no man ought ever to willfully sacrifice another man's life as a means to any other end . . ." Peter
refused to respond to questions about his belief in a Supreme
Being by saying that it depended on the definition of the term.
He believed in Reverend John Haynes Holmes' definition of religion as "the consciousness of some power manifest in nature
which helped man in the ordering of his life in harmony with its
demands . . ." Peter added that he supposed "you could
call that a belief in a Supreme Being or God. These just do not
happen to be the words I use." [18]

17.  50 U.S.C.A.App. § 456(j).

18.  *United States v. Seeger*, 380 U.S.
163, 85 S.Ct. 850, 13 L.Ed.2d 733
(1965).

The question presented to the Court was whether Seeger, Jakobson, and Peter's objections to service were based on "religious training or belief" or were unacceptable because they were "essentially political, sociological or philosophical views or a merely personal code." The Court decided unanimously that Seeger, Jakobson and Peter's beliefs were "parallel" to religious beliefs, i. e., that their notions of morality occupied the same place in their lives as did religion in the lives of others. The Court declined to confine conscientious objector status to those affiliated with established pacifist churches or even to those affiliated with recognized, organized sects, conceding that moral beliefs could be strongly held yet not derive from formal religious affiliation.

> . . . We believe that . . . the test of belief "in relation to a Supreme Being" is whether a given belief that is sincere and meaningful occupies a place in the life of its possessor parallel to that filled by the orthodox belief in God of one who clearly qualifies for the exemption. . . .[19]

The Court did attempt to salvage something of the distinction which Congress tried to make between religious belief and a "merely personal moral code."

> . . . We also pause to take note of what is not involved in this litigation. No party claims to be an atheist or attacks the statute on this ground. . . .

> . . . The use by Congress of the words "merely personal" seems to us to restrict the exception to a moral code which is not only personal but which is the sole basis for the registrant's belief and is in no way related to a Supreme Being. . . .

> . . . The statute does not distinguish between externally and internally derived beliefs. Such a determination would . . . prove impossible . . .

19. Ibid., at 165–166.

and we have found that Congress intended no such distinction.[20]

The Seeger decision avoided the potential pitfall for the Court of having to decide what is and what is not a religion, or of having to establish distinctions among religious beliefs as to which qualified for the conferral of conscientious objector status. It raised, however, some very practical problems, since it became, at least in the eyes of those who favored compulsory military service for as many young men as possible, and all too easy out for would-be draft evaders. To placate critics, Congress, in the 1967 amendments to the Selective Service Act, reiterated the distinction between religious and merely personal beliefs as a requirement for conscientious objector status:

> Religious training and belief does not include essentially political and sociological and philosophical views, or a merely personal code.[21]

Despite this, however, the Court continued to be generous in its interpretation of what constituted religious rather than personal moral convictions, as evidenced by the *Welsh* case.

In 1964 Elliott A. Welsh had requested conscientious objector status but had crossed out the words "religious training" on his application. His request had been denied at all administrative levels of the Selective Service System for lack of proof of religious basis for his ideas. Welsh, indicating that he believed "the taking of life—anyone's life—to be morally wrong" ultimately had refused induction and had been sentenced to a three year prison term. On appeal, the United States Supreme Court in a 5–3 decision, reversed Welsh's conviction.

In an opinion written by Justice Black, the Court, while recognizing that the Selective Service Act required a religious basis for conscientious objector exemption, indicated that some personal beliefs could be held so strongly as to take on the quality

20.  Ibid., at 173, 186.

21.  Military Selective Service Act of 1967, § 6(j), 50 U.S.C.A.App. § 456(j).

of religious beliefs. Pointing out the parallel to the *Seeger* case where both Seeger and Welsh strongly believed that killing in war was wrong, unethical and immoral, but where both felt they could neither definitely affirm or deny a belief in a Supreme Being, the Court noted:

> . . . Their objection to participating in war in any form could not be said to come from a "still, soft voice of conscience"; rather, for them that voice was so loud and insistent that both men preferred to go to jail rather than serve in the Armed Forces. There was never any question about the sincerity and depth of [their] convictions . . . but in both cases the Selective Service System concluded that the beliefs of these men were in some sense insufficiently "religious" to qualify them for conscientious objector exemptions under the terms of § 6(j). . . .[22]

Thus the Court concluded that despite the fact that Welsh himself in the course of the litigation had specifically denied that his objection to war was predicated on religious belief, Welsh was entitled to conscientious objector status because

> . . . very few registrants are fully award of the broad scope of the word "religious" as used in § 6(j)
>
> . . .
>
> . . . That section exempts from military service all those whose consciences, spurred by deeply held moral, ethical, or religious beliefs, would give them no rest or peace if they allowed themselves to become part of an instrument of war.[23]

Justices Douglas, Brennan and Marshall joined in Black's opinion, but Harlan concurred only in the result. Appalled by what he saw as a perverse interpretation of 6(j), Harlan accused

22. *Welsh v. United States*, 398 U.S.     23. Ibid., at 341, 344.
333 at 337, 90 S.Ct. 1792–1795, 26
L.Ed.2d 208 (1970).

his brethren of having performed a lobotomy on the Congressional statute. It was quite clear to him, he declared, that Congress intended to restrict the granting of conscientious objector status to those who followed a theistic religion, and meant to exclude precisely those individuals like Welsh, whose beliefs stemmed from a personal moral system of belief. To interpret section 6(j) in any other manner was to fly in the face of its plain meaning. That however, was the problem. If 6(j) were interpreted as he, Harlan, thought it should be, i. e., as giving conscientious objector status to religious believers and denying it to the nonbelievers, then the statute would be unconstitutional as a violation of the Establishment Clause, in that it conferred benefits on the religious which were denied to the nonreligious.

The constitutional question that must be faced in this case is whether a statute that defers to the individual's conscience only when his views emanate from adherence to theistic religious beliefs is within the power of Congress. Congress, of course, could, entirely consistently with the requirements of the Constitution, eliminate *all* exemptions for conscientious objectors. . . . However, having chosen to exempt, it cannot draw the line between theistic or non-theistic religious beliefs on the one hand and secular beliefs on the other. . . .

. . . [The statute] not only accords a preference to the "religious" but also disadvantages adherents of religions that do not worship a Supreme Being. The constitutional infirmity cannot be cured, moreover, even by an impermissible construction that eliminates the theistic requirement and simply draws the line between religious and nonreligious. This in my view offends the Establishment Clause . . . [24]

Under the circumstances, Harlan concluded regretfully, he would have to vote to uphold Welsh's claim to avoid the painful neces-

24.   Ibid., at 356–357.

sity of striking down 6(j) altogether as a violation of the Establishment Clause.

Justices White, Burger, and Stewart shared Harlan's distaste for the statutory interpretation expressed in the Black opinion. They, however, did not share his reservations about the constitutionality of 6(j) if it indeed conferred benefits on the religious which it withheld from the nonreligious. They dissented, indicating that they would have permitted Welsh's conviction to stand. In the first place, they argued, if Congress *had* conferred the benefit of conscientious objector status only on those with religious affiliations or beliefs, then Welsh himself had no standing to sue inasmuch as by his own declaration his desire to avoid military service did not stem from religious belief.

> . . . for as long as Welsh is among those from whom Congress expressly withheld the exemption, he has no standing to raise the establishment issue . . .[25]

But, even if Welsh did have standing to sue, his conviction should be upheld because Congress clearly intended that those whose objections were moral but nonreligious should be denied exemption. Such a statutory distinction, moreover, did not offend the Establishment Clause for at least two reasons. Religious conscientious objectors may have been exempted because Congress felt that they would be of little value in combat. Their exemptions thus, would be on purely practical grounds, with no intent to further the cause of religion. In the absence of such intent there could be no violation of the Establishment Clause. Secondly, to force religious conscientious objectors to serve might violate the Free Exercise Clause, or at least create grave problems in that respect. The dissenters went on to explain why despite previous opinion that the Free Exercise Clause did not mandate the establishment of conscientious objector exemption, Congress' failure to do so might well be considered a violation of the Free Exercise Clause.

25.   Ibid., at 368.

*Welsh,* for the majority at least, was a problem in how far Congress could go in protecting freedom of conscience under the Free Exercise Clause, without, at the same time, establishing religion in preference to nonreligion.  For the dissenters, and for the country as a whole, however, *Welsh* presented a very different problem: the demands the government might make on citizens in the interest of national defense.  The outcome of the case could not be such that the military needs of the country would be unduly hampered.  It is perhaps for that reason that the next conscientious objector cases to come to the Court, *Gillette v. United States* and *Negre v. Larsen* [26] were decided in a manner sharply at variance with *Welsh.*  Gillette was convicted of willful failure to report for induction into the armed forces.  He had indicated his willingness to participate in a war defending the United States, or in a United Nations peace-keeping operation, but he had refused to participate in the Viet Nam War because he felt it was "unjust  .  .  .  based on a humanist approach to religion  .  .  ." [27]  Negre, a devout Catholic, had tried to obtain his discharge from the United States Army after having completed basic training and having been ordered to Viet Nam.  He believed it his duty as a faithful Catholic to discriminate between "just and unjust wars."  Both petitioners claimed a right to conscientious objector status under the provisions of Section 6(j).  The Court accepted, without question, the sincerity of both Gillette and Negre's beliefs, but held that such scruples, in order to fall under the protection of 6(j), must relate to participation in any war and all wars.

Justice Marshall, writing for the majority, held that under any reading, the plain meaning of 6(j) was that the applicant for conscientious objector status must be opposed to war in general.  Nothing in the text of the statute, nor its legislative history could lead to any other conclusion.  Further, the religious basis for petitioners' beliefs was not relevant, since the issue presented was not whether the basis for the belief was religious

26.  401 U.S. 437, 91 S.Ct. 828, 28 L.    27.  Ibid., at 439.
Ed.2d 168 (1971).

training or a personal moral code, but whether the statute intended for applicants to pick and choose among wars. Thus, the Court dismissed the arguments by the petitioners that to deny them relief under 6(j) would violate both the Establishment and the Free Exercise Clauses.

Marshall went on to discuss the other side of the argument, the right of the Government to raise an army in a fair and equitable manner. Quoting from the Government's brief, he said:

> Apart from the Government's need for manpower, perhaps the central interest involved in the administration of conscription laws is the interest in maintaining a fair system for determining "who serves when not all serve."
>
> .   .   .   The claim to relief on account of such [selective conscientious] objection is intrinsically a claim of uncertain dimensions, and   .   .   .   granting the claim   .   .   .   would involve a real danger of erratic or even discriminatory decision making in administrative practice.
>
> .   .   .   There is considerable force in the Government's contention that a program of excusing objectors to particular wars may be "impossible to conduct with any hope of reaching fair and consistent results." [28]

In short, for the majority in *Gillette,* the religious issue was irrelevant because the pragmatic necessities of a government in wartime overrode the obligation to excuse draftees who objected on any grounds, religious or nonreligious, to the prosecution of this particular war, as opposed to the prosecution of all wars.

Thus, by a moderate use of semantic legerdemain, the Court majority attempted to rid itself of the First Amendment question. Justice Douglas however, was not to be deterred from raising the central issue: the right, perhaps the duty of a citizen in a democracy to refuse to do what he conceived to be evil.

28. Ibid., 455–456.

The question, Can a conscientious objector, whether his objection be rooted in "religion" or in moral values, be required to kill? has never been answered by the Court.   .   .   .[29]

Although the First Amendment speaks of freedom of religion and freedom of the press, the implied meaning of that Amendment was the protection of the right of conscience, and if that was so, for Douglas at any rate, no statute could constitutionally require a man to go to war when his conscience forbade that he do so. Relying on the brief of the prominent Catholic scholar, Dr. John T. Noonan, Jr., Douglas declared that a Catholic has a moral duty not to participate in "unjust" wars. In a footnote, he quoted from Pope John XXIII's encyclical, *Pacem in Terris*:

"Since the right to command is required by the moral order and has its source in God, it follows that, if civil authorities legislate for or allow anything that is contrary to that order and therefore contrary to the will of God, neither the laws made nor the authorizations granted can be binding on the consciences of the citizens, *since we must obey God rather than men.*" (emphasis in original) [30]

Douglas' point was well taken, but the majority refused to be deterred by the ghost of Nuremberg. The wartime needs of the military simply overrode philosophical considerations. As Holmes wrote so long ago, "The life of the law has not been logic: it has been experience. The felt necessities of the time .   .   . have had a good deal more to do than the syllogism in determining the rules by which men should be governed." *

29.  Ibid., at 464.

30.  Ibid., at 470.

* Though Gillette and Negre lost their cases, in the end, it was the government which gave way and the protestors who prevailed: the war became impossible to prosecute in the face of mounting moral outrage. In wartime, the courts cannot effectively protect minority rights that conflict with military necessity. Only the larger society can do that, after the war is over, if it is to be done at all. Cf. the Japanese Exclusion Cases: *Korematsu v. United States*, 323 U.S.

*Freedom of Religion: The Establishment Clause*

Cases arising under the Establishment Clause generally involve the attempts of particular religious groups to use the secular power of the government to strengthen their own organizations. Although it is *governmental* action which is challenged in these cases, the impetus for these actions usually lies with private religious groups that have acquired sufficient political power to obtain favorable legislative or administrative action. While the religious groups in question may, at times, constitute a majority of the electorate, more frequently they are a minority, albeit a large and militant one. Thus, while free exercise cases commonly involve individuals whose religious beliefs are unpopular and even despised, establishment cases relate to beliefs that are relatively widely held and whose exponents, therefore, feel them worthy of public support. These kinds of cases fall generally into three categories: those relating to religion and religious practices in the public schools; those relating to state laws which help some or all religions as opposed to nonreligion; and, those involving the use of public funds to support religious activities.

*Religion and the Public Schools*

During the nineteenth century the public schools were strongly Protestant in tone, so much so that they were offensive to Jews and Roman Catholics. While the protests of the tiny number of Jews were muted and inconsequential, those of the growing number of Catholic immigrants, especially in the cities of the eastern seaboard were quite another matter. Despite popular abuse and even physical violence, Catholics struggled during the nineteenth and early twentieth centuries to remove Protestant religious teaching from the curriculum. They succeeded eventually in secularizing instruction, but since their preferred goal was the propagation of Catholicism, they simultaneously built an extensive, and expensive network of Catholic schools in

214, 65 S.Ct. 193, 89 L.Ed. 194 (1944) and *Hirabayashi v. United*   *States,* 320 U.S. 81, 63 S.Ct. 1375, 87 L.Ed. 1774 (1943).

which children could be taught Catholic dogma along with the standard elementary and high school curriculum.  The original aim of the Church was to have a place in a Catholic school for every Catholic child, but this proved to be financially impossible, and many Catholic children attended the public schools.  Thus, by the end of World War II, the Church was anxious to introduce into the public schools some opportunity for religious instruction.  At the same time, it attempted to get government subsidies from tax funds to defray the costs of its own parochial schools.  These attempts were vigorously resisted by those who saw such subsidies as an establishment of religion forbidden by the First Amendment.  *Everson v. Board of Education,* a case raising this issue, came before the United States Supreme Court in 1947.[31]

In 1941 the State of New Jersey amended its State Education Law to permit local Boards of Education to reimburse parents for transportation of pupils to all nonprofit schools, public, private, and parochial.  Accordingly, the Board of Education of Ewing Township, a suburb of Trenton, voted to reimburse the parents of children attending Catholic high schools in Trenton. Ewing was too small to maintain its own high school and all students were bused at their parents' expense to high schools in Trenton.  Prior to 1941 only the parents of those children attending the public high school were reimbursed for the cost of transportation.  After 1941, however, parents of parochial high school children were reimbursed as well.  A taxpayer's suit was mounted by one Arch R. Everson against the use of public funds for this purpose.  Mr. Everson argued that such use of tax funds constituted an establishment of religion in that the state was, in effect, making it easier for the church to maintain its schools, thus aiding the cause of religion.

In a 5–4 decision, the United States Supreme Court ruled against Mr. Everson on the ground that the payments were not in aid of religion but were simply benefits extended to school

31.  330 U.S. 1, 67 S.Ct. 504, 91 L.Ed. 711 (1947).

children for which all school children in the area were eligible. The First Amendment, said Justice Black, commanded a wall of separation between church and state but did not command hostility to religion. In a much quoted passage the Court attempted to define the limits of the Establishment Clause:

> The "establishment of religion" clause of the First Amendment means at least this: Neither a state nor the Federal Government can set up a church. Neither can pass laws which aid one religion, aid all religions, or prefer one religion over another. Neither can force nor influence a person to go to or remain away from church against his will or force him to profess a belief or disbelief in any religion. No person can be punished for entertaining or professing religious beliefs or disbeliefs, for church attendance or non-attendance. No tax in any amount, large or small, can be levied to support any religious activities or institutions, whatever they may be called, or whatever form they may adopt to teach or practice religion. Neither a state nor the Federal Government can, openly or secretly, participate in the affairs of any religious organizations or groups and *vice versa.* In the words of Jefferson, the clause against the establishment of religion by law was intended to erect "a wall of separation between church and State." [32]

Nevertheless, the First Amendment did not command hostility to religion. Children must not be denied benefits simply because of their religious observance. Just as it was permissible for the state to provide policemen to protect children at school crossings near their parochial schools, along with police and fire protection and water and sewer services, the state might help parents to get these children along with all other school children, to and from their schools with safety and convenience.

---

32.　Ibid., at 15–16.

The dissenters, led by Justice Rutledge, objected that the cost of transportation was no different from the cost of textbooks, athletic equipment or teachers' salaries or buildings. Public money was being used to defray the costs of parochial school education, to make it easier for parents to send their children to religious schools rather than to the public schools. Such use constituted an establishment of religion forbidden by the First Amendment.

After *Everson* the issue of tax fund aid to parochial schools lay dormant, at least at the United States Supreme Court level, for twenty years. Another issue relating to the public schools, however, came before the high court almost immediately. The Catholic Church was instrumental in the adoption in various localities of programs to provide religious instruction for elementary school pupils during regular school hours. In some of these programs, religious instructors, including garbed priests and nuns, were brought into the schools; in others, the children were released early so that they might receive religious instruction in church or some other outside facility. Two challenges to such programs reached the Court.

In the first of these cases, *McCollum v. Board of Education*,[33] the Superintendent of the Public Schools of Champaign, Illinois, arranged for instructors to come into the public schools for 30 to 45 minutes each week to give students religious instruction. The children were divided into Catholic, Protestant and Jewish groups and were sent to separate rooms for instruction. While the program was in theory voluntary, there was considerable testimony that pressures were brought to bear on individual children to participate, that the class might have a "100% record." One Vashti McCollum, a militant atheist,* and the moth-

---

33.  333 U.S. 203 (1948).

* The term "militant" as applied to Mrs. McCollum is not an exaggeration. The tone of Mrs. McCollum's petition is revealing. "Religious worship is a chronic disease of the imagination contracted in childhood . . . Religion is born of fear, ignorance and superstition . . . One of said instructors in religious education teaches a doctrine that there is a supernatural and divine being, person or

er of Terry McCollum, a ten year old student in the Champaign public schools brought suit claiming that by bringing clergy into the schools and using students in the public schools as kind of a captive audience, the state was unconstitutionally violating the Establishment Clause.

The United States Supreme Court agreed with Mrs. McCollum. Justice Black, writing for the majority, said that it was impermissible for the state to use its buildings for the dissemination of religion and the compulsory attendance machinery of the public schools to provide students for religious instruction. Justice Frankfurter, (joined by Jackson, Burton, and Rutledge) concurred, adding that the program had undermined the primary integrative function of the public schools, and instead had introduced a divisive note.

> . . . Designed to serve as perhaps the most powerful agency for promoting cohesion among a heterogeneous democratic people, the public school must keep scrupulously free from entanglement in the strife of sects. . . .[34]

The mere fact that children could be excused from the program if their parents desired, did not mitigate the evil. The pressure on a child to conform was there, the grouping of children by religious preference was introduced, and the preferential treatment for believers over nonbelievers was apparent.

> . . . That a child is offered an alternative may reduce the constraint; it does not eliminate the operation of influence by the school in matters sacred to con-

thing, call 'God'; that there is a relationship between mankind and said alleged God, whereby all earthly persons are dependent upon said God. She also establishes in the minds of pupils a certain sectarian theory that said God is of masculine gender . . . and that said God and a female person named 'Mary' . . . were the father and mother of a male child, called 'Jesus Christ'; . . . " Excerpts from petition of Vashti McCollum as quoted in Pfeffer, *Church, State and Freedom,* pp. 402–403.

34. *McCollum v. Board of Educ.,* 333 U.S. 203, at 216–217, 68 S.Ct. 461, 467–468, 92 L.Ed. 649 (1948).

science and outside the school's domain. The law of imitation operates, and nonconformity is not an outstanding characteristic of children. The result is an obvious pressure upon children to attend. . . .[35]

Only Justice Reed dissented, arguing that this particular form of aid to religion was permissible because merely incidental to the operation of the school system. The First Amendment, said Justice Reed, did not bar "every friendly gesture between church and state."

Four years after the invalidation of the Champaign program, the United States Supreme Court agreed to review the constitutionality of a somewhat different released time program in New York City. Instead of clergy being brought into the public schools for the instructional period, pupils were released from school one day a week, an hour prior to the normal dismissal time to attend formal religious instruction at a religious institution of their choice. (This program had been in effect in New York State since the early 1940's and had been described to the *McCollum* Court in an *amicus* brief. Justice Reed had also discussed it at some length in his dissent.) While on its face Black's *McCollum* opinion seemed to preclude the permissibility of any instructional program involving the machinery of the public schools, Justice Frankfurter, in a concurring opinion had stated:

> We do not consider, as indeed we could not, school programs not before us which, though colloquially characterized as "released time," present situations differing in aspects that may well be constitutionally crucial. . . .[36]

Thus, when the New York program was challenged after *McCollum*, its defenders pinned their hopes on Frankfurter's ambiguous comment. They were not disappointed. In *Zorach v.*

35.  Ibid., at 227.          36.  Ibid., at 231.

*Clauson*[37] the Court, 6–3, upheld the constitutionality of the New York program.

The *Zorach* case was brought by Tessim Zorach, a parishioner of the Holy Trinity Episcopal Church and Esta Gluck, a Jew. Both Zorach and Gluck had children who were pupils in the Brooklyn, New York public schools. Under the New York program, local religious institutions, together with interested parents, organized programs of religious instruction. The religious institution then issued cards which were signed by the parents and delivered to the principal of the public school. The cards requested that the children involved be released for one hour each week to attend instruction on the premises of the religious institution. Each borough of the city was assigned a different day of the week for religious instruction. While the public school authorities did not assume responsibility for seeing that the children actually attended religious instruction, clergymen, nuns and other religious personnel were permitted access to the school grounds for the purpose of receiving the children and the institutions involved kept attendance records which were forwarded to the public schools so that absent pupils might be marked truant.

Technically, the school authorities had little if any role to play in either furthering or hindering the implementation of the program. In fact, there was considerable evidence that in many New York schools, as in the Champaign schools, the authorities exerted considerable pressure on children to participate in the program, and shamed or ridiculed those who did not participate. Much of this evidence was in the form of individual depositions from parents, students, teachers, and other school personnel. The American Jewish Congress, which was instrumental in handling the *Zorach* case, sought to introduce these affidavits as evidence, but the trial court judge refused to admit them and their contents were not considered by any subsequent court. Both sides conceded that during the period of released time no signifi-

37. 343 U.S. 306, 72 S.Ct. 679, 96 L. Ed. 954 (1952).

cant instruction took place for the remainder of the children who chose not to attend religious instruction, and it was customary for the students in those parochial schools where the released time children were to receive instruction to release their own students one hour earlier to make room for the public school children.

Zorach and Gluck contended that the released time program violated the First Amendment in that, as in *McCollum*, the machinery of the public school system and the compulsory attendance laws were being used to establish and maintain a religious program impermissible under the Establishment Clause. The United States Supreme Court disagreed. In an opinion written by Justice Douglas for the six man majority, Douglas declared that the program violated neither the Free Exercise nor the Establishment Clauses of the First Amendment. No pupil was compelled to participate and no pupil was pressured to refrain from participating. Neither was the incidental aid given to the program an establishment of religion. It was instead, simply a neutral contact between the church and the school. The First Amendment, said Douglas, did not demand hostility or alienation between church and state. There were many instances in which the government is tangentially concerned with religious matters: the practice of holding opening prayers in legislative and court sessions, the appointment of chaplains for the Armed Services and for prisons, religious mottoes on coins, etc. Such contacts do not violate the First Amendment.

> . . . The First Amendment . . . does not say that in every and all respects there shall be a separation of Church and State. Rather, it studiously defines the manner, the specific ways, in which there shall be no concert or union or dependency one on the other. . . . Otherwise the state and religion would be aliens to each other—hostile, suspicious, and even unfriendly. . . .
>
> We are a religious people whose institutions presuppose a Supreme Being. . . . When the state en-

courages religious instruction or cooperates with religious authorities by adjusting the schedule of public events to sectarian needs, it follows the best of our traditions. For it then respects the religious nature of our people and accommodates the public service to their spiritual needs. . . .[38]

The majority rationale, even though written (rather uncharacteristically) by Douglas, one of the more liberal members of the Court, failed to persuade Black, Frankfurter, and Jackson. Black protested that *McCollum* should be controlling, that the differences between the released time program in New York and Champaign were insignificant and that the central fact remained that the school authorities were using the public school system to provide recruits for a religious training program. Jackson concurred with Black's dissent in vigorous and often biting language:

> . . . schooling is more or less suspended during the "released time" so that the nonreligious attendants will not forge ahead of the churchgoing absentees. [The school] serves as a temporary jail for a pupil who will not go to Church. It takes more subtlety of mind than I possess to deny that this is governmental constraint in support of religion. . . .[39]

In response to the suggestion that opposition to a released time program was necessarily atheistic or antireligious, Jackson observed, "It is possible to hold a faith with enough confidence to believe that what should be rendered to God does not need to be decided and collected by Caesar."[40] In a final swipe at what he saw as the irrationality of his brethren in the majority he remarked, "'Today's judgment will be more interesting to students of psychology and of the judicial processes than to students of constitutional law."[41]

38. Ibid., at 312–314.          40. Ibid., at 324–325.

39. Ibid., at 324.          41. Ibid., at 325.

The *Zorach* decision was greeted with pleasure by Catholics, and with resentment by Jews and most Protestants. The program, which has never been reconsidered by the Court is still in force. Another public school issue, however, which reached the Court a decade later, proved to be even more controversial. Two cases came to the United States Supreme Court, challenging religious observances which were part of the public school curriculum: in New York, recitation of a short prayer; in Pennsylvania, reading from the Bible. The decisions of the high court proved to be so unpopular with a large segment of the public that serious, though unsuccessful, attempts were made to reverse the decisions through a Constitutional amendment.

The New York State Board of Regents in 1951, had composed a short nondenominational prayer which it recommended that children recite at the commencement of each school day together with the pledge of allegiance to the flag, in the hope that such opening exercises would inspire in the children both respect for law and the faith of their fathers as taught in their homes.

The text of the prayer itself could hardly have been less offensive:

> Almighty God we acknowledge our dependence upon Thee, and we beg Thy blessings upon us, our parents, our teachers and our country.

Nevertheless, the introduction of the prayer with its accompanying promotion of religion in the schools created a storm of controversy. While Catholics generally approved, many Protestant groups protested that the attempt to make the prayer palatable to all had so watered down the essentials of Christian prayer as to rob it of all meaning. Some Lutheran leaders called the prayer "an abomination and a blasphemy." [42] A few Protestant groups accepted the prayer; Jews were unanimous in their opposition to religious observances of any sort in the schools.

42. As cited in Pfeffer, *Church, State, and Freedom*, p. 462.

The Regents prayer was not mandatory and was not adopted in every school district across the state. The school board of New Hyde Park on Long Island, however, did adopt the prayer with the proviso that children who did not wish to participate could remain silent. In *Engel v. Vitale*,[43] parents in the district, aided by the New York Civil Liberties Union, brought suit in state court to have the prayer exercise declared unconstitutional. The parents lost their suit in the state courts, which upheld the validity of the program on the ground that the prayer was non-sectarian and thus did not favor any one religious group; and since children were free not to participate, the prayer did not constitute an establishment of religion.

On appeal to the United States Supreme Court, however, the losers in *Zorach* became winners: the judgment of the lower court was reversed. Justice Black, for the majority, held that by composing an "official prayer" the state authorities had violated the First Amendment ban on the establishment of a religion. The Establishment Clause he said:

> . . . must at least mean that in this country it is no part of the business of government to compose official prayers for any group of American people to recite as a part of a religious program carried on by government.[44]

Even though there was no coercion exerted on the pupils to participate, the composition and use of a state-sponsored prayer was nevertheless an establishment of religion. While claims of infringement of the Free Exercise Clause might require a demonstration of coercion on the part of state authorities, in establishment cases the mere showing of sponsorship was sufficient to demonstrate infringement of the Establishment Clause.

> [The] first and most immediate purpose [of the Establishment Clause] rested on the belief that a union of

43. 10 N.Y.2d 174, 218 N.Y.S.2d 659, 176 N.E.2d 579 (1961).

44. *Engel v. Vitale*, 370 U.S. 421 at 425, 82 S.Ct. 1261–1264, 86 L.Ed.2d 601 (1962).

government and religion tends to destroy government
and degrade religion.   .   .   .   Another purpose of the
Establishment Clause rested upon an awareness of the
historical fact that governmentally established religions
and religious persecutions go hand in hand.

.   .   .   [Though] the governmental endorsement
of [the Regents] prayer seems relatively insignificant
when compared to governmental encroachments upon
religion which were commonplace 200 years ago.
.   .   .   it may be appropriate to say in the words of
James Madison   .   .   .:   "[I]t is proper to take
alarm   at   the   first   experiment   on   our   liberties.
.   .   ." 45

Only Justice Stewart dissented, arguing that simply permitting
those who wanted to, to pray, was not an establishment of religion any more than was the daily invocation to God in the Supreme Court, prayers in Congress, or "In God We Trust" on our
coins.

Following close on the heels of *Engel* was *School District of
Abington v. Schempp,*[46] in which the Unitarian parents of three
pupils challenged a Pennsylvania law which required Bible reading as part of the opening exercises in the public schools but
permitted children who so requested to be excused from participation.   As in *Engel* the parents argued that compulsory Bible
reading was a constitutionally impermissible establishment of religion;   the state responded that the exercise was voluntary, non-
sectarian and in keeping with the overall religious traditions of
the American people.   The *Schempp* case ultimately reached the
United States Supreme Court along with a companion case, *Murray v. Curlett,* a suit brought by Mrs. Madeline Murray, an atheist, who challenged the daily Bible reading and recitation of the
Lord's Prayer in the schools of Baltimore, Maryland.   Mrs. Murray's child had been excused from participation at her request;

---

45.  Ibid., at 431–432, 436.          46.  374 U.S. 203, 83 S.Ct. 1560, 10
                                        L.Ed.2d 844 (1963).

Mr. Schempp had decided against requesting such exemption lest his children's relationships with their classmates be affected.

The Court in an 8–1 vote, ruled in favor of the parents in both cases. Justice Clark, for the majority, held that if the primary purpose or effect of a statute was either the advancement or inhibition of religion, then the law was invalid as an establishment of religion regardless of whether or not there was coercion of individuals to participate. Since both of the statutes challenged were intended to advance the cause of religion, both were unconstitutional notwithstanding the fact that children could be excused from participation. The prohibition against Bible reading in the public schools did not violate, moreover, the free exercise rights of those who wished to read the Bible.

> The conclusion follows that in both cases the laws require religious exercises and such exercises are being conducted in direct violation of the rights of the appellees and petitioners. Nor are these required exercises mitigated by the fact that individual students may absent themselves upon parental request, for that fact furnishes no defense to a claim of unconstitutionality under the Establishment Clause.   .   .   .
>
> Finally, we cannot accept that the concept of neutrality, which does not permit a State to require a religious exercise even with the consent of the majority of those affected, collides with the majority's right to free exercise of religion. While the Free Exercise Clause clearly prohibits the use of state action to deny the rights of free exercise to *anyone,* it has never meant that a majority could use the machinery of the State to practice its beliefs.   .   .   .[47]

Once again Justice Stewart dissented. While he conceded that Bible reading might be construed a religious exercise, he felt that to forbid this type of nonsectarian, nonpreferential religious exercise in the public schools would be a rigid and mechanical

47.   Ibid., at 224–225, 225–226.

interpretation of the Establishment Clause which inevitably must lead to infringement of the Free Exercise Clause. As long as there was no coercion of individual children to participate there could be, for Stewart, no establishment.

Stewart's dissent sufficiently disturbed the majority that at least one of their number, Brennan, devoted his concurring opinion to refuting the contention that *Schempp* implied there could be no permissible accommodation between church and state and that the Free Exercise Clause was necessarily violated by the majority's interpretation of the Establishment Clause. After pointing out that the programs in question served no substantial secular purpose and that the excusal procedure was invalid because by requiring a virtual proclamation of a student's disbelief, it infringed on a nonbeliever's free exercise rights, Brennan went on to give what he considered examples of permissible church-state involvement. These included:

1. Situations where strict adherence to the Establishment Clause would seriously violate the Free Exercise Clause, e. g., the failure to appoint chaplains in the armed forces and in prisons would leave no way for members of these organizations to obtain the services of clergy.

2. Formal opening exercises for groups composed of adults sufficiently mature to refrain from participation without trauma, e. g., legislative sessions.

3. Secular academic teaching of religion and the Bible.

4. Uniform tax exemptions available to many types of nonprofit groups which are incidently available to religious organizations.

5. Religious actions which have acquired secular meanings, as for example, the mottoes on coins.

*Engel* and *Schempp* (particularly the former) produced an unexpectedly sharp public reaction. Spokesmen for the Catholic Church and members of Congress from the South were particularly outraged by the decisions which they interpreted as an attempt by the Supreme Court to "secularize" the United States, to "make God unconstitutional," to "tamper with the soul of America." There were dark predictions that this was but the first step in bringing Russian style atheism to the United States, and many deplored removing from the classroom the wholesome influence of simple religious practices, such as nondenominational prayers and the reading of the Bible without comment or further instruction. In vain, did the supporters of the decision protest that parents had ample opportunity for the religious instruction of their children outside school hours, and that the Court ruling was not antagonistic to religion *per se,* but only to religious practices in the public schools.

The Court did not attempt to reconsider the issues, however, despite a storm of criticism sufficiently violent to engender calls for the impeachment of Earl Warren, and an energetic campaign for a constitutional amendment to permit prayer in the schools. There was also considerable evidence that in some areas of the country the decision was simply ignored, principally in smaller communities where parents overwhelmingly supported prayer and Bible reading in the public schools. While there still may be a considerable number of such communities today, in the large cities, *Schempp* and *Engel* have been complied with. There have been no acts of open defiance in any sizeable community, and state authorities have moved to insure compliance when violations have been brought to their attention. The issue is not yet one that has passed into obscurity; for some groups it is still a cause which they see as not totally lost. But for those who live in urban, heterogeneous areas, the secularism of the school curriculum has been preserved.

*The Support of Religion in Preference to Nonreligion*

Contemporaneous with the *Schempp and Engel* cases were four cases involving still another question arising under the Establishment Clause: were Sunday closing laws an infringement of the First Amendment? Many states have laws which limit commercial activity on the Christian Sabbath. Historically, of course, these laws originated in church restrictions on public activities that were forbidden in keeping with the Biblical admonition to "Remember the Sabbath day and keep it holy." Through the years, however, these laws had acquired a patchwork quality as new sections were added and other sections either deleted or ignored. In New York State, for example, during the 1950's one could sell cooked meat but not raw meat, gasoline but not kerosene, cigarettes but not pipes. Movies were unaffected, but the statute then on the books had been interpreted in earlier times to forbid movie and theatrical performances on the Sabbath. (The interpretation of the statute had since been modified, but the text remained unchanged.) These statutes aroused considerable opposition principally from two groups: merchants who wished to expand their business activities and take advantage of potential customers who might shop on Sundays; and, adherents of faiths observing a day other than Sunday as their Sabbath who were forced to restrict their commercial activities on two days a week rather than one. The latter groups were principally Jews and Seventh Day Adventists who observed their Sabbath on Saturday and hence could not work or shop on either Saturday or Sunday.

In 1961 the United States Supreme Court decided four cases known collectively as the Sunday Closing Cases. Two of these cases, *McGowan v. Maryland* [48] and *Two Guys from Harrison-Allentown Inc. v. McGinley* [49] were brought by the owners of discount department stores who wished to remain open seven days a week; the other two cases, *Gallagher v. Crown Kosher Supermarket of Massachusetts* [50] and *Braunfeld v. Brown* [51] were brought by kosher butchers whose shops were closed on Saturday and who therefore objected to complying with the Sunday closing law which forced them to close on Sunday as well. *Mc-*

---

48.  366 U.S. 420, 81 S.Ct. 1101, 6 L. Ed.2d 393 (1961).

49.  366 U.S. 582, 81 S.Ct. 1135, 6 L. Ed.2d 551 (1961).

50.  366 U.S. 617, 81 S.Ct. 1122, 6 L. Ed.2d 536 (1961).

51.  366 U.S. 599, 81 S.Ct. 1144, 6 L. Ed.2d 563 (1961).

*Gowan* and *Two Guys* asserted that Sunday closing laws, being religious in origin, constituted an establishment of religion which impermissibly interfered with their business operations. *Crown* and *Braunfeld* contended that the statutes in question infringed on their free exercise of religion since it imposed an economic penalty on them by forcing them to cease operations for the Christian as well as the Jewish Sabbaths. The states in question defended their laws by denying that religious purpose or intent underlay the statutes. The purpose of the Sunday laws was entirely secular: to provide the community with a common day of rest which would allow surcease from the noise and commotion of the working week and an opportunity for families to be together.

In all four cases the Court upheld the claims of the state. In an 8–1 opinion written by Chief Justice Earl Warren, the Court struck down the challenges of the discount department store owners, agreeing that the statutes were not an establishment of religion because their intent was not to further the cause of religion. While originally intended to promote observance of the Christian Sabbath, they had, through the years, become secular in purpose. The state had a legitimate interest in promoting a common day of rest for its residents, and the fact that the Christian Sabbath was the day most suitable for that purpose did not mean that Sunday closing laws were therefore an establishment of religion. Justices Frankfurter and Harlan concurred, arguing that only when the purpose or effect of a statute was to promote religion was it an unconstitutional establishment. Only Douglas dissented. For him any religious practice that had the sanction of law behind it was an establishment and therefore impermissible.

The orthodox Jewish butchers fared a little better than the discount department store owners but not enough to give them a victory in the high court. By a decision of 6–3, again written by Chief Justice Warren, the Court declared that while the freedom to hold religious beliefs was absolute, the challenged statute did not infringe on free exercise since its effect on the appellants' religious practice was only indirect.  Unlike the flag salute cases, it did not command an act forbidden by religion, nor, as in the polygamy cases, forbid an act that was commanded by religion.  The conduct regulated was secular in nature as was the states' purpose in enforcing the statute.  In a cosmopolitan society such as the United States it would be impossible to forbid all actions indirectly affecting religion.  The Court could not say that a state would not be justified in using this means to accomplish a legitimate purpose of establishing one day of rest per week.

Three justices, Brennan, Stewart, and Douglas dissented, arguing that the preferred position of the First Amendment precluded infringement on the right of free exercise of religion except for the most weighty purposes.  The Court should not exalt the administrative convenience of the states involved in such a way as to make the practice of their religion economically disadvantageous to orthodox Jews.

While the Court thus upheld the right of communities to declare the Christian Sabbath a secular day of rest, and to forbid much commercial activity on that day, time, has to some extent, rendered the decisions obsolete.  Increasingly states and localities have repealed or simply failed to enforce Sabbath closing laws, and in many areas Sunday is becoming one of the busiest shopping days of the week.  In 1976, in New York City, the large Fifth Avenue and Herald Square department stores for the first time in their history opened for business on Sunday.  The public reaction to this development was mixed: some greeted it as an opportunity for working people to shop at their leisure; others deplored the loss of a communal day of rest.  What was most notable, however, was that the controversy was no longer along religious lines.  Both the proponents and opponents of the new development advanced secular rather than religious arguments in support of their positions.  The limits of the First Amendment were no longer at issue.

*The Use of Public Funds To Support Religious Activities*

By the mid 1970's most church-state issues in the United States had either been resolved or were in abeyance. The ending of the war in Viet Nam put an end to the conscientious objector controversy. The cultural pluralism and generally more permissive standards of personal conduct made the flag salute question anachronistic and faintly ridiculous. The furor over Bible reading and prayer in the schools had not entirely dissipated but had been muted by concern over broader issues of public morality such as those raised by the Watergate controversy. The stigma for not participating in released time programs had lessened and with it the opposition to such programs had waned. Sunday closing laws were fast becoming obsolete. Only one issue was still of serious concern to the public at large: the question of whether tax funds could be used to support church-supported schools and other religious institutions. This issue came to a head with the passage of the Federal Elementary and Secondary Education Act of 1965, because, with the passage of this act, for the first time in American history, large sums of federal money became available for the support of elementary and secondary schools. Under ESEA, moreover some of the money became available to nonpublic schools including schools maintained by religious institutions.

Since the Civil War attempts had been made to enact federal legislation which would aid the states in meeting their obligations to provide free elementary and high school education. Most of the proposed measures provided for aid to public, i. e., tax supported, schools only, and either specifically, or by implication, forbade any of the proposed funds to be used for church related schools. Due in large part to the implacable and intense opposition of the Catholic Church, no such federal legislation was ever enacted. The Catholic Church, hard pressed for funds with which to maintain its parochial school system was bitter at what it saw as the use of tax money in such manner as to deny Catholics their share. In its view its members, like all taxpayers, contributed to the general treasury, and to restrict federal aid to the elementary and secondary schools to the public schools meant in effect that Catholics were doubly taxed, once for the support of the public schools and then again for the support of their own parochial school system. This, of course, was already true on the state and local level and Catholic opposition to recreating the situation on the federal level was bitter.

The majority position, taken by Protestants and Jews, was that the public schools were a community obligation. They were open to all children whose parents wished to send them, and they were an obligation to be paid for by all taxpayers regardless of whether the taxpayer had children who could or would attend the schools, had children who attended parochial or other private schools, or indeed had no children at all. The support of the schools was thus an undertaking in aid of the community, not primarily for the benefit of individual parents. As such, the support of the schools had to fall on every taxpayer regardless of the use he personally might make of the facilities provided.

Prior to 1965, thus, government support for education was almost entirely at the state and local level. Almost all funds expended were exclusively for the public schools, the only exception being the relatively small sums expended on services such as transportation, hot lunches for needy children, and rudimentary public health services, such as vaccinations, etc. Such expenditures had been approved by the United States Supreme Court in the *Everson* case under the "child benefit" theory. Another exception was the very large sums of money expended by the Federal government after World War II to aid returning veterans to attend college. Under the "G.I. Bill of Rights" enacted in 1943, the government paid for tuition and made small subsistence grants to veterans attending college. Included among the colleges eligible to enroll G.I.s were church supported colleges. No serious challenge was mounted to this program on church-state grounds. The program was widely conceived to be a program for the benefit of veterans rather than the institutions involved; in fact, the G.I. Bill resulted in wide scale expansion and strengthening of colleges throughout the country, particularly smaller church related schools.

By 1965, however, for a whole complex of reasons, it became politically possible for the first time to enact federal legislation that would provide direct, though limited federal aid, to all elementary and secondary schools in the United States, public, private, and parochial. The election (and later martyrdom) of John F. Kennedy as the first Roman Catholic president of the United States had done much to allay the fears of non-Catholics of the aggressiveness of the Catholic Church. The Church, also had modified its claims to tax support for its schools. In the discussion preceding the passage of the 1965 act, Cardinal Spellman disclaimed any demands for general financial aid to parochial schools and asked only for what, in effect, was an enlargement of the child benefit theory: aid for transportation, school books, and the like. Further, the ecumenical spirit promoted by Pope John XXIII led to an outreaching of the Church toward its Protestant neighbors which created pressure on the Protestants to make some compromise on the issue of aid to parochial schools. These factors, taken together with the fear that the Soviet Union might become technologically more advanced than the United States, produced a climate of opinion in which it was possible for Congress to enact the 1965 Act.

The principal provisions of ESEA were contained in three titles: Title I authorized the expenditure of more than one billion dollars for grants for general educational purposes, such as the construction of schools or the hiring of teachers, provided that the money was used to meet the needs of educationally deprived children of low income families. Poor, educationally deprived children who were enrolled in nonpublic schools, moreover, were permitted to share in these benefits proportionate to their numbers, provided that the specific services to be furnished were approved by the United States Commissioner of Education. Title II provided funds for the purchase of library books, text books and other instructional materials, and Title III provided money for supplementary educational services, such as guidance, coun-

seling and remedial instruction.  In all these areas specific provision was made for the allocation of funds to private schools
servicing the subject population of poor, educationally deprived
children.  The Act itself makes no mention of religious schools,
and benefits could theoretically have been restricted to private
secular schools.  No attempt, however, was made to do so, and
the law was extended immediately to cover religious schools.

Several groups, among them Protestants and Other Americans
United for Separation of Church and State (POAU) and the
United Parents Association (UPA), considered that the 1965 Act
violated the Establishment Clause in that it impermissibly aided
church schools.  As federal taxpayers they brought suit to en-
join federal expenditures under the Act on the ground that Congress had violated the First Amendment prohibition against the
establishment of religion.  The suit, *Flast v. Cohen,* was heard
initially by a three-judge federal court which held that the appellants lacked standing to sue, because since the 1923 case of
*Frothingham v. Mellon* [52] the federal courts have refused to en-
tertain taxpayer suits.  (The *Frothingham* case involved a taxpayer, Mrs. Frothingham, who challenged a federal law providing grants-in-aid to states which established clinics to care for
mothers and babies, on the ground that the Constitution did not
delegate power to Congress to establish such programs.  In order for Frothingham to assert her claim, however, she had to
have "standing to sue" i. e., the courts had to recognize her
right to appear before them.  The procedural rules of the federal
courts require that for a litigant to have standing to sue, he or
she must have suffered a personal injury.  In this case Mrs.
Frothingham's injury was to her pocketbook—she felt that the
funds she had contributed to the federal treasury had been improperly spent.  The Court dismissed her claim on the ground
that her contribution to the federal treasury was minuscule, a
trifle, and *de minimis non curat lex* (the law does not concern itself with trifles).  The Court, thus, ruled out the possibility of

---

52.  262 U.S. 447, 43 S.Ct. 597, 67 L.
Ed. 1078 (1923).

taxpayer suits. Whatever the merits of the legal reasoning for this decision, the practical considerations were overwhelming. Were the decision otherwise, there would be a real possibility of challenges to the spending of every dollar in the federal budget, which could effectively paralyze all federal activity.)

*Flast v. Cohen* was a taxpayer suit. Flast's attack on ESEA was based on her claim that her tax money, like Mrs. Frothingham's, had been improperly spent, in that Congress had had no right to expend tax funds for the support of church-related schools. There was, however, one difference between the Frothingham and Flast claims. Where Mrs. Frothingham claimed that it was beyond the power of Congress *(ultra vires)* to finance the construction of well-baby clinics, Mrs. Flast's contention was that the 1965 Act was not only beyond the power of Congress, but was an action (the establishment of religion) directly *forbidden* by the First Amendment. It was this difference which proved determinative of the outcome of the case. The United States Supreme Court reversed the ruling of the lower federal courts and held that where a taxpayer is challenging an act directly contravening a Constitutional mandate, he has standing to sue in the federal courts.[53]

Following their procedural victory in the *Flast* case, the opponents of the 1965 Act then sought to reinstitute suit on the merits of the case. Literally dozens of cases challenging ESEA were introduced into the federal courts, but by the beginning of 1977 no case had proceeded beyond the federal district court level. In March 1977, the National Coalition for Public Education and Religious Liberty (PEARL) succeeded in obtaining approval of its motion that a three-judge federal court be impanelled to hear a suit entitled *National PEARL v. Califano,* which challenged the provision of ESEA which made possible the assignment of public school teachers on the public payroll to parochial schools for remedial work with parochial school students.

53. *Flast v. Cohen,* 392 U.S. 83, 88 S.Ct. 1942, 20 L.Ed.2d 947 (1968).

ESEA has thus survived court challenge (if only by default) for at least the first twelve years after its passage. The impact of this legislation, however, has not been confined to its direct effects on local education. Following in its wake, have been a whole host of state laws which attempted to use the child benefit —aid to the disadvantaged rationales of ESEA, to overcome the political and legal obstacles to direct aid to local church-related schools. These state programs used a variety of devices, such as lending text books to parochial school children, and paying salaries of parochial school teachers who taught secular subjects. Many of these programs have been challenged in the courts, with mixed results. One of the earliest cases, *Board of Education v. Allen,*[54] involved a New York State law which required the state to lend, without charge, textbooks to every child in grades 7 through 12 in every school—public, private and parochial—in New York State. The law was upheld by the New York State Court of Appeals against the assertion that it constituted an establishment of religion. The United States Supreme Court agreed that the intent of the legislation was the extension of benefits in a neutral fashion to all children in the state. Only secular books were involved in the program, and parochial schools benefited no more than other types of schools. Thus, the intent was not to aid religion but simply to help all children in the state. Justices Black, Douglas, and Fortas dissented, pointing out that books, unlike bus transportation in the *Everson* case, were capable of being used for religious purposes, and as long as parochial schools had the option of requesting specific books, albeit on secular subjects, the state would be aiding religious schools to promote religious purposes.

Another challenge was mounted in *Lemon v. Kurtzman*[55] which involved Rhode Island's 1969 Salary Supplement Act. This law provided for a 15 percent salary supplement to be paid

---

54. 392 U.S. 236, 88 S.Ct. 1923, 20 L.Ed.2d 1060 (1968).

55. 403 U.S. 602, 91 S.Ct. 2105, 29 L.Ed.2d 745 (1971) (together with *Early v. DiCenso* and *Robinson v. DiCenso.*)

to teachers in nonpublic schools in which the average per pupil expenditure on secular education was below the average in public schools. Teachers were limited to teaching secular subjects, using materials used in the public schools. Also reviewed was Pennsylvania's Nonpublic Elementary and Secondary School Act of 1968 which authorized the state to reimburse parochial schools directly for teachers' salaries, textbooks, and instructional materials used for secular education. Both statutes were struck down by the United States Supreme Court on the ground that it would be impossible effectively to supervise the expenditure of state funds to insure their being used for strictly secular purposes. Though textbooks might be religiously neutral, the way a teacher handles a subject in the classroom might not be; the statutory schemes involved too much entanglement between government and religion. In similar fashion, a New York State law providing for reimbursement to nonpublic schools for the expenses of administering and grading examinations and the maintenance of pupil enrollment and health records was struck down, as was another New York law providing for direct money grants to some nonpublic schools for maintenance and repair of facilities and equipment to insure the students' health, welfare, and safety. In both cases the laws were held to constitute an aid to religion.[56]

The same day the *Lemon v. Kurtzman* case was decided, the Supreme Court also decided *Tilton v. Richardson*,[57] a case involving a federal law, the Higher Education Facilities Act of 1963. This law provided construction grants for college and university facilities, provided that such facilities were not used for sectarian instruction or religious worship for a period of twenty years. If the facilities were so used, then the government was entitled to a recovery of the funds expended. The act

---

56. *Levitt v. Committee for Public Educ. and Religious Liberty*, 413 U.S. 472, 93 S.Ct. 2814, 37 L.Ed.2d 736 (1973); *Committee for Public Educ. and Religious Liberty v. Nyquist*, 413 U.S. 756, 93 S.Ct. 2955, 37 L.Ed.2d 948 (1973).

57. 403 U.S. 672, 91 S.Ct. 2091, 29 L.Ed.2d 790 (1971).

was challenged as an impermissible use of tax funds for the support of religious institutions, but the United States Supreme Court disagreed, holding that the act was constitutional except for that portion which provided for the twenty year limit on the religious use of the facilities. The intent of the statute was to provide across-the-board benefits to all American colleges, rather than to advance the cause of religion. Further, the Court felt that subsidies for college buildings, unlike those of teachers' salaries, did not create the probability of undesirable entanglement between church and state. The buildings were nonideological in character, and the subsidy was a one-time, single-purpose grant unlike the continuing payments under the Rhode Island and Pennsylvania statutes.

Justice White, in a separate opinion, concurred with the majority in *Tilton,* but objected to the distinction made between the financing of college buildings for church-based colleges and the payment of supplementary salaries to teachers for the teaching of secular subjects. He could see no reason why, in the Rhode Island case, the Court refused to believe that religion could be kept out of the classroom during the period of time paid for by tax funds, but at the same time, it was persuaded that religion would be kept out of buildings similarly financed.* Douglas, Black, Marshall, and Brennan dissented, finding that the program did indeed aid religion, thus violating the Establishment Clause. As part of the majority in *Lemon,* they like White, saw no distinction between the two cases, but they would have invalidated both.

---

* White also noted the distinction that has consistently been made in funding colleges and universities on one hand, and elementary and secondary schools on the other. The G.I. Bill of Rights (1943), the National Defense Education Act (1958) and the Higher Education Act of 1963, all enacted prior to ESEA in 1965, were passed by Congress with little controversy over the First Amendment issue, though all provide benefits to church-related colleges. The decisions in *Lemon* and *Tilton* are consistent with this distinction. The reasons for differential treatment are largely political and sociological, rather than legal or constitutional.

In cases like *Lemon* and *Tilton,* the Court has no doubt been made aware that the political price of federal funding for public education may be some form of federal and state aid to church-related schools. To date, the issue is still unresolved. There is no accurate estimate of how much aid has been given to parochial schools under permissible state programs, and while church connected schools have received benefits under all three titles of ESEA, the constitutionality of ESEA itself has yet to be tested in the courts. An uneasy peace exists between the protagonists on both sides, with neither quite as angry as in former years, but neither quite willing to accept the *status quo.*

While the aid to education issue was being litigated, a new issue emerged which potentially had far greater significance for the future of all religious institutions in the United States. In 1970, in *Walz v. Tax Commission* [58] a New York taxpayer challenged the property tax exemption granted by the state to a religious organization for property which it owned and used for religious purposes only. Such exemptions have been commonly granted throughout the United States as part of a general governmental policy of aiding the work of, and encouraging contributions to, non-profit organizations devoted to the public good. Walz contended that while the state might have a right to exempt secular organizations from tax payments, to exempt and thus aid religious organizations would constitute an establishment of religion forbidden by the First Amendment. The implications of the suit were tremendous: if Walz' view prevailed, the entire financial base of American religious institutions was threatened. Not only would religious groups have to raise additional funds to pay state, federal and local taxes, but contributions to those organizations would presumably no longer be tax deductible and might well decline sharply.

Walz' threat to the religious establishment was short lived; the United States Supreme Court, in an opinion written by Chief Justice Burger, rejected his claims. The test under the First

58.   397 U.S. 664, 90 S.Ct. 1409, 25 L.Ed.2d 697 (1970).

Amendment said Burger, was whether the act in question was intended to either establish or interfere with religion or had the effect of doing so. "The legislative purpose of the property tax exemption is neither the advancement nor the inhibition of religion . . ." [59] Quoting Justice Holmes' famous remark, "A page of history is worth a volume of logic," Burger pointed out that two centuries of tax exemption had not led to the establishment of religion and, on the contrary had promoted free exercise. Justice Harlan concurred, adding,

> . . . As long as the . . . exemption includes groups that pursue cultural, moral, or spiritual improvement in multifarious secular ways, including, I would suppose, groups whose avowed tenets may be antitheological, atheistic and agnostic, I can see no lack of neutrality in extending the benefit of the exemption to organized religious groups. [60]

Only Justice Douglas dissented. To him a tax exemption was the equivalent of a subsidy, a subsidy was a payment from tax funds for the support of a church, and the support of a church was precisely the kind of establishment of religion that is forbidden by the First Amendment. Regardless of the fact that churches performed welfare work for the community that was secular in nature, such as the care of the sick, neither the states nor the federal government had the right to extend financial help to religious organizations. This kind of help, Douglas argued, could not be justified as an extension of the child benefit theory since the aid in question was given directly to the church rather than to individuals. "The financial support rendered here is to the church, the place of worship. A tax exemption is a subsidy." [61]

Douglas' dissent raises the interesting question of whether *Walz* would permit the direct subsidization of religious organizations. Despite his declaration that a tax exemption is the same

59.  Ibid., at 672.          61.  Ibid., at 704.

60.  Ibid., at 697.

as a subsidy, it is doubtful that subsidies would be constitutionally permissible. While tax exemptions may be the *financial* equivalent of subsidies (a position in which Justice Harlan concurred), there is at least one essential difference. A tax exemption can be given only to a going organization which already has income or owns property that can benefit from tax exemption. A subsidy, on the other hand, can be given to any individual or organization at any stage in its existence. Thus, tax exemption can benefit only a church already in existence, i. e., one that has already gotten and retained support from private sources. The initiative for starting and maintaining the organization came from outside the government. A subsidy, on the other hand, is far more dangerous because it permits the initiative to come from the government itself, or from individuals with no outside base of support, but with good contacts in the government funding agency.

In retrospect, church-state issues have not played as important a role in American history as have controversies over economic regulations, race relations, or freedom for political dissenters, nor have they aroused the sustained intense partisanship other issues have. For the most part, religion in America has been something that is there, to be taken or left according to individual preference. Nevertheless, cases involving church-state issues have been very important because in deciding them, the United States Supreme Court has repeatedly been forced to rethink and reevaluate the terms of the social contract by which America is governed—to redefine important dimensions of the relationship of man to the state. They are important, not least, because they are *civilized,* having transferred to the courts, controversies that historically were so often settled with bloodshed on the streets.

# Chapter IV

# CRIMINAL PROCEDURE

"The history of liberty has largely been the history of the observance of procedural safeguards."

Felix Frankfurter, *McNabb v. United States*

"A policeman's affidavit should not be judged as an entry in an essay contest."

Abe Fortas, dissenting, *Spinelli v. United States*

"The progress of science in furnishing the government with means of espionage is not likely to stop with wire-tapping."

Louis Brandeis, *Olmstead v. United States*

The interest of the United States Supreme Court in the rights of criminal defendants has gained momentum in the last fifteen years. While criminal procedure decisions have been handed down from time to time throughout the entire history of the Court, since World War II their number has been increasing, and in the last decade and a half, they have formed a significant part of the Court's case load. The earliest decisions in this area attracted little public attention; others, particularly in the area of confessions and the right to counsel, have been quite controversial and have attracted attention from the public at large, as well as from those directly involved in the law enforcement field. A large number of these decisions have been concerned with the legality of various kinds of police procedures, such as how and under what circumstances the police may arrest a suspect, or search him or his home; whether wiretapping or electronic eavesdropping is permissible; how rigorously the police may

140

question a suspect for the purposes of obtaining incriminating information; how voluntary a "voluntary" confession must be; and when a suspect is entitled to confer with counsel. While police procedure probably constitutes the largest single category of criminal procedure decisions made by the Supreme Court, several other important issues have also been of concern: the conglomeration of rights that ensure a fair trial, such as the right to a jury selected without class or racial prejudice, and the right to be free from excessive prejudicial publicity; the right to reasonable bail; the right not to be placed in double jeopardy; and the right not to be subjected to cruel and unusual punishment. All of the cases in the above areas considered by the United States Supreme Court have raised new questions even while they have settled others. Basically, these cases, while seemingly concerned with the technicalities of criminal procedure, are really concerned with the kind of world we wish to live in. The questions that are left unanswered relate not only to the way this world will look, but whether such a world is even possible to achieve.

*Search and Seizure*

The restriction on the right of the police to arrest is the hallmark of a free society. The basic condition for freedom, as far as any individual is concerned, is that he cannot legally be seized in an arbitrary or capricious manner at the discretion or whim of any government official. It is customary to refer to the writ of *habeas corpus,* the "Great Writ," as the guarantor of personal freedom in a democracy. The reference is correct; but it should be noted that *habeas corpus* is merely a method of *remedying* wrongful administrative action. The writ of *habeas corpus* is a challenge to an arrest or other detention *which has already occurred* and which may have been illegal. The statutory and constitutional standards for the making of an arrest are of crucial importance because they *prevent* police action which may be very harmful to the individual. Furthermore, by establishing a standard for *legal* police action, they make it possible to obtain *habeas corpus* relief from other kinds of action.

No other constitutionally guaranteed personal rights are meaningful in the absence of strict controls on the right of the police to arrest. To say that the individual enjoys freedom of speech or freedom of religion when he may be arbitrarily arrested for exercising either freedom is a contradiction in terms. In the United States, historically, purely political arrests have been relatively infrequent, at least as compared to the vast numbers of arrests that have been made for criminal activity. It is very important, nevertheless, that stringent controls be maintained over the right to arrest, for at least three reasons: (1) the Constitution exists for criminal suspects just as much as for any other individuals, and it is important that their rights be protected; (2) erosion of rights in one area leads to erosion of rights in other areas, and the protection of the criminal suspect's rights is essential for the protection of other people's rights; and (3) many activities which are political in nature, such as street assemblies, picketing, and mass demonstrations of all kinds, also fall afoul of the criminal law, and it is essential for political freedom that standards for the enforcement of the criminal law be strict and evenhanded.

The Fourth Amendment of the United States Constitution is the source of constitutional protection from arbitrary arrest.

> The right of the people to be secure in their persons, houses, papers, and effects, against unreasonable searches and seizures, shall not be violated, and no warrants shall issue, but upon probable cause, supported by oath or affirmation, and particularly describing the place to be searched, and the persons or things to be seized.

As interpreted by the courts, the standard for a legal arrest is "probable cause." Probable cause has no precise definition but has been described as something more than mere suspicion and something less than "beyond a reasonable doubt." The policeman, therefore, can arrest only if he has sufficient reliable information to establish a fair degree of certainty in his mind that a particular individual has committed an offense warranting an arrest. Similarly, he may search either a suspect or the premises to which a suspect has had access only on the basis of probable cause, rather than on mere suspicion or a hunch, and when he does search he may normally do so only for certain categories of evidence: the instrumentalities of a crime, the fruits of a crime, or contraband (that which it is illegal to possess, such as heroin, or policy slips).

Searches and seizures may be made either with or without a warrant. A warrant is an order issued by a magistrate who in effect certifies as to the soundness of the policeman's judgment that probable cause exists. If time and circumstances permit, warrants must be obtained prior to arrests or searches. Frequently, however, the fleeing of a criminal caught in the act or the threat that important evidence will be destroyed will necessitate on-the-spot police action. Such proceedings without benefit of warrant are legal, providing the police officer had probable cause for his actions.*

The Constitution forbids unreasonable searches and seizures, but it does not define the term "unreasonable." The courts have held, however, that at a very minimum, an *illegal* search is unreasonable, hence unconstitutional. Theoretically, the police are thus deterred from making any but legal searches and seizures. Practice, unfortunately, does not conform with theory. The police have made in the past, and continue to make at present, thousands of illegal arrests and searches each year. The justification offered for this illegal activity varies with individual cases, but the chief reason is probably that, in the opinion of the officer, the act was necessary in order for him to fulfill his function of maintaining law and order. In the practice of his profession the policeman acquires an expertise which leads him to look upon certain kinds of people in certain circumstances as suspects

* Most arrests are, in fact, made without a warrant, since arrests usually take place during or immediately following the commission of a crime. On the other hand, searches not incident to arrest are normally made with warrants.

and to take action against them.  The fact that his standards for action vary from the legal standards established by the courts does not deter him, because in his eyes, his standards are both more relevant and more binding than the court's standards which, after all, were established by a judge who likely had never walked a beat.  Where there has been a particularly nasty rape, for example, and the victim describes her attacker in general terms, it makes sense to many policemen to round up everyone in the immediate area who looks anything like the assailant.  This may or may not result in the arrest of the real culprit;  it positively *will* result in the arrest and detention of many entirely innocent people.  The courts, presumably, weigh the claims of the community for security from rapists against the need of individuals for freedom from arbitrary arrest.  The policeman, however, is not a social scientist, nor does he ordinarily wax philosophical.  His job is to find criminals, and he frequently goes about it in the most direct way he knows.

Another reason for the frequency of illegal arrests and procedures in this country is that police forces often see themselves as the agents of the most politically powerful groups in the community—the establishment.  And while they treat members of these groups with respect and even deference, they may treat politically impotent individuals, such as blacks, hippies, petty criminals, homosexuals, and drug users with contempt or brutality.  Occasionally, the illegality of police methods can be attributed to corruption within the police force.  This is less frequent, however, than illegality resulting from the distortions of the police role due to faulty perception of their function and place in society.

Whatever the reasons, however, it is unfortunate but true that American law enforcement, especially at the local level, has in the past been notorious for the frequency with which police officials utilized illegal methods.  It was in an attempt to remedy this condition that the "exclusionary rule" was developed and adopted by the courts.  In 1914, for the first time, the United States Supreme Court ruled that evidence seized in an illegal search could not be used in federal courts.* The purpose of this ruling was obvious: to deter federal agents from making illegal searches by removing the incentive, that is, by forbidding the use of the seized evidence in obtaining a conviction. Thus, since 1914, no convictions have been obtained in federal courts on the basis of illegally seized evidence. Federal agents have continued however, to make some illegal searches and seizures. The evidence thus obtained has either been used for the purpose of obtaining leads or informers, or, when appropriate, has been turned over to state law enforcement officials for use in the state courts.

Contrary to federal practice, up until 1950 relatively few states employed an exclusionary rule to deter police lawlessness. In 1949, police in Colorado illegally broke into the office of one Wolf, a physician who was suspected of being an abortionist. They seized his appointment book, which was subsequently used to obtain Wolf's conviction in state court. Wolf appealed on the ground that the use of illegal evidence by the state to obtain a conviction denied him due process of law and thus contravened the Fourteenth Amendment. Essentially, Wolf's claim was that for the state to break the law in order to convict him was basically unfair. A majority of the Supreme Court, in a decision written by Felix Frankfurter, agreed that an illegal search was contrary to the concept of "ordered liberty" and fell within the protection offered by the Fourteenth Amendment, but that the exclusionary rule was not *per se* required of the states. If the states chose to use the exclusionary rule as a method of disciplining their police forces they were free to do so, but there was no constitutional requirement for them to follow the federal

---

* *Weeks v. United States*, 232 U.S. 383, 34 S.Ct. 341, 58 L.Ed. 652 (1914). *Weeks* excluded illegal evidence only if seized by *federal* agents. Illegal evidence seized by state law enforcement officials could be turned over to federal agents and was admissible in federal courts. This so-called "silver platter" doctrine was declared unconstitutional by the United States Supreme Court in *Elkins v. United States*, 364 U.S. 206, 80 S.Ct. 1437, 4 L.Ed.2d 1669 (1960), which held that no matter who seized the evidence, if the seizure was illegal, its use in federal court was not permitted.

practice adopted in the *Weeks* case. Frankfurter pointed out that, as of 1949, only seventeen states were in agreement with the *Weeks* doctrine.[1]

The force of Frankfurter's reasoning was considerably weakened when, three years later he wrote a somewhat contradictory opinion in *Rochin v. California*.[2] Rochin was a suspected narcotics dealer whose house the police entered illegally. When they entered they found Rochin in his bedroom, partially dressed, sitting on his bed where his wife was lying. On the night table were two capsules which Rochin seized and swallowed upon seeing the officers. Assuming that the capsules contained illegal narcotics, the police grabbed the suspect, rushed him off to the hospital, and had his stomach pumped. The recovered evidence was used to obtain a conviction. Rochin appealed on the same grounds as Wolf: that the state's use of illegally seized evidence was a violation of the Fourteenth Amendment. This time Frankfurter agreed, not only that the search was a violation of the Fourteenth Amendment, but that the fruits of the search could not be used in court. The police-directed stomach pumping, Frankfurter said, was conduct that shocked the conscience.

*Wolf* and *Rochin,* taken together, present a confusing picture. The use of illegally seized evidence was clearly a violation of the Fourteenth Amendment and the evidence could—or could not— be used in state courts to obtain a conviction. The confusion was further compounded when the court held, in *Irvine v. California*,[3] that evidence obtained by *repeated* illegal entries by the police into the premises of the accused was admissible for purposes of obtaining a conviction. There seemed to be very little rhyme or reason behind these declarations of admissibility or non-admissibility, except perhaps the use of physical force on the defendant. Even this rationale was not clear, since the

1.  *Wolf v. Colorado*, 338 U.S. 25, 69 S.Ct. 1359, 93 L.Ed. 1782 (1949).

2.  342 U.S. 165, 72 S.Ct. 205, 96 L. Ed. 183 (1952).

3.  *Irvine v. California*, 347 U.S. 128, 74 S.Ct. 381, 98 L.Ed. 561 (1954).

Court upheld a conviction based on blood samples, drawn without consent from the accused, to prove his intoxication.*

There was, moreover, considerable protest both within and outside the United States Supreme Court against the notion that the states were free to do what was forbidden to the federal government. Many commentators felt that standards of due process must be comparable for state and federal authorities; that is, what is sauce for the goose must be sauce for the gander. The dissenters in the *Wolf* case, moreover, protested that to hold a search illegal but not apply the exclusionary rule was ridiculous, because the exclusionary rule was what made the Fourth and Fourteenth Amendments guarantees against illegal seizures a reality. After several years of confusion and heated controversy, the Court finally resolved the issue in the *Mapp* case [4] by declaring unconstitutional the use of illegally seized evidence in state courts.

Dolree Mapp was a Cleveland woman whose home was entered by the police acting on the basis of a tip that Miss Mapp was hiding a fugitive and/or a large amount of policy paraphernalia in her two-story home. When the officers initially demanded entry, Miss Mapp, after telephoning her lawyer, refused to admit them without a search warrant. Three hours later the police reappeared and forcibly entered the premises. When Miss Mapp demanded to see their warrant, a paper was held up by one of the officers. She snatched the paper and placed it in her bosom, whence it was immediately forcibly retrieved by a police officer who then handcuffed her. In the course of the ensuing search, neither the policy slips nor the fugitive was found. Some obscene literature was discovered in a basement trunk, and on the

---

* *Breithaupt v. Abram*, 352 U.S. 432, 77 S.Ct. 408, 1 L.Ed.2d 448 (1957). In all fairness it should be noted that the blood sample was drawn by appropriate medical personnel from an unconscious (and therefore unprotesting) patient. It is conceivable that had the defendant kicked, screamed or otherwise struggled, or had the sample been taken by police rather than physicians, the decision of the Court might have been otherwise.

4. *Mapp v. Ohio*, 367 U.S. 643, 81 S. Ct. 1684, 6 L.Ed.2d 1081 (1961).

basis of this evidence Miss Mapp was subsequently tried and convicted of the crime of possession of obscene literature. On appeal, the Supreme Court held that her conviction must be set aside because the requirements of the Fourth Amendment, as incorporated in the Fourteenth, made unconstitutional the use of illegally seized evidence. The Court specifically required the states to apply the exclusionary rule to illegally seized evidence. In *Mapp*, the majority apparently bought the argument of the dissenters in *Wolf:* that the exclusionary rule was the only effective method of deterring police lawlessness and effectuating constitutional guarantees. The Court also noted that by 1961, more than one-half of the states had adopted the exclusionary rule.

While the *Mapp* decision put an end to confusion over the admissibility of illegally seized evidence, it did not, unfortunately, end the problem of illegal law enforcement. Critics claimed that only some of the worst excesses and the more blatant disregard of the procedural niceties were curbed, but other procedures of dubious legality continued unchecked, such as the time-hallowed police custom of indiscriminately stopping and searching "suspicious" people on the street. The police argued that to perform their function of maintaining the peace through preventing crime, they must be permitted to stop and question individuals who look or act "wrong," and they held that the professional expertise gained from years of on-the-street observation gave them a rational basis for such judgment. Others charged that to give the police such wide discretion in the matter of on-the-street stops might expose everyone who was either unconventional or disliked by the police to harassment.

In 1968, three cases came to the United States Supreme Court questioning the constitutionality of such on-the-spot searches and questioning. *Terry v. Ohio*[5] involved a suspect who was stopped and searched by an experienced police officer who had observed the suspect apparently "casing" a store for robbery.

5.   392 U.S. 1, 88 S.Ct. 1868, 20 L.
Ed.2d 889 (1968).

*Sibron v. New York* [6] concerned a patrolman who questioned, and then reached into the pocket of a man whom he had observed over a period of eight hours to be in conversation with known drug addicts. In *Peters v. New York* [7] the suspect was collared and searched by an off-duty veteran policeman who saw Peters prowling around his (the policeman's) apartment house hallway. In each of these cases incriminating evidence was found: Terry had a gun, Sibron had heroin, and Peters had burglar's tools. Each defendant moved to suppress the incriminating evidence on the grounds that the police in each case had not had probable cause to make either the stop or the search.

In deciding these cases the Court was faced with a number of difficulties, some conceptual and some practical. If the Court were to declare that under certain circumstances policemen need not have probable cause in order to conduct a stop and search, then how much meaning would be left in *Mapp v. Ohio?* If probable cause was not to be the clear-cut constitutional standard for legality in searches and seizures, what standard would take its place? On the other hand, if the Court were to insist on a far higher standard for action than the police had traditionally observed for on-the-street stops and searches, would, or even could, the police obey such a decision? Were the police, in fact, correct in maintaining that a more flexible standard for street questioning was essential for proper law enforcement?

The Court decided that an on-the-street stop for brief questioning accompanied by a superficial search or patting down of external clothing was something less than a full-scale arrest and search in the constitutional meaning of those terms, and therefore, could be conducted on grounds somewhat less than the traditional probable cause. In *Terry,* the Court felt that the policeman's expertise, acquired through thirty-four years on the job, invested his decision to stop and search Terry with sufficient reasonableness to pass constitutional muster. In *Peters,* the

6. 392 U.S. 40, 88 S.Ct. 1889, 20 L. Ed.2d 917 (1968).

7. 392 U.S. 40, 88 S.Ct. 1889, 20 L. Ed.2d 917 (1968).

Court split on the question of whether the patrolman had probable cause, or only reasonable suspicion as a justification for his
search and seizure of the suspect.* All the justices agreed, however, that the search under the circumstances was not unreasonable. In *Sibron,* however, the Court agreed with the defendant's
contention that the policeman had insufficient grounds for his
search of Sibron's pocket. The state had justified the patrolman's search on the ground that an experienced officer could
logically have deduced from Sibron's lengthy conversation with
known addicts that Sibron was selling drugs, since only selling
and the negotiations connected with such sales would have required such protracted interaction. The Court rejected this argument and held that the officer had no reasonable grounds for
the search.

Very few working policemen would have agreed with the
Court's finding in *Sibron,* and many policemen saw the police action in this case to be fully as reasonable as the police action in
*Terry* or *Peters.* This suggests that something more than reasonableness or unreasonableness was behind the divergent result
in *Sibron.* *Terry* and *Peters* were concerned with crimes of violence or potential violence; *Sibron,* however, involved infraction
of a morals law. Perhaps, in balancing the equities, that is, the
need of the community for protection against the right of the individual to be free from police harassment, the Court was willing to tip the balance in favor of community protection only
where violent crime was concerned, especially in cases where the
policeman had reason to fear for his own safety. In *Sibron,* the
alleged offense was not a violent one, and traditionally it has
been in the area of the enforcement of morals legislation that
the greatest amount of police harassment of suspects has occurred. In the eyes of the Court, thus, *Sibron* may have ap-

* "It is difficult to conceive of
stronger grounds for an arrest
short of actual eyewitness observation of criminal activity." Warren, C. J., *Peters v. New York,* at

66. "I do not think that Officer
Lasky had anything close to probable cause to arrest Peters." Harlan, J. (concurring), at 74. Truth
is in the eye of the beholder.

peared to be a case where neither the community nor the policeman was endangered by a *violent* criminal suspect, and the alleged offense was of such nature than an unchecked police force might resort to considerable illegal harassment of suspects. The Court therefore, tipped the balance in favor of the defendant, apparently concluding that Sibron was more likely to need protection from the police than the community from Sibron.

To the criticism that in *Terry* and *Peters* the Court was backing away from the *Mapp* decision, Justice Warren responded,

> . . . Street encounters between citizens and police officers are incredibly rich in diversity. . . . Encounters are initiated by the police for a wide variety of purposes, some of which are wholly unrelated to a desire to prosecute for crime. Doubtless some police "field interrogation" conduct violates the Fourth Amendment. But a stern refusal by this Court to condone such activity does not necessarily render it responsive to the exclusionary rule. . . . it is powerless to deter invasions of constitutionally guaranteed rights where the police either have no interest in prosecuting or are willing to forego successful prosecution in the interest of serving some other goal.[8]

The Court said, in short, that no purpose would be served by too slavish an adherence to the exclusionary rule since the exclusionary rule only deterred the police *to the extent that the police wished to carry a case to the courts for prosecution.*

There are many reasons why a policeman may arrest or search other than a desire to prosecute the offender for a crime. The most important of these, perhaps, is that often when a policeman detains a minor offender, he is not so much interested in arresting him as in obtaining him as an informant. Once incriminating evidence is found, it matters little to the suspect that the search was illegal; the path of least resistance is to purchase freedom by supplying the police with information on

8. *Terry v. Ohio*, at 13–14.

more important criminals.  Even in important cases, moreover, where prosecution rather than information is the controlling consideration, the finding of contraband, for example, inevitably shifts the balance of forces against the suspect.  Courts tend to rationalize the legality of police behavior when the results in terms of evidence proved the police to have been correct in their original suspicions.  The norms of police organization also put pressure on the police to confiscate harmful objects such as narcotics or weapons, so that even if prosecution fails, the policeman feels that at least he has protected the community to the extent of removing dangerous commodities from circulation.  For all these reasons, the exclusionary rule is only a partially effective deterrent to illegal police action, and the *Terry, Peters,* and *Sibron* decisions were not so much a backing away from *Mapp* as a recognition of the realities and necessities of police procedure.[9]

Other Warren Court decisions continued the Court's tendency to approve dubious police procedures which, however, led to obtaining hard objective evidence of the guilt of the accused.  In *Davis v. Mississippi,*[10] a 1969 case, the Court indicated that even a dragnet fingerprinting campaign might be permissible if the police had prior permission from a judge.  The Court had earlier also permitted the use as evidence of a robber's clothing—"mere evidence"—as opposed to the usual fruits of the crime, instrumentalities of a crime, or contraband.[11]  The Court, during this period, also lowered the standards for the use of wiretap evidence and non-testimonial evidence, such as blood and urine samples drawn from the body of the accused.  (The use of body fluids as evidence presents Fifth Amendment as well as Fourth Amendment problems.  At least one justice—Black—consistent-

9. For further discussion of this point, see Jerome H. Skolnick, *Justice Without Trial* (New York: Wiley, 1966), Chap. 10.

10. 394 U.S. 721, 89 S.Ct. 1394, 22 L.Ed.2d 676 (1969).

11. *Warden, Md. Penitentiary v. Hayden,* 387 U.S. 294, 87 S.Ct. 1642, 18 L.Ed.2d 782 (1967).

ly held that if a man's conversation cannot be used to convict him, then neither can his blood, urine, or exhaled breath. Black's concept of *self*-incrimination extended to the flesh as well as the spirit.)

For five years after *Terry, Peters,* and *Sibron,* very few decisions were made by the United States Supreme Court in the area of procedurally defective searches and seizures. In 1973, however, the Court headed by Chief Justice Burger, handed down three decisions, *Cupp v. Murphy,*[12] *Schneckloth v. Bustamonte,*[13] and *U. S. v. Robinson,*[14] all of which continued the Warren Court policy of permitting the police moderate deviations from procedural norms for the purpose of producing non-testimonial evidence of the suspect's guilt. The decision in *Robinson,* moreover, seemed to eliminate the distinctions the Warren Court was willing to recognize in *Sibron.* While all three cases were decided in favor of the police by a majority of the Court, in *Cupp,* Justices Douglas and Brennan dissented, and in *Schneckloth* and *Robinson,* Justices Douglas, Brennan, and Marshall dissented.

In *Cupp v. Murphy,* the estranged wife of Daniel Murphy was found at home, dead from strangulation, with abrasions and lacerations on her throat. Murphy voluntarily appeared at the police station accompanied by his attorney. When the police observed a dark spot on Murphy's finger they asked whether they could take a sample of scrapings from his fingernails. Murphy refused, but the police nevertheless, took samples that turned out to contain bits of blood, skin, and fabric from the victim's nightgown. This evidence, introduced at the trial, resulted in Murphy's conviction. On appeal, the United States Supreme Court sustained the conviction on the ground that the police had had probable cause to arrest Murphy, and therefore, even though no arrest had in fact been made, the search was never-

12. 412 U.S. 291, 93 S.Ct. 2000, 36 L.Ed.2d 900 (1973).

13. 412 U.S. 218, 93 S.Ct. 2041, 36 L.Ed.2d 854 (1973).

14. 414 U.S. 218, 94 S.Ct. 467, 38 L. Ed.2d 427 (1973).

theless reasonable especially since the evidence might have been destroyed had the search been delayed.

In *Schneckloth v. Bustamonte,* a California police officer, while on routine patrol at 2:40 A.M. stopped a car operating with a burned out headlight and license plate light. Of the six occupants of the car, only one had identification, and the driver could not produce an operator's license. Two additional police officers then arrived, and when the officer asked whether he could search the car, one of the men said, "Sure, go ahead," and even helped by opening the trunk and glove compartment. Under the left rear seat the police found three checks previously stolen from a car wash. Arrests were made, and at the trial the defendant moved to suppress the evidence on the ground that while consent is one of the specifically established exceptions to the probable cause requirement for a search, consent had not been established inasmuch as no showing was made that the suspect knew he had a right to refuse the officer's request. The defendant was convicted, and on appeal the United States Supreme Court sustained the conviction, accepting the state's argument that the defendants, though poor and uneducated, and alone on a road with three armed policemen in the early hours of the morning could reasonably be supposed to be capable of knowing and exercising their right to refuse to permit a police search of their car.

*United States v. Robinson* was a Washington, D.C. case stemming from the arrest of Willie Robinson at 11 P.M. in an automobile which the police had reason to believe was being driven without Robinson's having an operator's license. In fact, Robinson was driving with a revoked permit, an offense for which District of Columbia law permits a full scale arrest. Robinson was arrested, taken to the station house and searched. In a cigarette package, the police found 14 capsules of heroin. Robinson moved to suppress the evidence on the ground that custodial arrest for a traffic offense was unnecessary and unusual and constituted insufficient legal ground for a complete search. The police also had had no right to open and look inside the cigarette package in Robinson's possession, which could simply have been removed from him.  Both the trial court, and ultimately the United States Supreme Court disagreed, accepting the counter-arguments of the state: the full-scale arrest was permissible under the statute and therefore was legal.  Further, when the police assumed custody of the suspect, they assumed total responsibility for him and therefore needed total control.  Such control necessitated a complete search, including a detailed inventory of the suspect's possessions so that he might have his property returned at the proper time.

In all three of these 1973 search and seizure cases, the Burger Court denied the claims of defendants, denials which were probably justified from a technical legal point of view.  In *Cupp,* the facts strongly suggested probable cause to arrest, and therefore to search, and the fact that the search was made prior to the arrest, was not necessarily significant.  In *Schneckloth,* though there was a question as to whether the consent given was truly informed, to have required the police to prove that the defendant knew he had a right to refuse, might in the real world have eliminated the possibility of any consent searches whatever, since a defendant, after the fact, could simply claim that his consent was uninformed.  In *Robinson,* however unusual an arrest for a traffic offense might have been, it was clearly permissible under the statute, and once the defendant was in custody, the police were obliged in the name of safety, to search him thoroughly.  Nevertheless, the three cases taken together created the impression that the Burger Court was not only continuing the pattern of the Warren Court—lowering procedural standards for the police in the interest of obtaining reliable evidence of guilt—but was encouraging the police to make questionable arrests and searches on increasingly technical grounds.[15]  This impression was heightened in 1976 by two more decisions in this

15.  For a full discussion of this issue, see Ruth G. Weintraub and Harriet Pollack, "The New Supreme Court and the Police," in Arthur Niederhoffer and Abraham Blumberg (eds.) *The Ambivalent Force,* 2nd ed., New York: Praeger, (1976), pp. 257–268.

area: *U. S. v. Watson* [16] and *U. S. v. Martinez-Fuerte.* [17] *Watson,*
a rather complex case, involved an informer who told United
States postal authorities that Watson had stolen credit cards in
his possession. An arrest was made, and the cards were found,
(though in Watson's car rather than on his person). The legal
problem was that the arrest and search were *warrantless,* even
though the authorities had had ample time and grounds to obtain a warrant. *Martinez-Fuerte* involved an arrest of illegal aliens who were found in a routine stop of the defendant's car by
customs officials at a check point north of the Mexican border.
While customs officials do not need probable cause to stop cars
at the border, the question in this case was whether they could
stop cars and question occupants routinely *inside* the border.
(Because of the physical difficulty of patrolling the entire United States-Mexican border, check points have been established
well within the United States where side roads leading from
Mexico converge with main United States routes). The Burger
Court decided both cases in favor of the government, and went
on to decide a third case which further restricted the rights of
defendants. In *Stone v. Powell,* [18] the Court in a 7–2 decision,
ruled that where a state has provided an opportunity of fully
and fairly litigating a Fourth Amendment claim of illegal search
or seizure, a state prisoner may not be granted *habeas corpus*
access to the federal courts for purposes of litigating that claim.
The Court, in effect, was removing itself (at least in Fourth
Amendment cases) as an overseer of the administration of justice in the states, provided that the state courts made provision
for determining whether searches and seizures met constitutional standards.

The Burger Court clearly does not like the exclusionary rule.
Like Cardozo, they deplore letting the criminal go free because
the constable has blundered. Some members of the Court, the

16. 423 U.S. 411, 96 S.Ct. 820, 46 L.
Ed.2d 598 (1976).

17. 428 U.S. 543, 96 S.Ct. 3074, 49
L.Ed.2d 1116 (1976).

18. 428 U.S. 465, 96 S.Ct. 3037, 49
L.Ed.2d 1067 (1976).

Chief Justice in particular, have indicated their feeling that communities are paying too heavy a price in loss of security for holding the police to what they see as excessively high technical standards. Yet, the Court has not overruled *Mapp*. For all its defects, and for all the attempts to modify it, the exclusionary rule still stands. The lessons of history have not been lost even on such conservatives as the Burger Court majority. The police excesses that *Mapp* was designed to curb were neither minor nor technical, but gross and flagrant. If police performance and legality have improved markedly in recent years, the much abused exclusionary rule must be given a good part of the credit.

*Wire-tapping and Electronic Eavesdropping*

In considering the constitutionality of government wiretapping and electronic eavesdropping, the basic problem is that the authors of the Constitution were not acquainted with telephone taps or electronic microphones. The Constitution talks of invasions of privacy in terms of unreasonable searches and seizures, referring obviously to physical entries by police officials into private premises. With the advent of modern electronic devices, snooping without physical penetration of the premises became a reality, and the question immediately arose whether a search for evidence via a tapped wire, or by means of an electronic listening device, was a search within the meaning of the Fourth Amendment. In *Olmstead v. United States*,[19] a case involving wiretapped evidence against a bootlegger, Chief Justice Taft, writing for a majority of the United States Supreme Court, held that a wiretap was not a search within the meaning of the Fourth Amendment, since there was no seizure of a tangible object, and since the evidence in question was obtained through the sense of hearing rather than by the usual physical act of searching. Four justices dissented vigorously, including Brandeis who protested that the intent of the founding fathers was obviously to protect the right of privacy—the right to be let

19.  277 U.S. 438, 48 S.Ct. 564, 72 L.
Ed. 944 (1928).

alone—and that the Fourth Amendment must, therefore, be interpreted broadly enough to handle problems stemming from technological advances. Holmes was repelled by the "dirtiness" inherent in wiretapping and the unattractive role that governmental officials were forced to play.

> .  .  . We have to choose, and for my part I think
> it is a less evil that some criminals should escape than
> that the government should play an ignoble part.[20]

Six years later, the question of whether a wiretap was a search within the meaning of the Fourth Amendment was mooted when Congress passed the Federal Communications Act, Section 605 of which provides:

> No person not being authorized by the sender shall intercept any communication and divulge or publish the existence, contents, substance, purport, effect, or meaning of any such communication to any person.

The courts subsequently interpreted this passage as applicable to both state and federal agents as well as private persons, and to messages both within the state or between two states.[21]  While the average English-speaking layman might thus conclude that wiretapping was made illegal for everyone all over the United States, the United States Department of Justice and the Federal Bureau of Investigation read Section 605 and came to the conclusion that unauthorized interception of telephone messages was permitted *if no divulgence takes place.*  Moreover, divulgence in the Department's lexicon was interpreted as to forbid publication or use in evidence but to permit use by agents in the preparation of cases for prosecution (that is, as leads).  As a result of this somewhat unusual interpretation of Section 605, federal agents continued to use wiretapping as a method of gathering evidence in federal cases.  In 1939, the United States Supreme Court held that neither interception nor divulgence was

---

20.  Ibid. at 470.

21.  *Nardone v. United States*, 302
U.S. 379, 58 S.Ct. 275, 82 L.Ed. 314
(1937).

permissible, and that even leads developed from wiretaps could not be used in federal courts.[22] State agents however, continued to wiretap despite Section 605, and in 1952, in *Schwartz v. Texas*,[23] the United States Supreme Court held that while Section 605 forbade such state action, the state courts were nevertheless not constitutionally compelled to exclude such illegally gathered evidence. Five years later this decision was modified slightly in *Benanti v. United States*,[24] when Chief Justice Warren held that the federal courts must exclude wiretap evidence illegally gathered by state agents, even if there was no collusion between the two sets of law enforcement officials. (Left undecided was the question of whether such evidence could be used in state courts.)

In a very real sense, however, the *Nardone, Benanti,* and *Schwartz* decisions were irrelevant, since both the United States Department of Justice and most of the states continued their operations in total disregard of what the United States Supreme Court had to say. The United States Department of Justice ordered wiretaps from 1931 at least until the start of the Carter administration in 1977 with the exception of a brief interval in 1941, and justified this practice by the idiosyncratic interpretation of Section 605 cited above. To criticisms that the Department ought not be doing what the Supreme Court so plainly said was illegal, the Departmental response was a bland statement that it wiretapped only when "national security" was involved. The United States Supreme Court was so ineffective in curbing wiretapping that some states passed laws specifically permitting what federal law prohibited.

The best known of these state laws is that of New York, which authorizes the state courts to issue orders which permit the tapping of wires for a specified length

**22.** *Nardone v. United States*, 308 U.S. 338, 60 S.Ct. 266, 84 L.Ed. 307 (1939).

**23.** 344 U.S. 199, 73 S.Ct. 232, 97 L. Ed. 231 (1952).

**24.** 355 U.S. 96, 78 S.Ct. 155, 2 L. Ed.2d 126 (1957).

of time. . . . The Supreme Court of the United States held in 1957 that every New York policeman who taps a wire under one of these orders and subsequently repeats what he has heard is guilty of a federal crime. But, despite the Supreme Court's clear statement that this is a federal crime, New York courts continue to issue wiretap orders, New York police continue to tap wires and to testify in court and the Department of Justice continues to look the other way.[25]

No one today knows how many illegal wiretaps were ordered in the past by state and federal officials, but it is clear that the occasional official figures issued far understated the real numbers, and there is evidence that thousands of wiretaps were authorized annually by law enforcement officials, and in addition, thousands of unauthorized, totally illegal wiretaps were placed by private individuals. To complicate matters even more, the use of electronic devices such as hidden microphones ("bugs") or parabolic receivers, became increasingly popular in contrast to the older method of physical intrusion on telephone wires. For a long time, electronic eavesdropping where there was no physical trespass was covered neither by Section 605 nor the Fourth Amendment,[26] and as a result, eavesdropping by anyone, including private persons, was legal under federal law and in all but seven states until 1968. In six of these seven states, moreover, eavesdropping was legal if done by authorized persons on court order.

In an attempt to remedy the more obvious abuses inherent in this state of statutory and constitutional anarchy, the United States Supreme Court struggled for years to restrict electronic eavesdropping practices without going back to the ultimate constitutional question which had been decided so unsatisfactorily in *Olmstead:* Was eavesdropping by a government official on a private individual's conversation a prohibited search within the

25. Edward Bennett Williams, *One Man's Freedom* (New York: Atheneum, 1962), pp. 113–114.

26. *Goldman v. United States*, 316 U.S. 129, 62 S.Ct. 993, 86 L.Ed. 1322 (1942).

meaning of the Fourth Amendment? To avoid upsetting the *Olmstead* decision the Court went so far (in *Silverman v. United States* [27]) as to assert that sticking a spike microphone into a party wall a short distance until it made contact with a heating duct in a house was a physical trespass forbidden by the Fourth Amendment, even though the physical penetration of the microphone into the premises of the defendant was miniscule.

The Court also developed the principle that an unauthorized disclosure of a confidential communication is permissible if the disclosure is made by or with the consent of one of the parties to the conversation. In *On Lee v. United States*,[28] an undercover agent of the Federal Narcotics Bureau entered the defendant's premises with the latter's consent and, while conversing with him, elicited several incriminating statements. The narcotics agent had on his person an electronic transmitter which conveyed On Lee's statements to another agent outside the premises. Similarly, in *Lopez v. United States*,[29] an Internal Revenue agent who falsely represented himself as willing to accept a bribe, instead recorded Lopez's illegal offer on a pocket tape recorder. In both cases the Court reasoned that when the defendants made their incriminating statements to parties who subsequently turned out to be undercover agents, they assumed a risk that the other party to the conversation might not be trustworthy. The rationale was a kind of *caveat emptor* policy with relation to conversations. Thus, when James Hoffa made incriminating statements to an undercover government informer who had entered Hoffa's hotel suite under false pretenses, the Court held that Hoffa should not have been so naive as to trust the informer. The majority of the Court felt that the evidence had been obtained not by an invasion of Hoffa's privacy, but rather because of Hoffa's misplaced confidence in the undercover agent.

27. 365 U.S. 505, 81 S.Ct. 679, 5 L. Ed.2d 734 (1961).

28. 343 U.S. 747, 72 S.Ct. 967, 96 L. Ed. 1270 (1952).

29. 373 U.S. 427, 83 S.Ct. 1381, 10 L.Ed.2d 462 (1963).

.   .   .   The argument is that Partin's failure to
disclose his role as a government informer vitiated the
consent that the petitioner gave to Partin's repeated entries into [Hoffa's hotel] suite, and that by listening to
the petitioner's statements Partin conducted an illegal
"search" for verbal evidence.

Where the argument fails is in its misapprehension
of the fundamental nature and scope of Fourth Amendment protection.   What the Fourth Amendment protects is the security a man relies upon when he places
himself or his property within a constitutionally protected area, be it his home or his office, his hotel room
or his automobile.   .   .   .

.   .   .   Partin was in the suite by invitation, and
every conversation which he heard was either directed
to him or knowingly carried on in his presence.   The
petitioner, in a word, was not relying on the security of
the hotel room;  he was relying upon his misplaced confidence that Partin would not reveal his wrongdoing.
.   .   .

Neither this Court nor any member of it has ever expressed the view that the Fourth Amendment protects
a wrongdoer's misplaced belief that a person to whom
he voluntarily confides his wrongdoing will not reveal
it.   .   .   .[30]

Despite the earnest efforts of the Court to avoid reevaluating
*Olmstead,* the question of whether information obtained by
eavesdropping or wiretapping therefore was obtained by an un-

---

30.   *Hoffa v. United States,* 385 U.S.
293 at 300–302, 87 S.Ct. 408, 412,
413–414, 17 L.Ed.2d 374 (1966).
There was vigorous dissent from
Justices Warren and Douglas who
felt it was basically unfair for the
government to use a paid informer
as a stool pigeon, especially when,
as was true of Partin, he was in

prison facing indictment for serious crimes.   Douglas remarked
that a man may have to assume
the risk that a friend will turn
against him, but the planting of
an undercover agent constituted an
unlawful breach of privacy by the
government.

constitutional search simply would not go away. Finally, in 1967, in *Berger v. New York*,[31] the Court overruled *Olmstead* by holding that conversations are protected by the Fourth Amendment, and an eavesdrop is a constitutionally impermissible search. Berger was convicted of conspiracy to bribe the chairman of the New York State Liquor Authority on evidence obtained by a series of wiretaps placed by the District Attorney of New York County. The wiretaps were placed pursuant to a New York State law, which authorized certain administrative officials to request a court order for a wiretap if there were reasonable grounds to believe that evidence of a crime might thus be obtained. The persons to be eavesdropped on and the telephone number involved had to be specified, and the order was effective for only two months unless renewed. Berger appealed his conviction by challenging the constitutionality of the New York State statute under the Fourth Amendment. The Court reversed Berger's conviction on the ground that the sweep of the New York statute was far too broad. To pass constitutional muster, reasonable ground would have to be the equivalent of probable cause, and the crime, the place to be searched, and the conversations to be seized would also have to be specified.

The *Berger* decision freed Berger, at least temporarily, but it clearly opened the door to the legalization of wiretapping and electronic eavesdropping. While the decision did much to end the absurdities and strained interpretations forced on the Court by the *Olmstead* decision, nevertheless, by bringing conversations under the protection of the Fourth Amendment, the Court paradoxically opened the door to legalized electronic surveillance. The Court defined its position even more clearly in *Katz v. United States*,[32] decided shortly after *Berger*. Katz was convicted of transmitting betting information in violation of federal law, on the basis of evidence obtained from an FBI bug of a public telephone. Once again, the conviction of the defendant was reversed because of procedural irregularities. (In this case, al-

31. 388 U.S. 41, 87 S.Ct. 1873, 18 L. Ed.2d 1040 (1967).

32. 389 U.S. 347, 88 S.Ct. 507, 19 L. Ed.2d 576 (1967).

though the FBI had had sufficient grounds for the search, and had carefully limited the scope of its surveillance, no proper warrant had been obtained.) At the same time, the Court clearly indicated that electronic eavesdropping is constitutionally permissible under restrictions similar to those required for traditional searches.

In 1968, Congress, taking advantage of the broad hints dropped by the Court in *Berger* and *Katz,* enacted, as Title III of the Omnibus Crime Control and Safe Streets Act, a series of regulations establishing guidelines for legal wiretapping and eavesdropping. The Act is quite complex, but the substance of it tries to create as close a parallel as possible with the traditional restrictions on the usual kinds of physical searches and seizures, that is, the person and place to be searched must be specified, the application must be made by an administrative official to a judge, and the evidence procured may be used only for specific purposes.

Although *Berger, Katz,* and Title III made contributions towards bringing order into the chaos of the wiretapping and eavesdropping field, confusion, constitutional and otherwise, was still the order of the day. The establishment of legal guidelines did not end the prevalent police custom of illegally tapping and snooping electronically, nor did it end the totally unauthorized, completely illegal use of eavesdropping by private individuals. Worse yet, the legal guidelines established in Title III had so many loopholes that it is questionable whether any effective control over law enforcement officials had been established at all. For one thing, there could not be any advance notice to the subject that his premises were about to be searched, as there is when the warrant is produced in a conventional search. For another, although Title III required the termination of a tap after thirty days (unless an extension is obtained from the court), how could such termination be enforced and/or verified? Was overhearing a conversation a search or a seizure, or both? If a conversation was heard, but not used, was the tapping or bugging a seizure, or merely a search? Could there be such a thing as an overheard conversation that was not used? How could a defendant protect himself against a tap that had been tampered with? What controls were there over the police to ensure that the tape recording introduced into evidence was accurate and intact? Was a tap which was conducted over a period of time a single intrusion into the suspect's privacy, or a series of intrusions? If it was a series of intrusions, could it be legally justified on the basis of only one showing of cause? What about the rights of innocent third persons who might have been party to the conversations under surveillance? Were not the rights of such persons infringed far more than would have been the case in a traditional search?

The inadequacies of Title III were perhaps most glaringly revealed, however, in the national security field. The Act provided for eavesdropping without a warrant for 48 hours in cases involving either national security or organized crime. (After 48 hours the search could be continued only after a warrant had been obtained from a court.) The definition of the terms "national security" and "organized crime" was left largely to administrative discretion however, and most serious of all, the loose wording of the Act encouraged the Nixon administration to claim and exercise investigatory powers unprecedented in American history. This claim was finally challenged in *United States v. United States District Court*,[33] a case involving right-wing political extremists charged with conspiring to destroy government property. In seeking evidence against the defendants, the government had tapped their telephones without a court order, relying on Section (3) of Title III which stated that none of the Act's requirements shall

> . . . limit the constitutional power of the President to take [necessary measures to protect] against the overthrow of the Government by force or other unlawful means, or against any other clear and present

33. 407 U.S. 297, 92 S.Ct. 2125, 32 L.Ed.2d 752 (1972).

danger to the structure or existence of the Government.

The Justice Department, headed by Attorney-General John S. Mitchell, argued that in national security matters, the President had an inherent right to protect the nation that was not limited by the customary requirements of the Fourth Amendment; that the President could order electronic surveillance at any time of any person if he, in his uncorroborated judgment, felt national security was endangered. The United States Supreme Court unanimously disagreed, finding that the section of Title III relied upon did no more than declare that Title III did not "legislate with respect to national security surveillance." The government, (in this case, the executive branch), most assuredly was bound by the standards of the Fourth Amendment—in domestic security cases even more than in others—since such cases presented even greater jeopardy to constitutionally protected speech. In somewhat offended tones, the Court rejected the Justice Department's contention that only the executive branch was capable of handling the problems presented by political extremists.

We cannot accept the Government's argument that internal security matters are too subtle and complex for judicial evaluation. Courts regularly deal with the most difficult issues of our society. There is no reason to believe that federal judges will be insensitive to or uncomprehending of the issues involved in domestic security cases. Certainly courts can recognize that domestic security surveillance involves different considerations from the surveillance of "ordinary crime." If the threat is too subtle or complex for our senior law enforcement officers to convey its significance to a court, one may question whether there is probable cause for surveillance.

Nor do we believe prior judicial approval will fracture the secrecy essential to official intelligence gathering. The investigation of criminal activity has long involved imparting sensitive information to judicial officers who have respected the confidentialities involved. Judges may be counted upon to be especially conscious of security requirements in national security cases. . . .[34]

The *District Court* case was followed closely by the Watergate scandal and the forced resignation of President Nixon. Since then, no president has asserted his claim to unspecified inherent powers in the area of national security. With the revelation of decades of shocking illegal activities by the FBI and CIA,[*] a major effort by the Carter administration has been to draw up legislation which will prevent abuse of the intelligence gathering and law enforcement powers of the government. A bill was introduced in May, 1977 which would extend and strengthen the warrant requirement for electronic surveillance in national security cases and which specifically did not recognize the inherent power of the President to authorize such activity outside the provisions of the bill.[35] This bill, along with several other similar measures are, as of this writing, still under consideration.

Wiretapping, as Justice Holmes said so long ago, is a dirty business. It is probably impossible to conduct a wiretap without violating the civil liberties of the defendant, and the opportunities for lawless police work, harassment, and invasion of privacy are almost unlimited. It is a procedure which raises the hackles of every civil libertarian, but which traditionally has been defended as an efficacious tool in law enforcement which police and prosecutors have maintained they could not dispense with, and should not be asked to give up. Recently, however, critics have suggested that not only is wiretapping "dirty" and danger-

34. Ibid., at 320–321.

* Government records indicate that the FBI illegally spied on the Socialist Worker's party for well over 30 years, monitoring their mail, wiretapping, bugging, and burglarizing their offices!

35. *New York Times*, May 19, 1977, p. 1.

ous to civil liberties, but it is also far less effective in the fight against crime and subversion than its defenders would have the public believe. Herman Schwartz, Professor of Law at the State University of New York at Buffalo, maintains that wiretapping has had only a very limited impact on organized crime, and none at all on street crime.[36] From the time of the enactment of Title III in 1968 to 1976, federal and state governments installed 5,495 legal taps or bugs and listened in on 3.6 million conversations between 282,429 people for law enforcement purposes, not including hundreds of thousands of people eavesdropped upon ostensibly for national security purposes. Of those placed under surveillance, over half were suspected of illegal gambling activities, and one-quarter of dealing in drugs. In 1975 and 1976, over 80 percent of the taps were on small time gamblers and drug peddlers. These taps, moreover, were costly: $11,000 for the average gambling tap, $20,000 for a drug tap, exclusive of the cost of police, prosecutors' and judges' time in preparing and processing the applications.

The breakdown shows that in only 7 percent of the federal cases, none of which involved major crimes, were there convictions for other federal crimes. On the state level, the classic example is that of Special Prosecutor Maurice Nadjari of New York who installed a tap that "operated for almost three months, overheard 123 people in 625 conversations, cost at least $110,000 . . . and never produced a single arrest." [37]

Schwartz also suggests that legislative attempts to prevent indiscriminate eavesdropping in national security cases by strict enforcement of the warrant and "probable cause" requirements are futile. In reviewing the operations under Title III, he found that while the applications for authorizing wiretaps had to show "probable cause," in the period from 1969 through 1976 only 15 out of 5,563 applications for wiretaps were rejected in both fed-

36.  Herman Schwartz, *Taps, Bugs, and Fooling the People* (New York: Field Foundation, 1977), (a pamphlet).

37.  Ibid., at 16.

eral and state courts.  As long as permission to eavesdrop can be granted in cases where no *criminal* activity is suspected, abuses are likely to persist.  It should be noted, moreover, that in the last few years under two Congresses and two Administrations, no one has been able to make a case that non-criminal standards for intelligence eavesdropping are essential for national security. Both Secretary of Defense Harold Brown and CIA Director Stansfield Turner have stated that their respective agencies could function within the Fourth Amendment and that the departure from the Fourth Amendment protections was "principally an FBI requirement."

No happy or simple solution suggests itself at this point to the problems raised by wiretapping.  Perhaps the best that can be hoped for is a political culture and climate of public opinion that frowns upon police harassment of individuals and unnecessary intrusions into their private lives.  Technology is not an unmixed blessing.

*Confessions and Right to Counsel*

In 1649, John Lilburn, on trial for treason, refused to answer questions, saying, "I am upon Christ's terms, when Pilate asked him whether he was the Son of God, and adjured him to tell him whether he was or no; he replied, 'Thou sayest it.'  So say I: thou, Mr. Prideaux, sayest it, they are my books.  But prove it." The right not to be forced to testify against oneself is historically very old.  Talmudic law, a compilation of ancient Hebrew legal dicta, practices and precedents predating the Christian Era, records the maxim *ein adam meissim atsmo rasha,* a man cannot represent himself as evil.[38]  The same notion appears in the Common Law a thousand years later as *nemo tenetur seipsum accusare,* no one is obliged to testify against himself.  The principle reappears in the Canon Law of the Catholic Church, and in the Fifth Amendment of the United States Constitution.

---

38. For an excellent discussion of the origins of the right against self-incrimination, see Leonard W.  Levy, *Origins of the Fifth Amendment* (New York: Oxford University Press, 1968).

The idea that a man should not be forced to incriminate himself in a criminal investigation no doubt arose in reaction to the inquisitorial practices of governmental authorities seeking to root out treason, heresy, subversion, or whatever offense or mode of thought seemed most threatening to the *status quo* of the time. Whether the issue involved Catholics rooting out apostate Protestants, Protestants searching for heretical Catholics, the Spanish Inquisition looking for Jews and disbelievers, or the Stuart kings investigating political opponents—whatever the issue historically, investigators and prosecutors have used physical torture to elicit confessions from hapless defendants. It was in reaction to this type of proceeding that the notion of a right against self-incrimination developed. It was the memory of what had gone before that led the founding fathers to incorporate into the Fifth Amendment the phrase "nor shall any person be compelled in any criminal case to be a witness against himself." As Chief Judge Calvert Magruder once said, "Our forefathers, when they wrote this provision into the Fifth Amendment of the Constitution, had in mind a lot of history which has been largely forgotten today." [39]

Traditionally, the United States Supreme Court has excluded physically coerced confessions on the ground that such confessions might very well be unreliable or untrue because of the duress used against defendants to produce them. *Brown v. Mississippi*,[40] in 1936, was the first Fourteenth Amendment due process confession case decided by the United States Supreme Court. The conviction of the defendant was reversed when the record was found to indicate that the deputy who had presided over the beating of the defendants conceded that one of them had been whipped, but "not too much for a Negro; not as much as I would have done if it were left to me." The Court, rejecting the law officer's evaluation of black psychology, decided that even a slipshod whipping might make the resulting confession unreliable, and therefore inadmissible. In 1944 the Court reject-

---

39. Levy, p. viii.

40. 297 U.S. 278, 56 S.Ct. 461, 80 L. Ed. 682 (1936).

ed a confession obtained after thirty-six hours of continuous interrogation of the defendant by the police.[41] The exclusion of such confessions was, at least in part, an attempt by the Court to discipline lawless police officers by refusing them the conviction they had worked to obtain.

As the quality of police work improved in the years after World War II, the use of severe physical torture by the police declined, at least insofar as cases seeking Supreme Court review were concerned. More recent cases have concerned the use of psychological, rather than physical, pressure on defendants. In *Spano v. New York*[42] the accused was questioned for eight hours by six police officers in relays and was told falsely that the job and welfare of a friend who was a rookie cop depended on his confession. He was also refused contact with his lawyer. The Court reversed Spano's conviction by holding his confession inadmissible because involuntary, but a reading of the majority opinion shows that the Court was moving away from the old unreliability rationale to a new rationale of fairness. There was not sufficient physical force used against Spano to warrant the conclusion that his confession was untrue; but the use of such a confession was repugnant to the Court because it was obviously not a voluntary statement.

> The abhorrence of society to the use of involuntary confessions does not turn alone on their inherent untrustworthiness. It also turns on the deep-rooted feeling that the police must obey the law while enforcing the law; that in the end life and liberty can be as much endangered from illegal methods used to convict those thought to be criminals as from the actual criminals themselves. . . .[43]

In *Spano* the Court was adding a new dimension to the old unreliability standard: the importance of the state and its agents

41. *Ashcraft v. Tennessee*, 322 U.S. 143, 64 S.Ct. 921, 88 L.Ed. 1192 (1944).

42. 360 U.S. 315, 79 S.Ct. 1202, 3 L. Ed.2d 1265 (1959).

43. Ibid., at 320–321.

observing the decencies of civilized behavior. Even if a defendant's confession is reliable and can be independently verified, it must not be used if the defendant was coerced, psychologically or otherwise, into making it. Though this fairness rationale may be new in terms of Supreme Court jurisprudence, it probably hews more closely to the thinking of the old Talmudists than does the unreliability standard, in that the purpose of the old Talmudic law was primarily the preservation of the dignity and integrity of the defendant as a human being. As Dean Erwin Griswold of Harvard (later Solicitor General of the United States) has said,

> We do not make even the most hardened criminal sign his own death warrant, or dig his own grave, or pull the lever that springs the trap on which he stands. We have through the course of history developed a considerable feeling of the dignity and intrinsic importance of the individual man. Even the evil man is a human being.[44]

The state, in short, may convict and punish a defendant, but it must not force him to condemn himself out of his own mouth. The current interpretation of the self-incrimination clause of the Fifth Amendment thus enhances a constellation of values: lawful law enforcement, the reliability of evidence used for conviction, and the preservation of the dignity of the accused.

The exclusion of coerced confessions, like the exclusion of illegally seized evidence, is an only partly effective sanction against undesirable police and prosecutorial practices. Unless all confessions are to be eliminated, there is no means of excluding the confession which results from the fear induced in the defendant by the very circumstances surrounding the process of arrest and arraignment. Only the most experienced and hardened criminal can fail to be terrified when surrounded by armed policemen in a strange and forbidding environment, cut off from communication with friends and family, and faced with an accusation,

---

44. As quoted in Williams, p. 127.

which, if proved, may lead to severe punishment. Even the most secure defendant feels panic and bewilderment. Under these circumstances, any questioning by the police is threatening, and any statement by the accused, especially if he is not completely aware of his legal rights, is not really a voluntary statement given with consent based on knowledge. An example of this is the case of Danny Escobedo: [45]

On the night of January 19, 1960, Escobedo's brother-in-law was fatally shot. At 2:30 A.M. Danny was arrested without a warrant and questioned. He made no statement to the police, and was released fourteen and one-half hours later, after a lawyer retained by his family had secured a writ of *habeas corpus*. Because of the testimony of one DiGerlando, another suspect who had fingered Danny for the murder, Danny and his sister, the widow of the deceased, were arrested and taken to police headquarters. With his hands handcuffed behind his back, as Danny later testified without contradiction, the "detectives said they had us pretty well, up pretty tight, and we might as well admit to this crime," to which Danny replied, "I'm sorry but I would like to have advice from my lawyer." His request was denied, even after the lawyer arrived and requested permission to see his client.

Escobedo was questioned for several hours, handcuffed and standing up. Finally, a Spanish-speaking police officer suggested to him that, if he pinned the murder on DiGerlando, he could be released. Escobedo, in a face-to-face confrontation with DiGerlando, accused the latter, saying "I didn't shoot Manuel, you did it." By his statement, Escobedo for the first time admitted some knowledge of the crime, and also acknowledged complicity, an admission which, under Illinois law is as damaging as firing the fatal shot. On the basis of this and other statements made by Escobedo, he was ultimately convicted. At no point during his questioning had anyone advised him of his right to remain

45. *Escobedo v. Illinois*, 378 U.S. 478, 84 S.Ct. 1758, 12 L.Ed.2d 977 (1964).

silent, and it was apparent that he was unaware of the legal implications of his statement accusing DiGerlando.  His conviction was appealed to the United States Supreme Court on the ground that the police denial of his request to speak to his lawyer made the statement elicited in the subsequent statement inadmissible, because the defendant had, in effect, been denied his right not to incriminate himself.  The United States Supreme Court agreed, saying that where

> .  .  .  the investigation is no longer a general inquiry into an unsolved crime but has begun to focus on a particular suspect, the suspect has been taken into police custody, the police carry out a process of interrogations that lends itself to eliciting incriminating statements, the suspect has requested and been denied an opportunity to consult with his lawyer, and the police have not effectively warned him of his absolute constitutional right to remain silent, the accused has been denied "the Assistance of Counsel" in violation of the Sixth Amendment to the Constitution as "made obligatory upon the States by the Fourteenth Amendment," *Gideon v. Wainwright* and that no statement elicited by the police during the interrogation may be used against him at a criminal trial.[46]

While the Court based its decision on Escobedo's Sixth Amendment right to counsel, the real thrust of the decision was to protect the defendant's *Fifth Amendment right not to incriminate himself*.  What the Court was saying, in effect, was that to make the right against self-incrimination a reality for a suspect detained in police custody, the services of an attorney are essential; that most accused persons are too scared, too ignorant, too flustered, and too bewildered to utilize effectively the protection offered by the Fifth Amendment without the support and advice of an attorney trained in the law.  The decisions rendered in *Mi-*

46.  Ibid., at 490–491.

*randa* and its companion cases * two years later add very little conceptually to *Escobedo*. They simply set down in fairly explicit form the guidelines for lawful police procedure: that a suspect must be warned of his right to remain silent; that he must be told of his right to consult with a lawyer, and have his lawyer with him during interrogation: that if the suspect indicates that he wishes counsel, questioning must stop until counsel is present; and that if the accused is without funds to obtain a lawyer, a lawyer will be appointed for him.

Very few people aware of the realities of police procedure will disagree with the Court on the need for counsel if the accused is to be effectively protected in his right to silence.** The *Escobedo* and *Miranda* decisions have, nevertheless, created a tremendous furor in law enforcement circles, largely on the ground that the presence of counsel will so inhibit the responses of the accused as to virtually forestall any possibility of a confession or even of information helpful to the police in their investigation. The police, in short, are afraid that if suspects are protected from having to answer questions relating to the crime, investigations will be so hamstrung that the solution of crimes will become impossible.

* *Miranda v. Arizona, Vignera v. New York, Westover v. United States,* and *California v. Stewart,* 384 U.S. 436, 86 S.Ct. 1602, 16 L.Ed.2d 694 (1966). Miranda was charged with rape, Vignera, Westover, and Stewart with robbery. In each case, the accused was questioned for several hours while in custody. While some of the defendants had been informed of some of their legal rights, none had been effectively informed of either his right to remain silent, or his right to have a lawyer present during questioning. No evidence of physical coercion was introduced, but in *Miranda,* there was some evidence that the "confession" was in police language rather than Miranda's own words. In each case, there was probably sufficient independent evidence for conviction without the use of a confession.

** John Griffiths and Richard E. Ayres, "A Postscript to the Miranda Project: Interrogation of Draft Protesters," *Yale Journal,* 77, (1967):300. The authors report the results of a study of twenty-one Yale faculty, staff members, and students who were interviewed in their homes by FBI agents in connection with their having turned in their draft cards as a gesture of protest against the Viet Nam war. The authors found that even where the suspects were highly educated,

While it is impossible to determine accurately how damaging *Miranda* and *Escobedo* have been to the police and prosecutorial processes, such evidence as has been gathered by studies of police practices in the eleven years since *Miranda* (1966) indicates that there is not too much factual basis for these fears.[47] For one thing, suspects frequently feel a strong need to talk to the police, either as a form of emotional catharsis, or because of a desire to explain away seemingly incriminating evidence or circumstances. Many suspects, even when warned, could not grasp the significance of what they were told, or in any event could not apply what they were told to the situation at hand. Furthermore, the police, even when they gave the required warnings, implied by their tone of voice, or by the selection of the words used, that the warnings were a routine formality and of no great consequence. They encouraged suspects to disregard the warnings and proceed with their statements. In a fair number of cases the police simply ignored the *Miranda* requirements entirely and failed to issue any warning to the suspects. Several conclusions can be drawn from these studies. One could argue that the statistics showing little change in the pre- and post-*Miranda* rate of convictions in selected precincts were due to the non-implementation of *Miranda* by the police, but there is also considerable data to suggest that first, suspects talk even when warned (and possibly even after consultation with counsel); and second, that confessions are not always crucial in obtaining convictions.[48]

articulate, reasonably mature, and strongly motivated individuals who were questioned in their own homes by experienced professional FBI men, the suspects were unable to understand and make effective use of their constitutional rights. The authors found that "nervousness decidedly impaired their judgment and behavior, and that questioning did not cease even when they stated that they did not wish to answer any further questions."

47. For an excellent brief discussion of the effect of Miranda on police practice, see "The Impact of *Miranda* in Practice" in Yale Kamisar, Wayne R. LaFave, and Jerold H. Israel, *Modern Criminal Procedure*, 4th ed. (St. Paul, Minn.: West Publishing Co., 1974, pp. 592–596.

48. Nathan R. Sobel, *New York Times*, November 20, 1965, p. 1. Also note "Interrogations in New

Despite the lack of evidence that *Miranda* warnings are adversely affecting police and prosecutorial functions, public opinion generally is still hostile to the concept of protecting the rights of the suspect in custody largely because many people attribute the increase in crime to the fact that the Courts are too "soft" on criminals.[49] When the Burger Court acquired a majority of conservative justices, many critics of the criminal justice system hoped and expected that *Miranda* (along with *Mapp*) would be overturned. Although the Chief Justice himself is apparently in favor of such a move, that has not yet happened, and the advent of the more liberal Carter administration makes it less likely to occur in the future when Carter appointees take their place on the Court.

*Miranda* has, however, been modified to some extent, principally in four cases decided by the Court since 1970: *Harris v. New York,*[50] *Oregon v. Hass,*[51] *Michigan v. Mosely,*[52] and *Oregon v. Mathiason.*[53] In *Harris v. New York,* the Court, in a 5–4 decision, held that a statement given to the police by an unwarned suspect, while not admissible as part of the prosecution's case, might be brought in as part of the cross-examination of the defendant, should he elect to testify in his own behalf. (The defense, however, presumably could then introduce the circumstances under which the statement was obtained). The Court reaffirmed this line of reasoning four years later in *Oregon v. Hass* which involved a suspect who had been taken into custody and given *Miranda* warnings. The suspect, Hass, indicated to

Haven: The Impact of Miranda," *Yale Law Journal,* 76 (July 1967): pp. 1521–1648.

49. For a discussion of the relationship of procedural protections, the urban courts, and the inadequate handling of criminal suspects, see Alexander B. Smith and Harriet Pollack "The Courts Stand Indicted in New York City," *Journal of Criminal Law and Criminology,* 68 (June 1977): pp. 252–261.

50. 401 U.S. 222, 91 S.Ct. 643, 28 L. Ed.2d 1 (1971).

51. 420 U.S. 714, 95 S.Ct. 1215, 43 L.Ed.2d 570 (1975).

52. 423 U.S. 96, 96 S.Ct. 321, 46 L. Ed.2d 313 (1975).

53. 429 U.S. 492, 97 S.Ct. 711, 50 L. Ed.2d 714 (1977).

the police that he would like to telephone his lawyer, but was told he could not do so until he reached the police station. Before reaching the station house, Hass made incriminating statements, which, while not used by the prosecutor as part of the state's case, were used to impeach Hass' credibility when he took the stand in his own defense. The United States Supreme Court, per Justice Blackmun, affirmed the conviction. Brennan, joined by Marshall dissented, protesting that

> . . . after today's decision, if an individual states that he wants an attorney, police interrogation will doubtless now be vigorously pressed to obtain statements before the attorney arrives. . . . [54]

Some months later, the Court considered *Michigan v. Mosely,* a case involving a robbery suspect who, after having been given *Miranda* warnings at the time of his arrest, exercised his right to remain silent. Mosely was then placed in a cell, where, two hours later, a police officer, after again giving him *Miranda* warnings, proceeded to question him about an unrelated holdup murder. This time Mosely neither asked for a lawyer nor indicated that he wished to remain silent. He made several incriminating statements which were subsequently used to convict him. On appeal, the United States Supreme Court in a 7–2 decision affirmed the conviction, holding that while *Miranda* required that interrogation must cease when the suspect indicates he wishes to remain silent, it did not forbid a second interrogation directed toward an unrelated crime. Again Brennan and Marshall dissented sharply.

> . . . Today's decision . . . virtually empties *Miranda* of principle, for plainly [it] encourages police asked to cease interrogation to continue the suspect's detention until the police station's coercive atmosphere does its work and the suspect responds to resumed questioning. . . . [55]

**54.** 420 U.S. 714 at 725, 95 S.Ct. 1215–1222, 43 L.Ed.2d 570 (1975).

**55.** 423 U.S. 96 at 118, 96 S.Ct. 321–333, 46 L.Ed.2d 313 (1975).

Two years later, the Court once again narrowed the scope of *Miranda*. In *Oregon v. Mathiason* a parolee was called into a police station, but was not told that he was a suspect or that he was under arrest. The police falsely told him that his fingerprints had been found at the scene of a burglary, whereupon Mathiason confessed. At his trial his attorney attempted, unsuccessfully, to suppress the confession because the defendant had not been properly given his *Miranda* warnings. The trial court admitted the confession which led to Mathiason's conviction. On appeal, the United States Supreme Court sustained the conviction, 6–3, on the ground that *Miranda* applied only to suspects who were in custody. Since Mathiason had not been formally arrested, he was not in custody, despite the fact that in the real world, most people (and parolees *a fortiori*) consider a request to appear at a police station an order, and a restraint on their liberty.

The *Mathiason* decision led some observers to predict that the Burger Court would shortly overturn *Miranda,* but only two months later, the Court, over the vigorous protests of the Chief Justice, and in a case involving a particularly revolting crime, reaffirmed its adherence to the basic *Miranda* holding that a suspect in custody must be protected from unwittingly incriminating himself. In *Brewer v. Williams,*[56] Williams, the defendant, on the advice of counsel, surrendered to the Davenport, Iowa police to face charges that he had kidnapped and murdered a 10 year old girl in Des Moines. After consultation between Williams' attorney and the Des Moines police, it was agreed that the Davenport officials would not question the prisoner while he was being transferred to Des Moines. The prisoner was then arraigned in Davenport and the *Miranda* warnings given. During the trip to Des Moines the prisoner expressed an unwillingness to be interrogated in the absence of his attorney but stated he would tell the whole story after seeing his attorney in Des Moines. However, responding to one of the arresting officers'

56. 430 U.S. 387, 97 S.Ct. 1232, 51 L.Ed.2d 424 (1977).

pleas that they stop and locate the body of the girl because her parents were entitled to a "Christian burial" for the girl who had been abducted on Christmas Eve, the prisoner made several incriminating disclosures and led the officers to the body. The prisoner was convicted on the basis of the evidence resulting from his disclosures.

In a 5–4 decision, the United States Supreme Court sustained the contention that the evidence in question had been wrongly admitted at the trial. The majority opinion by Justice Stewart held that the prisoner had been denied his constitutional right to the assistance of counsel under the Sixth and Fourteenth Amendments, and in light of the prisoner's assertion of his right to counsel, there was no reasonable basis for finding that the prisoner had waived that right. Among the dissenters, Chief Justice Burger contended that the prisoner had made a valid waiver of his rights, and his disclosures were therefore voluntary and uncoerced.

*Miranda*, like *Mapp*, is far from a perfect solution to the problem of curbing police and prosecutorial lawlessness without endangering the safety of the community by freeing dangerous criminals. The Burger Court, conservative by nature, and sensitive to the justifiable concern of the public over the increase in violent crime, has chipped away at both of these decisions, but it is fair to say that more has been preserved than has been struck down. To the relief of many liberals, and the disappointment of conservatives, the Burger Court, to date, has not overturned either *Mapp* or *Miranda* because for all their faults, no one has yet suggested a better way of preventing official incursion on personal rights that would be dangerous, not only to suspects in criminal cases, but to every person in the United States.

*Fair Trial and the Right to Counsel*

The right to counsel, as enunciated in *Miranda* and *Escobedo,* is an adjunct of the right not to incriminate oneself specified in the Fifth Amendment. This is a recent and innovative use of the right to counsel. Traditionally, this right concerned efforts to ensure counsel for the accused *at the time of the trial.* The Sixth Amendment to the United States Constitution provides that an accused shall "have the assistance of counsel for his defense." It is quite clear that this clause means, at the very least, that in a federal trial a defendant who wishes to provide himself with counsel may not be denied the privilege. What is not clear, however, is the degree of obligation on the part of the federal government to provide counsel for an accused too poor to pay for his own lawyer.

As early as 1790, in the Federal Crimes Act, Congress ordered the courts to assign counsel for the defendant in all capital cases. The obligation was not considered to extend to non-capital cases, however, and up until 1938, if a defendant charged in federal court with a non-capital crime could not or would not retain a lawyer for his trial, the federal government made no attempt to rectify the situation. In that year, in *Johnson v. Zerbst,*[57] the United States Supreme Court declared that the Sixth Amendment deprives the federal courts of the power to convict a defendant unrepresented by counsel, unless the defendant knowingly and intelligently waives the right. Since the *Johnson* case, counsel has been provided for all accused persons in federal courts.

The right to counsel in the state courts was initially established as a *federal* right in the first Scottsboro case. *Powell v. Alabama.*[58] The case involved seven teenage black boys charged with the rape of two white girls while all were travelling on a freight train through northern Alabama. The boys were charged in an atmosphere so hostile that it was widely understood that only the certainty that the defendants would be convicted and hanged prevented the local residents from lynching the defendants on the spot. The case first came to trial without counsel. A small group of interested black townspeople attempted to procure counsel for the defendants, who were terrified and virtually illiterate. When the attempt proved unsuccessful, the

57.   304 U.S. 458, 58 S.Ct. 1019, 82   58.   287 U.S. 45, 53 S.Ct. 55, 77 L.Ed.
      L.Ed. 1461 (1938).                       158 (1932).

trial judge appointed all the members of the local bar to act as counsel for the defendants.

In fact, the boys were unassisted by counsel when they went to trial on the capital charge of rape. News of the trial began to appear in the New York press, and the case became somewhat of a political *cause celebre* when the defendants were quickly found guilty and sentenced to death despite the very weak case presented by the prosecution. The NAACP, the Communist Party, and other interested groups raised funds on behalf of the Scottsboro boys which were used to retain Samuel S. Leibowitz (later appointed to the New York State Supreme Court) to defend the boys. Leibowitz appealed the verdict of the first trial on the ground that Powell had been denied due process of law when he was convicted of a capital crime without the assistance of counsel. The United States Supreme Court agreed that "the failure of the trial court to give [the defendants] . . . reasonable time and opportunity to secure counsel was a clear denial of due process." [59] Furthermore, the Court added, if the defendants were unable through their own efforts to procure counsel, it was incumbent upon the state to provide counsel for them. The Court refused to consider whether this obligation applied to all criminal trials or only to those involving capital offenses, but simply decided, on the basis of the facts of the *Powell* case, that the conviction could not stand.

> . . . Whether this would be so in other criminal prosecutions, or under other circumstances, we need not determine. All that is necessary now to decide, as we do decide, is that in a capital case, where the defendant is unable to employ counsel, and is incapable adequately of making his own defense because of ignorance, feeble mindedness, illiteracy, or the like, it is the duty of the court, whether requested or not, to assign counsel for him as a necessary requisite of due process of law. . . . [60]

59. Ibid., at 71.                 60. Ibid.

The *Powell* decision was too closely tied to the facts of that case to permit a substantial broadening of the right to counsel in state courts. Left unanswered were the issues of whether the right applied in non-capital cases as well as in capital cases, and whether it applied to defendants less helpless than the Scottsboro boys. Ten years later, in *Betts v. Brady*,[61] a Maryland case, an indigent defendant was convicted of robbery without benefit of counsel despite his request for legal representation at the trial. The Maryland law provided counsel for poor defendants in capital cases only. The United States Supreme Court held that Betts had not been denied due process of law by the failure of the state to provide him with counsel. The Sixth Amendment, the Court declared, was not automatically incorporated into the concept of due process of the Fourteenth Amendment, and therefore, counsel could be denied at the discretion of the state where it was felt that the trial on the whole, had been fundamentally fair.

Although the majority of the Court, in considering the *Betts* case, seemed to think that Betts was reasonably capable of defending himself in court, the facts when more closely examined do not support this conclusion. Although Betts was a man of normal intelligence, and grasped the principles of cross-examination, he was obviously incapable of analyzing the state's case against him, and pointing out its weaknesses.

For example, the robbery victim testified: The robber "had on a dark overcoat and a handkerchief around his chin and a pair of dark amber glasses . . . I told the police that I wasn't sure I could identify him without the glasses and the handkerchief, after seeing him when it was almost dark that evening." The *only* man in the line-up the day the victim came to the jail to identify the robber was Betts. And he could only be identified when he put on the dark coat, the smoked glasses and the handkerchief. . . .

61.   316 U.S. 455, 62 S.Ct. 1252, 86 L.Ed. 1595 (1942).

No coat or dark glasses or handkerchief was ever offered in evidence.   .   .   .   Although the matter is not entirely free from doubt—because neither trial judge nor prosecutor seemed to care much and Betts evidently failed to realize how this would weaken the State's case—a careful study of the record warrants the conclusion that the following occurred: The victim described to the police the various items the robber was supposed to have worn; the police obtained the requisite coat, glasses, and handkerchief and placed them on Betts; the victim then made his identification, based largely on the coat, glasses, and handkerchief the police had put on Betts.[62]

The realities of the criminal justice process are such that very few open-minded observers could accept the Court's reasoning in *Betts*.   It was obvious then, and became even more so with the passing years, that no one could receive a fair trial without the presence of his own attorney.   Certainly, no one suggested that middle-class or upper-class defendants would be likely to go voluntarily to trial without benefit of counsel.   After years of unhappiness with the *Betts* decision, and several decisions modifying the *dictum* therein, the Court finally seized upon an appeal *in forma pauperis* by one Clarence Gideon, from his conviction on a breaking and entering charge in Florida, as a vehicle for reconsideration of the *Betts* rationale.   Gideon had requested counsel at his trial and had been denied an attorney because Florida, like Maryland, provided counsel for indigents in capital cases only.   When his appeal reached the United States Supreme Court, the Court appointed Abe Fortas to argue the case for Gideon.   In deciding the case, the Court finally overruled *Betts*, holding that in a felony prosecution, the right to counsel is a fundamental right, and therefore an integral part of the concept of due process.   By implication the Court also held that the

62.   William B. Lockhart, Yale Kamisar, and Jesse H. Choper, *Constitutional Rights and Liberties*, 2nd ed. (St. Paul, Minn.: West Publishing Co., 1967), p. 225.

Sixth Amendment right to counsel is subsumed and made applicable to the states through the Due Process Clause of the Fourteenth Amendment.[63]

*Gideon*, (one of the few major criminal procedure decisions of the Warren Court to meet with general approval) left, however, certain issues unresolved. Gideon himself was charged with a felony. Did defendants charged with misdemeanors have similar rights to counsel at trial? In *Argersinger v. Hamlin*,[64] the Burger Court held that "no person may be imprisoned for any offense . . . unless he was represented by counsel at his trial." [65] Any defendant sentenced to jail or prison thus, must have counsel at trial. Expressly left open by the *Argersinger* majority, was the question of the right to counsel in prosecutions *not* involving imprisonment. The tenor of the decision, however, suggests that the Court is leaning towards a further extension of the right to counsel at trial.

Another related issue is the right of a defendant to conduct his own defense. May the state force a lawyer on a defendant who insists he does not want one? In *Faretta v. California*,[66] the United States Supreme Court held that an accused person has a constitutional right to defend himself if he wishes to. Justice Blackmun, along with Chief Justice Burger and Rehnquist, dissented, commenting:

> If there is any truth to the old proverb that "One who is his own lawyer has a fool for a client," the Court by its own opinion today now bestows a *constitutional* right on one to make a fool of himself.[67]

The *Gideon* decision was confined to a defendant's rights at his trial. Did the principle of providing equal access to justice for the rich and for the poor also apply to a defendant's rights

63. *Gideon v. Wainwright*, 372 U.S. 335, 83 S.Ct. 792, 9 L.Ed.2d 799 (1963).

64. 407 U.S. 25, 92 S.Ct. 2006, 32 L. Ed.2d 530 (1972).

65. Ibid., at 37.

66. 422 U.S. 806, 95 S.Ct. 2525, 45 L.Ed.2d 562 (1975).

67. Ibid., at 852.

to *appeal* his conviction?    As early as 1956, the United States Supreme Court, in *Griffin v. Illinois*,⁶⁸ held that all indigent defendants, under the Due Process and Equal Protection clauses, must be furnished free transcripts at least where allegations were made and not denied that manifest errors occurred at the time of the trial.    Justice Black observed

.   .   . There can be no equal justice where the kind of trial a man gets depends on the amount of money he has.    Destitute defendants must be afforded as adequate appellate review as defendants who have money enough to buy transcripts.⁶⁹

Seven years later, at the same time *Gideon* was handed down in 1963, the Court, in *Douglas v. California* ⁷⁰ extended *Griffin* to include not only the right to a free trial transcript and a waiving of the fees required for an appeal, but the right to an attorney for a first appeal made *as of right.* However, in *Ross v. Moffitt* ⁷¹ the Burger Court refused to intervene in those states where no provision was made to provide counsel for *discretionary* appeals.    Justice Rehnquist explained the reasoning of the Court.

.   .   . [A] defendant needs an attorney on appeal not as a shield to protect him against being "hailed into court" by the State and stripped of his presumption of innocence, but rather as a sword to upset the prior determination of guilt.    This difference is significant for, while no one would agree that the State may simply dispense with the trial stage of proceedings without a criminal defendant's consent, it is clear that the State need not provide any appeal at all.    The fact that an appeal *has* been provided does not automatically mean that a State then acts unfairly by refusing to provide

68.  351 U.S. 12, 76 S.Ct. 585, 100 L. Ed. 891 (1956).

69.  Ibid., at 19.

70.  372 U.S. 353, 82 S.Ct. 71, 7 L. Ed.2d 23 (1963).

71.  417 U.S. 600, 94 S.Ct. 2437, 41 L.Ed.2d 341 (1974).

counsel to indigent defendants at every stage of the way. Unfairness results only if indigents are singled out by the State and denied meaningful access to the appellate system because of their poverty. . . .[72]

As of the present moment, thus, every defendant in every criminal case in every court, state and federal, in the United States, if charged with an offense punishable by imprisonment, is entitled to the assistance of counsel at the trial stage of his case, and also at such times prior to the trial as are necessary for the effective preparation for the trial. He is also entitled to counsel for at least one appeal where state or federal law makes provision for such appeal. His rights to have counsel appointed for him for a discretionary appeal have no constitutional basis, however, and even if one rejects Rehnquist's argument that this is not an unfair discrimination against an indigent defendant, there are difficulties in equalizing access to the appellate process for defendants of modest means. Everyone, as Rehnquist pointed out, has a right to a trial, no matter how weak his case. Not every case presents an obvious ground for appeal, however, and the search for an attorney who can find the proper legal arguments for an appeal may well be expensive, and in many cases fruitless. For most defendants, the quest for justice must inevitably end at the trial court level.*

The presence of an attorney is not the only requisite for a fair trial for the defendant, of course. As important, if not more so, is the right of the defendant to be judged by a jury unprejudiced against him. The problem of prejudice in regard to juries stems basically from two sources: either the jury may be biased by

72. Ibid., at 610–611.

* The United States Supreme Court has not yet addressed itself to the right of an indigent defendant to the services of private investigators and/or expert witnesses such as handwriting experts, pathologists, psychologists, and the like. In some cases, such witnesses are essential to the defense case, as, for example in the Sheppard murder case, where the defendant after winning a new trial because of the inflammatory publicity surrounding his original trial, was able to establish his innocence largely on the basis of testimony given by pathol-

the race, religion, sex, or socio-economic status of the defendant; or its prejudice may stem from jurors' having fixed or relatively fixed opinions with regard to the guilt of the accused prior to the trial. Regarding bias which stems from race or class consideration, the most thorny problem of the American criminal justice system has been the persistent, widespread discrimination against blacks in the selection of juries.*

Following the Civil War, state laws that specifically restricted jury rolls to white males were struck down by the United States Supreme Court as violating the Fourteenth Amendment.[73] The Southern states then retreated to a policy of unofficial discrimination against blacks, whereby blacks were excluded from juries in practice though not in law. Thus, in the second Scottsboro case, *Norris v. Alabama*,[74] attorney Leibowitz was able to show through questioning hundreds of witnesses that no black had served on a jury in the Alabama county involved within the memory of the oldest living residents, white or black, and no such service by blacks appeared in any of the court records. He was also able to demonstrate that there were in the county a sizeable number of fully qualified blacks who had never been called for service. On appeal, the United States Supreme Court upheld Leibowitz's contention that discrimination against blacks could be established by inference from established practice, even though no express statutory prohibition existed.

ogists retained by the defense. A much more serious problem relating to the access of the poor to the courts, is the complete failure of most communities to provide any kind of free legal assistance to litigants in *civil* cases such as divorce proceedings, landlord-tenant disputes, consumer fraud cases and the like. Poor people in many areas are virtually excluded from the relief available from the courts by their inability to retain counsel.

No case presenting this issue directly has yet reached the United States Supreme Court.

\* For a further discussion of bias against blacks and women in jury selection, see Chapter 5, *infra*.

73. *Strauder v. West Virginia*, 100 U.S. 303, 25 L.Ed. 644 (1879).

74. 294 U.S. 587, 55 S.Ct. 579, 79 L. Ed. 1074 (1935).

Since the *Norris* case, it is clear that some blacks must appear on the jury rolls in every jurisdiction in which blacks reside. How many, of course, is another question, and there is some evidence that in rural areas tokenism has replaced the earlier policy of unofficial total exclusion, that is, one, or a handful of blacks will be added to the jury rolls in areas where the black population warrants far greater representation. The courts have thus far been unable effectively to cope with this kind of discrimination though the situation is far better than it was even 10 years ago. They have been able at least, to assure each defendant the right to be tried before a jury on which it was *possible* for blacks to sit. No defendant, however, has a right at this point to a jury on which one or more blacks *does* sit. From the point of view of black defendants (or conceivably even white defendants), it is probably unfair to be tried before a jury whose racial composition is not representative of the racial composition of the population at large. It is not clear, however, how the courts can remedy this situation, and most likely such conditions cannot be rectified in the absence of willingness on the part of administrative officials to do so.

Not only blacks are discriminated against by the jury selection system. Poor people are probably vastly underrepresented on all juries throughout the United States. The degree to which this is true depends on the particular jury system used, and systems vary not only from state to state, but from federal district to federal district. For many years, for example, federal jurors were chosen under the "key man" system, whereby a prominent member of the community recommended other outstanding citizens as veniremen. Another widely used method for both state and federal jury selection is the use of public records such as tax rolls, voting lists, telephone subscriber lists, and the like, all of which tend to represent propertied, employed, home-owning citizens rather than poorer people.

In 1949, during the prosecution of Eugene Dennis and his fellow leaders of the American Communist party, the defense attorneys tried to challenge the validity of the jury by establishing that poor people, women, Negroes, Jews, blue-collar workers, and members of the American Labor Party had been excluded from the jury rolls. The judge rejected their contention that the jury selection was invalid; nevertheless, the defense contention that the jury was unrepresentative was probably true. In March 1968, a federal jury reform act was passed, which requires a random selection of jurors from a "fair cross-section of the community," and forbids discrimination on the basis of race, color, sex, national origin, or economic status. How this is to be accomplished, however, is not altogether clear, and the courts have found it difficult to cope with the problem of socio-economic discrimination in jury selection.

Women present a somewhat special problem in terms of jury selection. Until recently, in many states women could not be compelled to serve on juries, and in some others were not even called for jury service unless they voluntarily entered their names on the jury rolls. Such regulations undoubtedly stemmed from concern for women's domestic responsibilities, especially in regard to the care of young children. Nevertheless, such practices created juries which by their very nature were unrepresentative. In 1975, however, the United States Supreme Court ruled, in *Taylor v. Louisiana* [75], that women could not be excluded as a group from jury service, nor called for service in a manner different from potential male jurors. This decision should result in juries that are more balanced in terms of their male-female ratio. There are, however, other less obvious factors which tend to make juries unrepresentative of the communities from which they are drawn. Judges tend to excuse from service those for whom such service is an economic hardship or a matter of great inconvenience, so that juries frequently have disproportionate numbers of government employees, or employees of large corporations willing to continue salary payments during the period of jury service. Self-employed people, teachers, and manual laborers, among others, are found on juries far less fre-

---

75.  419 U.S. 522, 95 S.Ct. 692, 42 L.
Ed.2d 690 (1975).

quently than public utility employees, clerical workers, and corporation officials. Another factor, frequently overlooked, is the manner in which both prosecutors and defense attorneys exercise their peremptory challenges. For a variety of reasons, blacks, women, and young people (along with unusually well-educated or prestigious individuals) are more often challenged than others and juries as finally selected are generally skewed in terms of the number of white middle-aged males.

Juries may also be prejudiced by the jurors having formed opinions as to the guilt or innocence of the accused before the trial. Prejudice on the part of individual jurors is normally handled reasonably effectively through the device of challenging, either for cause or peremptorily. Much more serious, however, is the problem which arises when the entire panel of veniremen may have attitudes antagonistic toward the accused, because of either strong local pre-trial sentiment stemming from the status of the defendant or from excessive ill-considered pre-trial publicity relating to the crime and the defendant. Some trials, such as the *Scottsboro* trial or the *Frank* trial in Georgia [76] in 1915, are conducted in an atmosphere so filled with hostility to the defendants as to be virtually legal lynchings. In the *Frank* trial, for example, the defendant was a New York born Jewish manager of the local textile mill, accused of raping a girl employee. The judge gave tacit recognition to the rampant xenophobia and anti-Semitism of the local population by requesting the defendant and his attorney to remain away from the courtroom when the verdict was brought in, lest there be a lynching if a verdict other than guilty as charged were returned. Frank was convicted, and appealed unsuccessfully to the United States Supreme Court on the ground that the atmosphere surrounding the trial had prevented him from receiving a fair trial. Some months later, while in prison awaiting execution, Frank was taken from the state prison farm by a mob and lynched. His perception of the atmosphere in which his trial was conducted was apparently accurate.

76. *Frank v. Mangum*, 237 U.S. 309,
35 S.Ct. 582, 59 L.Ed. 969 (1915).

It is unlikely that the United States Supreme Court today would be as insensitive to the claims of a defendant in circumstances similar to Frank's, as it was in 1915. Eight years later, in *Moore v. Dempsey*,[77] a case involving black sharecroppers accused of murdering white men who had terrorized the black community, the Court substantially agreed with Holmes' comment in the earlier *Frank* case that "lynch law [is] as little valid when practiced by a regularly drawn jury as when administered by one elected by a mob intent on death." [78]

More troublesome today are cases involving juries inflamed, not by the mere status of the defendant, but by extensive pretrial publicity unfavorable to him as a person and as a defendant. The ultimate in situations of this kind was the publicity given to the arrest of Lee Harvey Oswald for the assassination of President John F. Kennedy in 1963, in Dallas, Texas. It is highly questionable whether, had Oswald lived and gone to trial, an unprejudiced jury could have been impanelled anywhere in the United States, much less in Texas. The quantity and quality of mass media coverage of the crime, and the subsequent search for and arrest of the suspect had such enormous, almost universally felt impact that it is doubtful there existed twelve adult Americans of normal intelligence who had open minds as to the guilt or innocence of Oswald. The issue was not joined, of course, because of the assassination of Oswald himself, an act stemming in part, at least, from the self-same publicity.

Oswald's case, fortunately, is unique, but the problem of pretrial prejudicial publicity is not. More typical are cases such as *Irvin v. Dowd*,[79] where reports that the defendant offered to plead guilty if promised a ninety-nine year sentence were widely circulated. Local newspapers also described the accused as the "confessed slayer of six," a parole violator, and a fraudulent check artist. Some 90 percent of the veniremen, when ques-

77.  261 U.S. 86, 43 S.Ct. 265, 67 L.
Ed. 543 (1923).

78.  *Frank v. Mangum*, at 350.

79.  366 U.S. 717, 81 S.Ct. 1639, 6 L.
Ed.2d 751 (1961).

tioned, admitted to some opinion as to his guilt. In *Rideau v. Louisiana*,[80] shortly before the defendant's arraignment and trial, a local TV station broadcast, at three different times, a twenty-minute film of the accused in the presence of the sheriff and two states troopers, admitting in detail, in response to leading questions by the sheriff, the commission of various offenses. Most widely publicized of all was the case of Dr. Samuel Sheppard, a wealthy young osteopath accused of murdering his wife.[81]

Sheppard's family lived in a suburb of Cleveland and operated an osteopathic hospital in the vicinity. The Cleveland press quite early took the position that Sheppard was guilty, and that any investigatory action on the part of law enforcement officials pointing in any direction other than Sheppard's guilt was an attempt to shield wealthy and influential people from the processes of the law, and thus was evidence of corruption. The pre-trial publicity given the investigation was intense and virulent.

> . . . Charges and countercharges were aired in the news media besides those for which Sheppard was called to trial. In addition, only three months before trial, Sheppard was examined for more than five hours without counsel during a three-day inquest which ended in a public brawl. The inquest was televised live from a high school gymnasium seating hundreds of people. Furthermore, the trial began two weeks before a hotly contested election at which both Chief Prosecutor Mahon and Judge Blythin were candidates for judgeships.[82]

Not only was pre-trial publicity extensive and detrimental to the accused, but the trial was run in the atmosphere of a Roman circus. Reporters were permitted to sit inside the bar, and the goings and comings of the representatives of the mass media created so much confusion that not only could the testimony of

80.  373 U.S. 723, 83 S.Ct. 1417, 10 L.Ed.2d 663 (1963).

81.  *Sheppard v. Maxwell*, 384 U.S. 333, 86 S.Ct. 1507, 16 L.Ed.2d 600 (1966).

82.  Ibid., at 354.

witnesses not be heard, but Sheppard was forced to leave the courtroom to consult with his attorney.

> .   .   .   The fact is that bedlam reigned at the courthouse during the trial and newsmen took over practically the entire courtroom, hounding most of the participants of the trial, especially Sheppard.   .   .   . The erection of a press table for reporters inside the bar is unprecedented. The bar of the court is reserved for counsel, providing them a safe place in which to keep papers and exhibits, and to confer privately with client and co-counsel.   .   .   .   Moreover, the judge gave the throng of newsmen gathered in the corridors of the courthouse absolute free rein.   Participants in the trial, including the jury, were forced to run a gantlet of reporters and photographers each time they entered or left the courtroom.   .   .   .[83]

The names of the jurors, with their addresses and their pictures, appeared in the newspapers both before and during the trial, and the jury itself, although sequestered in the course of the trial, was permitted to make telephone calls freely to friends and relatives outside.

Sheppard was convicted of his wife's murder and, after ten years of motions and appeals (made possible, in part, by his personal wealth), finally succeeded in obtaining from the United States Supreme Court a reversal of his conviction on the grounds that he had not received a fair trial because of the uncontrolled prejudicial publicity surrounding his trial.   He was re-tried by the state of Ohio and acquitted.

In reaction to the Sheppard, Ruby, and Oswald cases, and to the potential for a miscarriage of justice inherent in the mass media coverage of each of them, a good deal of public discussion was engendered as to how such coverage could be restricted to best protect the rights of defendants.   In 1967, the Reardon Committee of the American Bar Association made a series of recom-

83.   Ibid., at 355.

mendations which would have severely restricted statements to the press by law enforcement officials—police, prosecutors, and court attachés—as well as by defense counsel. Such matters as the defendant's prior criminal record, statements including confessions which he might have made, the identity of witnesses, their potential testimony, and speculations as to the guilt or innocence of the accused—would all be prohibited. In general, only such details as might be necessary for the apprehension of a fugitive or for the protection of the community would be released. The obvious feeling of the committee was that the less publicity surrounding any trial the better. The proposed restrictions would be enforced either by internal departmental disciplinary procedures against law enforcement officials, or by bar association proceedings against private attorneys, or by the use of the contempt power of the judge against reporters and others.

Representatives of the mass media, understandably, disagreed with many of the suggestions of the Reardon Committee. For one thing, the use of the contempt powers of the courts against reporters, while in line with British practice, runs counter to American tradition. On the whole, the United States Supreme Court has been reluctant to sustain convictions of reporters for contempt, that is, publication that does not actually obstruct the business of the court. "A judge of the United States," as Justice Holmes once remarked, "is expected to be a man of ordinary firmness of character," [84] and presumably, therefore, able to shield his courtroom from unwarranted interference or influence by the press.

More important, however, the representatives feel that publicity is not only not necessarily evil, but is an essential good in a democratic society. While willing to concede that excesses and abuses frequently occur in the coverage of trials, they feel that to virtually do away with press coverage of police investigations and trials is to throw out the baby with the bathwater.

84. *Toledo Newspaper Co. v. United States*, 247 U.S. 402 at 424, 38 S.Ct. 560, 565–566, 62 L.Ed. 1186 (1918).

Public discussion of major problems in the court of public opinion has proved historically to be a far more potent method of correction of inbred evil or advocating needed change than legal processes limited to the courtroom alone. We should go slowly about adopting rules that would have prevented Attorney General Richmond Flowers of Alabama from commenting on the hand-picked Liuzzo murder jury, Estes Kevauver from exposing the violent crimes and corrupting influence of the Mafia, or Senator Walsh from denouncing the Teapot Dome Scandal. Nor do I think that Clarence Darrow's great debate on freedom of education in the period preceding the *Scopes trial* should have been stricken from our history.[85]

The critics of the ABA report correctly point out that the press is a watchdog against official corruption, and while harm may befall an individual defendant through improper press coverage, far greater harm may befall all defendants should public surveillance of police and prosecutorial practices be relaxed.

The point may be illustrated by a consideration of pretrial confessions. . . . If a confession is truly voluntary, it will be admitted at trial, and the damage that the press may bring about by prior publication will be inflicted against principle but not practicality. If, however, the confession is coerced and is *not* admitted at trial, then pretrial news of the confession may hurt the defendant's chances of getting an impartial jury. But it also constitutes a highly necessary and perhaps the only notice to the public of police misfeasance. There has been harm to the defendant, perhaps avoidable. But which was the greater harm to him, the coer-

85. Judge George C. Edwards, as quoted in Livingston Hall, Yale Kamisar, Wayne R. LaFave, and Jerold H. Israel, *Modern Criminal Procedure*, 3rd ed. (St. Paul, Minn.: West Publishing, 1969), p. 1180, Fn.

cion of a confession, or the publication that a confession was made? [86]

On balance, it would appear that excessive restriction of press coverage may well be a greater social evil than totally unrestricted press coverage. There seems no need, however, to select between two such dire alternatives. A recognition of the problem by attorneys, reporters, and law enforcement officials and willingness to set reasonable voluntary standards for restraints should do much to eliminate the worst excesses of the type in evidence at the Sheppard trial. Trial judges, moreover, have sufficient power, if they care to use it, to sequester and insulate the proceedings in their courtrooms from the adverse effects of prejudicial press coverage. Certainly, the circuses that were permitted to take place under the appellation of trials in the cases cited above have had a salutary effect in alerting all concerned to the dangers of improperly influencing the judicial process through unrestricted publicity.

The situation does not appear to be so unmanageable as to warrant officially imposed silence, which may lead to even graver evils. It is instructive to recall that at the height of the Watergate scandal, John Mitchell and Maurice Stans were acquitted in New York City of charges of obstruction of justice in connection with an investigation of illegal campaign contributions, even though the prosecution's case was fairly strong, and public opinion was quite hostile to the defendants. Similarly, although a predominantly black Washington, D.C. jury (blacks were considered to be very hostile to the Nixon administration) convicted Mitchell, Haldeman, and Ehrlichman of conspiracy to obstruct justice by covering up the Watergate break in, their co-defendant, Kenneth W. Parkinson was acquitted. Even jurors who have been exposed to extensive pre-trial publicity, can, apparently, if handled properly by the presiding judge, render a fair verdict.

86.   Alfred Friendly and Ronald L. Goldfarb, *Crime and Publicity*      (New York: Twentieth Century Fund, Inc., 1967), p. 240.

The issue, nevertheless, is troublesome and some judges attempt to restrict press coverage of cases brought before them. In a recent case in Nebraska [87] involving an accused mass-murderer who had received extensive adverse pre-trial publicity, the trial judge imposed a total ban on all news coverage of pre-trial procedures including the preliminary hearing and the selection of jurors. The press and broadcasting media were forbidden to report not only any statements made by the accused which might implicate him, but court proceedings which were open to the public.

The Nebraska Press Association appealed the gag order to the United States Supreme Court as an unconstitutional prior restraint on the press, and the high court, in an opinion written by the Chief Justice, unanimously reversed the Nebraska court. While some of the Justices were willing to examine the facts of the case to determine whether the circumstances warranted such press restriction, a majority seemed to express doubt that such prior restraint could ever be justified. While the press was understandably and justifiably relieved by the decision in the *Nebraska Press Association* case, nevertheless, the handwriting is on the wall. If news coverage becomes so inflammatory as to make the proper handling of defendants impossible, there will be further attempts at restraining the media, some of which may succeed. There is no reason to suppose, however, that the news media are incapable of responsible coverage of criminal proceedings, or that a *modus vivendi* between the courts and the newspapers is impossible to reach.

One last consideration in relation to a fair trial is that the right to a jury trial inheres in the seriousness of the punishment for the charged offense rather than the appellation given that offense within a particular penal code. The constitutional provisions regarding jury trial are clearly intended to protect accused persons from serious punishment until after adjudication by

87. *Nebraska Press Ass'n v. Stuart,* 427 U.S. 539, 96 S.Ct. 2791, 49 L. Ed.2d 683 (1976).

*juries.* Traditionally, this has been taken to mean that those prosecuted for felonies have a right to a trial by jury. Recently, however, the United States Supreme Court has broadened this concept to include the right of jury trials in misdemeanor cases where the permissible punishment may be as long as two years. In *Duncan v. Louisiana,*[88] the conviction of a defendant accused of simple battery, a misdemeanor punishable under Louisiana law by two years imprisonment and a three hundred dollar fine, was reversed because the accused's request for a jury trial had been denied by the trial judge. In reversing the conviction the Court, after some discussion of the relationship of the Fourteenth to the Sixth Amendment, recognized that some crimes are too petty to warrant jury trials, and defined this category as including at least those where the specified punishment was a maximum of six months imprisonment. The six months standard was later reaffirmed in *Baldwin v. New York.*[89] The *Duncan* and *Baldwin* decisions are regarded with some horror by state and local officials, not so much for the principles they have enunciated as for the practical problems they have created. With court calendars already filled to bursting, the prospect of large numbers of additional cases requiring jury trial is unattractive, to say the least. Should the situation become sufficiently desperate, there is some likelihood that certain misdemeanor punishments may be revised downward to remove them from the required jury trial category. However, two recent cases may have somewhat diminished the constitutional burden that the state courts must and should carry. *Williams v. Florida,*[90] held that a twelve-man jury was a historical accident, and accordingly, a six-man jury in criminal cases does not violate the Sixth Amendment, as applied to the states via the Fourteenth. *Apodaca v. Oregon,*[91] upheld the constitutionality of less-than-unanimous jury verdicts in state criminal cases.

---

**88.** 391 U.S. 145, 88 S.Ct. 1444, 20 L.Ed.2d 491 (1968).

**89.** 399 U.S. 66, 90 S.Ct. 1886, 26 L. Ed.2d 437 (1970).

**90.** 399 U.S. 78, 90 S.Ct. 1893, 26 L. Ed.2d 446 (1970).

**91.** 406 U.S. 404, 92 S.Ct. 1628, 32 L.Ed.2d 184 (1972).

*Double Jeopardy*

The notion behind the constitutional prohibition against double jeopardy is that the state may not get two bites at the apple. A defendant may be tried only once for a particular crime, and the state must then either convict him or forever hold its peace, so to speak. The principal complication that has arisen in the United States, however, stems from the fact that we live in a federal system where there is not one sovereign, but two; not merely federal law, but state law as well.

The Fifth Amendment says, "Nor shall any person be subject for the same offense to be twice put in jeopardy of life or limb." This means quite clearly that if John Robber holds up a federally insured bank in New York State, New York State may try him only once for the crime of bank robbery. The difficulty is, however, that such a robbery is also a federal crime. The federal government may also try Mr. Robber only once. Neither sovereignty has had "two bites of the apple;" nevertheless, Mr. Robber has been tried twice for the same offense. Thus far the United States Supreme Court has upheld the practice of double prosecutions by different sovereignties, as not violative of the Fifth and Fourteenth Amendments, although in *Benton v. Maryland* [92] the Court ruled that the double jeopardy clause of the Fifth Amendment is applicable to the states through the Fourteenth Amendment.* Double prosecutions are a very real problem and violate the spirit, if not the letter, of the Constitution. The federal government, for its part, has attempted administratively to remedy the situation by a voluntary decision on the part of all attorneys general since 1959 not to try federal

---

[92]. 395 U.S. 784, 89 S.Ct. 2056, 23 L.Ed.2d 707 (1969).

* On November 7, 1977, in *Rinaldi v. United States*, the majority of the United States Supreme Court held, 6 – 3, that the federal robbery conviction of a Florida man should be dismissed because he had already been convicted on state charges based on the same events, and the state verdict had been sustained on appeal. The Court acted on the recommendation of the United States Department of Justice which felt that such prosecutions wastefully duplicate state efforts and had the potential for unfairness to defendants.

cases where there has already been a state prosecution for substantially the same act.　The states, however, have not reciprocated, and continue double prosecutions not only where a federal prosecution has taken place, but even where local or municipal prosecution has taken place for an act that is simultaneously violative of a local or municipal code.

Another type of multiple prosecution sometimes occurs when the criminal act committed can actually be thought of as more than one act.　For example, if while robbing the bank, Mr. Robber takes money first from the teller and then from each of three customers standing in line, his bank robbery can be thought of as four separate criminal acts.　If the state were to prosecute him for the robbery of the teller and fail to convict him, should it have an opportunity to try him subsequently for the robbery of each customer?　A 1970 case that came to the United States Supreme Court illustrates this problem.　*Ashe v. Swenson* [93] arose out of a robbery of a group of poker players by three or four men.　Ashe had originally been charged with the robbery of player No. 1, a Mr. Knight.　The trial judge instructed the jury that if they thought that Ashe had been one of the robbers they must convict him, even if he had not personally robbed Knight.　The prosecutor's case was poorly presented and Ashe was acquitted.　Subsequently, Ashe was indicted for the robbery of player No. 2, a Mr. Roberts.　This time, the state's case was stronger and Ashe was convicted.　He thereupon appealed his conviction to the United States Supreme Court on double jeopardy grounds, contending that his acquittal at his first trial established that he was not one of the robbers, and therefore the state could not try him again, simply by switching victims.　The United States Supreme Court agreed, noting that the state, in its brief, had frankly admitted that it had treated Ashe's first trial and his acquittal merely as a dry run for the second trial:

　．　．　．　"No doubt the prosecutor felt the state had a provable case on the first charge and, when he lost,

93.　397 U.S. 436, 90 S.Ct. 1189, 25 L.Ed.2d 469 (1970).

he did what every good attorney would do—he redefined his presentation in the light of the turn of events at the first trial." . . . [94]

This is what the constitutional guarantee forbids. The general rule is that separate offenses require separate evidence for conviction; that is, if the evidence for all offenses is identical, only one conviction can be obtained.

Jeopardy normally attaches with the swearing in of the first juror at the beginning of the trial. When a person has been acquitted or convicted by a court of competent jurisdiction he may not be re-tried for the same offense. If, however, the jury fails to reach a verdict, or a mistrial is declared, the accused is not considered to have been placed in jeopardy, and trial proceedings may be reinstituted. (The prosecution may not, of course, for tactical reasons, interrupt the trial and ask for a mistrial if things are going badly for the state. Otherwise, any district attorney who detected an unfavorable response on the part of the jury could throw in the sponge and hope for better things with a subsequent jury.) If the court is later determined not to have had proper jurisdiction, or to have been improperly constituted in some way, the accused may also be re-tried.

*Conclusion*

In the last decade and a half, the United States Supreme Court has made more changes in criminal procedure than had been made by the Court in the previous 175 years of its existence. Critics of the Court, particularly under the stewardship of Chief Justice Warren, have charged bitterly that these changes have "coddled criminals" and have reflected an undesirable attitude of permissiveness toward bad conduct. A fair-minded review of what the Court has actually done will show that these contentions are not true. The Court has not created any new rights for criminals; it therefore cannot have coddled criminals or been permissive of their evil ways. *What the*

---

94. Ibid., at 447.

*Court has done is to equalize the rights of rich suspects and poor suspects.* The Court has not created any new rights, but it has extended to the poor, illiterate, and ignorant accused those rights which have long been known and enjoyed by the middle or upper-class defendant. The *Miranda* decision created not one right or privilege that was not known and used by defendants who were either experienced or sufficiently affluent to hire good counsel promptly.

Nevertheless, the critics are right in accusing the Warren Court of having created a revolution in the field of criminal procedure. By extending the rights of the rich to the poor, enormous *practical* problems have been created. *Poor people commit more, and more serious crimes, than rich people,* and by giving the poor the treatment that has traditionally been reserved for the rich, the Court is overloading to the point of breakdown our criminal justice system. It is also forcing our society to declare whether it really believes in equality before the law. Many citizens and public officials who are appalled at crowded court calendars, lengthy appellate proceedings, overcrowded prisons, and the need for more and better police work—all of which are to some extent the results of the higher standards enunciated by the Court—have evaded the fundamental issue through rather mindless criticisms of the Court as being soft on criminals. In fact, in many areas relating to criminal procedure, the United States Supreme Court has taken away rights that suspects previously enjoyed. The standards for legal searches and seizures have been lowered and made more flexible; the rules for the admission of evidence in criminal cases (outside of statements by the accused) have been made less rigid; and wiretapping and eavesdropping have been legalized.

Nevertheless, the record of the Warren Court with regard to criminal procedure is, on the whole, one of the high-water marks of American history. Despite the legitimacy of much of the criticism of the United States as a violent, machine-dominated, materialistic, inhuman society, the attempt to protect the rights of the most despised members of society—criminals—is surely an indication that we are more decent, more civilized, and more truly libertarian than many critics, both on the Right and the Left, are willing to admit.   After all, the point about *Miranda* is not what the decision did for Ernesto Miranda, but what it did for the rest of us.

# Chapter V

# EQUALITY BEFORE THE LAW

"We hold these truths to be self evident, that all men are created equal."

Declaration of Independence

"But in view of the Constitution, in the eye of the law, there is in this country no superior, dominant, ruling class of citizens. There is no caste here. Our Constitution is color-blind. . . ."

Justice Harlan, dissenting,
*Plessy v. Ferguson* (1896)

"Though the law itself be fair on its face and impartial in appearance, yet, if it is applied and administered by public authority with an evil eye and an unequal hand, so as . . . to make unjust and illegal discriminations between persons in similar circumstances . . . the denial of equal justice is still within the prohibition of the Constitution. . . ."

*Yick Wo v. Hopkins* (1886)

"Traditionally, . . . discrimination [against women] was rationalized by an attitude of 'romantic paternalism' which, in practical effect, put women not on a pedestal, but in a cage. . . ."

*Frontiero v. Richardson* (1973)

That ringing declaration of America's political faith, the Declaration of Independence, states forthrightly that all men are created equal. To deduce from this, however, that government, therefore, has an obligation to treat all persons equally would be incorrect. There is no obligation on the part of the authorities to treat everyone alike: rich or poor, black or white, male or female, young or old. Government can and frequently should treat disparate groups differently. What is required is that where unequal treatment exists, the inequalities must be rational, and related to a legitimate interest of the state. Thus, it is proper for Congress to levy a heavier income tax on the rich than on the poor because ability to pay is rationally related to the fairness of a tax, and taxation is a legitimate interest of the federal government. It would not be proper to base tax contributions on the color of an individual's eyes, on his religion, or on his sex, because these attributes bear no reasonable relationship to the problem of raising governmental funds. It might, however, be appropriate to base a water use tax on the number of faucets in an individual's home rather than his total income, since the utilization of the service provided may be rationally related to the amount of money a taxpayer should pay.

Almost all laws in the broadest sense create categories. A law imposing tolls on a bridge applies to those who use the bridge, but not to those who don't. A law punishing breaking and entering punishes burglars but not arsonists. Social security pensions are given to those who meet certain age or disability requirements but not to workers who do not, even if a younger able-bodied worker has contributed more to the fund than his older, or handicapped neighbor. Men are drafted into the armed forces but women are not. The question in every case is not whether the law should create categories. By the very nature of the governmental function, laws must create categories, because it is the creation of categories that is the real purpose of many laws. The Social Security law is designed to benefit the old at the expense of the young. The Selective Service Act is precisely that—selective service—it requires that the youngest and most fit males in the community defend the nation. Tolls are paid by bridge users only, precisely because the community at large does not wish to pay for a facility which may be used by some but not all. The question, thus, is not whether the law may treat people unequally, but whether the inequalities created are justifiable—in legal jargon, whether the person upon whom the law's burden falls has been denied equal protection of the law. Is it fair for only young men and not others to be drafted? Is it fair for only those over 62 to get pensions? Is it fair for only bridge users to pay for the cost of a bridge?

The standards for equal protection, like the standards for due process are not absolute, but relative. They vary with the social, political, and economic environment, and they change as that environment changes. In many countries in the world today women, as well as men, are drafted into the armed services, and it would be considered unreasonable to exempt them from service. Similarly, the age of retirement is far from fixed, and there is disagreement over the proper method of financing old age benefits. In some communities public improvements are paid for by bonds repaid out of general tax funds; in other communities, bonds are repaid out of fees paid by users of the facility financed by the bonds. In the largest sense, just as almost every law creates categories, the legislature, in passing it, makes a determination that those categories are fair.

The problem of equal protection arises when individuals disagree with the legislative judgment, or when the environment in which the law was originally conceived and passed changes so radically that the law itself becomes an anachronism. Thus, women, for example, have historically been treated very differently from men. While some women no doubt, objected contemporaneously to laws which in effect made them the wards of their fathers or husbands, the inequities inherent in such statutes only became more apparent as women became more capable of earning a living outside their homes, and increasingly financially independent of their male relatives.* When all blacks in

---

* Carl Degler, the American historian, points out that much of the opposition to extending the vote to women in the early twentieth century came from *women* who apparently preferred their different, and unequal legal status, and found it not unreasonable. See the *New York Times*, September 19, 1977, p. 35.

the United States were illiterate slaves, it seemed reasonable to white people that blacks were inferior to whites and should be treated accordingly. As the social and economic status of blacks rose, the reasonableness of such differential treatment became dubious.

In the United States two categories created by law have become increasingly suspect: those categories based on race, and those based on sex. The great majority of significant equal protection cases involve challenges to laws which separate persons by virtue of their color or their gender. Historically, challenges to racial discrimination started in the era after the Civil War and the emancipation of the slaves. Those relating to sexual discrimination are a relatively recent phenomenon, with most of the cases coming to the United States Supreme Court within the last ten years. There have been, of course, equal protection cases that related to groups other than women and racial minorities. Poor people, illegitimate children, aliens, and homosexuals, among others, have challenged legislation which they saw as discriminatory. Nevertheless, it is in the field of race and sex discrimination that the most important legal challenges have occurred, and the most significant changes in constitutional standards have taken place.*

*Discrimination Through Direct State Action: Orientals*

Although most racial discrimination in the United States has been against blacks, the discriminatory treatment of Orientals

---

* Strictly speaking, the Constitution forbids only discriminatory acts by *public* officials, state or federal. Private individuals are free, in constitutional terms, to discriminate against others in any way they see fit. Much private action, has, however, been limited by state or federal statutes (as for example, laws forbidding discrimination in housing or employment). Further, many private institutions are now quasi-public, as for example, universities which receive public subsidies, and are thus subject to constitutional restrictions. The first part of this chapter will deal with direct governmental discrimination; the second part will deal with the limitations on private action.

provides some insights into the legal problems in this area. Consider for example, the case of *Yick Wo v. Hopkins*.[1]

A San Francisco ordinance which purported to be a health and safety measure made it unlawful to operate a laundry without the consent of the Board of Supervisors unless the laundry was housed in a brick or stone building. Yick Wo, a Chinese alien, who had operated a laundry for 22 years and who had certificates of compliance from both health and fire authorities, was denied consent by the Board. He was subsequently fined ten dollars for operating the laundry without the required consent and jailed for nonpayment of his fine. The state conceded that

> . . . there were about 320 laundries in the city [and] about 240 were owned [by] subjects of China, and of the whole number, viz., 320, about 310 were constructed of wood, . . . petitioner, and more than 150 of his countrymen, have been arrested [for violating the ordinance] while those who are not subjects of China, and who are conducting 80 odd laundries under similar conditions are left unmolested. . . .[2]

Thus, Chinese aliens operating laundries in wood buildings were denied permission to continue in business, but white laundrymen similarly situated, were not bothered. The problem did not lie in the categories created by the law. It might have been quite reasonable for a number of purposes (such as fire safety or sanitation) for San Francisco to make a distinction between laundries housed in wood buildings and laundries housed in brick buildings. The problem, in *Yick Wo* was obviously in the administration of the statute rather than in the statute itself. The Board of Supervisors had in effect ignored the categories created by law, brick and wood buildings, and had instead created two other categories, Chinese laundrymen and non-Chinese laundrymen. On appeal, the United States Supreme Court declared

1. 118 U.S. 356, 6 S.Ct. 1064, 30 L. Ed. 220 (1886). 2. Ibid., at 358–359.

the *de facto* categories created by the Board of Supervisors to be unreasonable: in legal terms, a denial of equal protection of the laws.

> . . . [The] facts shown establish an administration directed so exclusively against a particular class of persons as to warrant and require the conclusion, that, whatever may have been the intent of the ordinances as adopted, they are applied . . . with a mind so unequal and oppressive as to amount to a practical denial by the State of [equal protection] . . . ..
> . . . [3]

Fortunately for Yick Wo, the discrimination against him as a Chinese was not only clear, but admitted by the authorities. Thus, the problem of proof, which was to prove so difficult in so many later cases, did not arise.

> . . . The fact of this discrimination is admitted. No reason for it is shown, and the conclusion cannot be resisted that no reason for it exists except hostility to the race and nationality to which the petitioners belong
> . . . . . . . [4]

Thus, the high court declared that racial discrimination based simply on community prejudice was forbidden by the Fourteenth Amendment. Left unanswered was the question of under what circumstances (if any), punitive categories based on race might be permissible.

A half century after *Yick Wo* the Supreme Court again had cause to review a case involving hostility to Orientals, this time, Japanese. Following Pearl Harbor, great concern was felt on the West Coast that there might be a Japanese invasion of Hawaii or even attacks on the mainland itself. One of the measures taken to contain the danger was the enforced evacuation of Japanese residents from the West Coast to concentration camps euphemistically labelled "relocation centers." Over

3.  Ibid., at 373.                    4.  Ibid., at 374.

100,000 Japanese, 70,000 of whom were American citizens, were involuntarily moved from their homes and businesses at a cost of untold personal anguish and a property loss of hundreds of millions of dollars. The internment of the Japanese was effected originally pursuant to an executive order issued in February 1942 by President Roosevelt and confirmed one month later by Congress, the rationale for which was military security. The military authorities considered all Japanese to be security risks, presumably because no matter how long their residence in this country, or whatever their legal status, their loyalty would be to Japan rather than to the United States. No evidence was put forth to support this hypothesis, and the President and Congress simply accepted the argument as the considered judgment of informed experts. In reality, the judgment of the military as to the loyalty of the Japanese dovetailed neatly with widespread prejudice on the West Coast against the Japanese, the roots of which stemmed more from economic competition than from political ideology.

More than a year passed before the Supreme Court reviewed the constitutionality of any part of this unprecedented use of governmental authority. In *Hirabayashi v. United States* [5] the Court upheld the conviction of a defendant on charges of failure to obey a curfew requiring all aliens and persons of Japanese ancestry to be in their homes between 6 P.M. and 8 A.M. The Court, deferring to the unsubstantiated judgment of the military, held that while racial classifications were normally unconstitutional because they fulfilled no legitimate legislative purpose, in time of war it was conceivable that those having "ethnic affiliation" with the enemy might be a greater source of danger than other Americans and could then be restricted.

*Hirabayashi* dealt only with the curfew question. The far more important evacuation and relocation issues were not reviewed for still another year. Finally, in 1944, *Korematsu v. United States* [6] upheld, 6 – 3, in an opinion written by no less a

5.　320 U.S. 81, 63 S.Ct. 1375, 87 L.　6.　323 U.S. 214, 65 S.Ct. 193, 89 L.
Ed. 1774 (1943).　　　　　　　　　　Ed. 194 (1944).

civil libertarian than Justice Black, the constitutionality of the internment program.  Korematsu, an American citizen of Japanese descent was convicted of remaining in San Leandro, California, a military area subject to evacuation regulations which required that all Japanese surrender themselves to the military authorities for the purposes of removal from the area.  No question was raised as to Korematsu's loyalty.  His offense consisted solely in failing to submit to evacuation.  Black, for the Court, conceded that racial classifications are normally highly suspect, and that the evacuation order created tremendous hardships for those subject to it.  Nevertheless, he concluded that it was not beyond reason that ethnic ties created a security problem and on that basis the judgment of the military upon which the executive order in question was based must be upheld.

> Here, as in *Hirabayashi*, " . . . we cannot reject as unfounded the judgment of the military authorities and of Congress that there were disloyal members of that population, whose number and strength could not be precisely and quickly ascertained.  We cannot say that the war-making branches of the Government did not have ground for believing that in a critical hour such persons could not readily be isolated and separately dealt with, and constituted a menace to the national defense and safety, which demanded that prompt and adequate measures be taken to guard against it." [7]

Rather weakly, the Court attempted to rationalize the racial basis for the exclusion order.

> . . . Korematsu was not excluded from the Military Area because of hostility to him or his race.  He *was* excluded because we are at war with the Japanese Empire . .  . . . . [8]

Concurring separately, Frankfurter supplied the "Amen" to Black's argument.  For the Court to uphold the constitutionality

7.  Ibid., at 218.                    8.  Ibid., at 223.

of the exclusion regulation, did not, he said, imply approval, but merely deference to the judgment of the military, Congress and the executive.

Roberts, Murphy, and Jackson dissented, each in a separate opinion. Roberts pointed out that the order excluding Korematsu from his home in San Leandro did not leave him free to relocate elsewhere in the United States, but instead required him to submit to forceable detention in a prescribed area. The case, therefore, could not be argued solely on the alleged military necessity of excluding Japanese from the coastal areas. Murphy did not hesitate to label the decision as an exercise in racism. For the government, in the absence of any demonstrable proof that Japanese persons were any more likely to be disloyal than other residents of the United States, to intern them in concentration camps was totally unreasonable and indefensible. No attempt had been made to establish the loyalty of the individuals involved, many of whom were children or elderly men and women. Jackson enlarged on Murphy's theme by pointing out that Korematsu, who was a native born American, had been deprived of his home and property although no one had ever questioned his loyalty. He had been "convicted of an act not commonly a crime," consisting of

> .   .   . merely of being present in the state whereof he is a citizen, near the place where he was born, and where all his life he had lived.

> Now, if any fundamental assumption underlies our system, it is that guilt is personal and not inheritable. .   .   . But here is an attempt to make an otherwise innocent act a crime merely because this prisoner is the son of parents as to whom he had no choice, and belongs to a race from which there is no way to resign. .   .   .[9]

Jackson then went on to discuss the military justification for the order and remarked that the test of any military order is

9.   Ibid., at 243.

not its legality but its success. He conceded that he was in no position to evaluate the soundness of the commanding general's assessment of the situation from the military point of view, but neither could he in good conscience place the imprimatur of constitutionality of what was essentially an exercise in expedience. The actions taken may have been permissible military procedures, but to Jackson it did not follow that they were constitutional.

> I should hold that a civil court cannot be made to enforce an order which violates constitutional limitations even if it is a reasonable exercise of military authority.
>
> .  .  .
>
> .  .  .  I do not suggest that the courts should have attempted to interfere with the Army in carrying out its task. But I do not think they may be asked to execute a military expedient that has no place in law under the Constitution.  .  .  .  [10]

In short, Jackson's position was that when a nation is at war there can be no civil liberties and no constitutional guarantees that can be sustained against the claims of the military.

It would be comforting to think of *Korematsu* as a shameful episode not likely to reoccur. Unfortunately, history bears out Jackson's point. Civil liberties are an early casualty of war. The problem presented by *Korematsu* is not dead, only dormant.

### Discrimination Through Direct State Action: Blacks

While *Yick Wo* and *Korematsu* are dispiriting commentaries on American treatment of Orientals, discrimination against blacks is and always has been the most serious equal protection problem in the United States. Prior to the Civil War blacks had, for all practical purposes, no civil rights, since chattel slavery was a legally permissible institution. This was true despite the fact that to a very limited extent blacks did have standing to

10. Ibid., at 247–248.

sue in the courts.* (The plaintiff in *Dred Scott,* for example, was a slave.) The victory of the North in the Civil War resulted in the adoption of the Thirteenth, Fourteenth, and Fifteenth Amendments, all of which were enacted primarily to grant to the newly freed slaves the civil rights and liberties of other residents of the United States.

The Civil War amendments forbade overt *de jure* racial discrimination against blacks. Thus, the Fifteenth Amendment made it unlawful for the states to deny the right to vote because of race, color, or previous condition of servitude. The Thirteenth Amendment abolished involuntary servitude, including of course, chattel slavery. The Fourteenth Amendment, more general in its terms, repeated the due process guarantees of the Fifth Amendment—"nor shall any state deprive any person of life, liberty, or property, without due process of law"—and added to it an equal protection clause—"nor deny to any person within its jurisdiction the equal protection of the law." ** Despite the enactment of these amendments, both *de jure* and *de facto* discrimination against blacks continued for at least a century, either in the form of direct state action, or as private action aided, abetted or permitted by the government. Early challenges to overt state discriminatory action were made in *Strauder v. West Virginia,*[11] where the state restricted jury service to whites, and *Plessy v. Ferguson,*[12] where the state imposed a re-

---

* For a full, very interesting discussion of the legal rights of blacks under slavery, see Eugene D. Genovese, *Roll, Jordan, Roll* (New York: Pantheon Books 1974). Genovese cites examples of court recognition of a slave's claim to extra compensation for increased working hours, and compensation for personal property confiscated or lost by the slave's owner.

** The Fourteenth Amendment also conferred national and state citizenship on the newly freed slaves, and forbade the states to deny any person "the privileges or immunities of citizens of the United States." Neither of these provisions, for a variety of historical and legal reasons has been as important in the struggle for racial justice as have the Due Process and Equal Protection clauses.

11. 100 U.S. 303, 25 L.Ed. 664 (1880).

12. 163 U.S. 537, 16 S.Ct. 1138, 41 L.Ed. 256 (1896).

quirement for separate railroad accommodations for blacks and whites. Private discriminatory action, however, was challenged in the *Civil Rights Cases* [13] which involved the refusal of hotel and theatre owners and the proprietors of common carriers to serve blacks. Each of these types of challenges historically has given rise to a host of cases, and for purposes of conceptual clarity it is easier to discuss each genre separately rather than to consider the general category of race discrimination cases chronologically. Thus, the question of the extent to which the state may legislate discrimination will be considered in an analysis of *Plessy, Strauder,* and their progeny; the extent of permissible, private discrimination will be considered in the discussion of the *Civil Rights Cases* and their aftermath.

*From Strauder v. West Virginia to Brown v. Board of Education: De jure Segregation*

In 1880, Strauder, a black man convicted in a West Virginia court of murder, appealed his conviction on the ground that he had been denied equal protection of the laws because West Virginia law forbade blacks from serving on grand or petit juries. His appeal was successful. The Court set aside his conviction— not because the jury which convicted him was all white, but because the law deliberately excluded all blacks from jury service. [14] Strauder had had no right to have blacks proportionately represented on the jury, but he did have a right to have members of his race eligible for jury service on the same terms as whites. "[T]he true spirit and meaning" of the Civil War amendments, said the court, was

> . . . securing to a race recently emancipated . . . the enjoyment of all the civil rights that under the law are enjoyed by white persons . . . .
>
> . . . What is this [equal protection but] that all persons, whether colored or white, shall stand equal before the laws of the States, and, in regard to the col-

13. 109 U.S. 3, 3 S.Ct. 18, 27 L.Ed. 835 (1883).          14. *Strauder v. West Virginia,* 100 U.S. 303, 25 L.Ed. 644 (1879).

ored race, for whose protection the amendment was primarily designed, that no discrimination shall be made against them by law because of their color? [15]

The West Virginia statute, said the Court, was clearly discriminatory and could not stand. While a state was free to "confine the selection [of jurors] to males, to freeholders, to citizens, to persons within certain ages, or to persons having educational qualifications," it could not exclude from jury service blacks, any more than it could exclude whites or "naturalized Celtic Irishmen." [16] In short, racial categories were inherently unreasonable and could not stand, at least absent a strong showing of necessity.

Despite this early victory in the Supreme Court, discrimination against newly freed blacks was only beginning, not ending. Until relatively recent times in many areas of the South blacks, in fact, were excluded from the possibility of jury service. The decision in *Strauder* was observed in the narrowest possible sense, i. e., the southern states did not pass laws forbidding blacks being called for jury service. However, just as the San Francisco Board of Supervisors arranged that only Chinese laundrymen were put out of business, southern administrative officials saw to it that blacks were simply not called. Whatever subterfuge may have been necessary to avoid black veniremen was employed, and in 1935, in the second Scottsboro case [17] Samuel Leibowitz appealed the conviction of Clarence Norris on the ground that in fact no black person had ever served on a grand or petit jury in the county in which the trial was held. Norris' appeal was successful and constituted a recognition by the Supreme Court of the *de facto* discrimination against blacks that was widely prevalent in the South. Since 1935, this type of discrimination has slowly declined, but not until the civil rights agitation of the 1950's and 60's did it become reasonably likely that blacks would appear in the venire from which jurors were

15.  Ibid., at 306–307.

16.  Ibid., at 310, 308.

17.  *Norris v. Alabama*, 294 U.S. 587, 55 S.Ct. 579, 79 L.Ed. 1074 (1935).

drawn. As late as 1967 the names of prospective jurors in Georgia were selected from records of the county tax office which were maintained on a racially segregated basis.[18]

Far more harmful, however, than the administrative subterfuges used in *Strauder* was the development of the "separate but equal" doctrine which became the accepted standard following the decision in *Plessy v. Ferguson*.[19] In 1890 Louisiana passed a law requiring that railway passenger cars have "equal but separate accommodations for the white and colored races." Plessy, who claimed that he was seven-eighths Caucasian and one-eighth African was arrested for riding in the white coach. He challenged his conviction as a violation of the Equal Protection Clause of the Fourteenth Amendment. Plessy argued that the establishment of racial categories was detrimental to him, and therefore, was forbidden by the Fourteenth Amendment, the obvious intent of which was to protect the full civil rights of all citizens, both black and white. The State of Louisiana responded that it had not discriminated against either race, but had made a rule which was applicable to both races. If Plessy was excluded from the white coach, white people by the same token, were excluded from the black coaches. The Court accepted Louisiana's argument, holding that while the object of the Fourteenth Amendment "was undoubtedly to enforce the absolute equality of the two races before the law  .   .   .  it could not have been intended to abolish distinctions based on color, or to enforce social, as distinguished from political equality." [20]

Justice Brown, for the majority, went on to say that while the same argument that was used to justify this type of segregation could be used to justify other unacceptable types of segregation, as for example, requiring "white men's houses to be painted white, and colored men's black," the test in every case was the reasonableness of the regulation. He saw no reason to doubt that the Louisiana statute in question had been passed in good

18. *Whitus v. Georgia*, 385 U.S. 545, 87 S.Ct. 643, 17 L.Ed.2d 599 (1967).

19. 163 U.S. 537, 16 S.Ct. 1138, 41 L.Ed. 256 (1896).

20. Ibid., at 544.

faith and for the promotion of the public good, rather than for the oppression of or injury to any group of citizens. Brown concluded by chiding Plessy gently for his paranoid interpretation of Louisiana's action.

> We consider the underlying fallacy of the plaintiff's argument to consist in the assumption that the enforced separation of the two races stamps the colored race with a badge of inferiority. If this be so, it is not by reason of anything found in the act, but solely because the colored race chooses to put that construction upon it. . . . [21]

Repeatedly in his opinion, Brown referred to the reasonableness of the state's recognition of the "established usages, customs, and traditions of the people." Because most whites saw blacks as inherently inferior, at least on a social level, it was not unreasonable for a state law to establish racial categories.

Justice Harlan, alone, dissented vigorously in an opinion which, along with his dissent in the earlier *Civil Rights Cases,* has established his claim to immortality. Harlan denied the right of the legislature to base legal categories on skin color, and challenged Brown's ingenuous description of the nonstigmatizing character of the law in question. A segregation law was indeed a badge of inferiority that the dominant white group had fastened on politically powerless blacks.

> It was said in argument that the statute of Louisiana does not discriminate against either race, but prescribes a rule applicable alike to white and colored citizens. [But] everyone knows that [it] had its origin in the purpose, not so much to exclude white persons from railroad cars occupied by blacks, as to exclude colored people from coaches occupied by . . . white persons. . . . [22]

21.  Ibid., at 551.                    22.  Ibid., at 556–557.

In a remarkably prescient passage Harlan went on to point out the possible consequences of permitting this type of legislative discrimination.

> . . . If a State can prescribe, as a rule of civil conduct, that whites and blacks shall not travel as passengers in the same railroad coach, . . . why may it not require sheriffs to assign whites to one side of a courtroom and blacks to the other? And why may it not also prohibit the commingling of the two races in the galleries of legislative halls . . . .*

(What seemed unthinkable to Harlan—that whites should sit on one side of the courtroom and blacks on the other—did, of course, come to pass.) In one of the most memorable passages of any Supreme Court decision, Harlan, in almost Biblical tones, expounded his view of what the Constitution ought to stand for in the United States.

> The white race deems itself to be the dominant race in this country. And so it is, in prestige, in achievements, in education, in wealth, and in power. So, I doubt not, it will continue to be for all time, if it remains true to its great heritage, and holds fast to the principals of constitutional liberty. But in view of the Constitution, in the eye of the law, there is in this

---

* *Plessy v. Ferguson*, 163 U.S. 537, at 557–558, 16 S.Ct. 1138, 1145–1146, 41 L.Ed. 256 (1896). Most people today imagine that segregation was a way of life in the South, accepted and unbroken from the day the first Negro slave arrived in Virginia until the passage of the Federal Civil Rights Act of 1964. This is not true. During the period of slavery, of course, blacks were segregated and their conduct regulated by Black Codes. Following the Civil War these Black Codes were repealed, and legal segregation was not imposed for a considerable period of time. The 1890 Louisiana Statute involved in Plessy was actually a reenactment of part of an old Black Code of pre-Civil War days, but this was a quarter of a century after the close of the Civil War. For a full discussion of this topic, see, C. Vann Woodward, *The Strange Career of Jim Crow*, 3rd edition (New York: Oxford University Press, 1974).

country no superior, dominant, ruling class of citizens. There is no caste here. Our Constitution is color blind. . . . [23]

Unfortunately for the United States, neither society nor the Constitution in 1890 were color blind and the decision in *Plessy v. Ferguson* was far more acceptable to most people than Harlan's dissent would have been, had it prevailed. The separate but equal doctrine became the established constitutional standard for better than a half century following. Segregation became the rule in all kinds of public and private places, primarily in the states of the old Confederacy, but also to a somewhat lesser extent in border states, such as Maryland, Kansas, and Missouri. Segregation was practiced in relation to theatres, hotels, restaurants, all types of public transportation, hospitals, prisons, rest rooms, and in almost any kind of situation where blacks and whites were likely to meet and mingle. In the northern and western states, while segregation was not mandated by law, it was frequently practiced, especially by private individuals, in relation to hotels, restaurants, and other types of public accommodations. As recently as the end of World War II in New York City, blacks could not be certain of being served in mid-town restaurants, or being able to rent a room in a mid-town hotel.

As stigmatizing as such practices were to blacks, and as destructive as they were to both black and white societies, perhaps the very worst kind of *de jure* segregation took place in the public schools. School segregation was the general rule in the United States, both before and after the Civil War in all sections of the country. Indeed, Justice Brown in his majority opinion in *Plessy* cited as an example of permissible racial segregation *Roberts v. Boston*,[24] an 1849 case in which the great Chief Justice Shaw upheld the validity of separate schools for blacks and whites. Following the Civil War, in the general movement to upgrade public education in the North, schools improved and laws requiring segregation were either relaxed or abandoned.

23.   Ibid., at 559.                    24.   59 Mass. (5 Cush.) 198 (1849).

In the South, which had had virtually no public school system before the Civil War, public schools were established for whites but little attention was paid to the needs of blacks. Higher education for blacks, limited as it was, was provided almost exclusively by private charities, such as the Baptist and Methodist churches, and private philanthropists, such as the Rockefellers and Rosenwalds. At the elementary school level, southern schools were on the whole underfunded, with black schools frequently getting less than half the amounts allocated for the support of white schools. As for high schools, in many communities such facilities for blacks were simply not provided.

The net result was, that in the field of education (as in transportation and public accommodations), facilities, though surely separate, were far from equal. Suits brought to challenge the inequality in the allocation of public funds to black and white schools were unsuccessful. In *Cumming v. Richmond County Board of Education*,[25] black taxpayers sued to restrain the school board from supporting a white high school while discontinuing the existing black high school. A unanimous Supreme Court, avoiding the segregation issue, denied that the discontinuance of the black high school violated the Equal Protection Clause, and concluded that an injunction which would close the white high schools would not, in any way, help blacks and was not the proper remedy. Even Justice Harlan felt that interference by the federal government in a matter of state concern, such as education, was warranted only in cases where constitutional rights had been clearly disregarded. Suits brought subsequent to 1899 were no more successful until the 1930's when for the first time the NAACP mounted a successful suit to achieve equality in educational facilities available to whites and blacks.

In *Missouri ex rel. Gaines v. Canada*,[26] Lloyd Gaines, a black student, sought admission to the state law school, which refused to admit him but offered instead to pay his tuition fees at a law school in any neighboring state where segregation was not en-

25.  175 U.S. 528, 20 S.Ct. 197, 44 L. Ed. 262 (1899).      26.  305 U.S. 337, 59 S.Ct. 232, 83 L. Ed. 208 (1938).

forced. Gaines refused this offer and insisted on his right to equal treatment, i. e., admission to the same school that would have been available to him were he white. The United States Supreme Court in an opinion written by Chief Justice Hughes upheld Gaines' position, agreeing that Missouri, by providing facilities for white law students, had incurred an obligation to provide equal facilities for its black citizens. Following the *Gaines* decision, Missouri and other southern states complied with its letter but not its spirit by setting up separate but inferior law schools. In 1950 the NAACP again successfully challenged this practice. In *Sweatt v. Painter*,[27] Sweatt, who had been denied admission to the University of Texas Law School, refused to go to the separate law school for blacks on the ground that it was substantially inferior to the school provided for whites. The Court agreed with Sweatt and compared the two schools in terms of prestige, faculty, student body, library facilities, alumni, etc. and concluded that it would be difficult to believe that any one who had a choice would select the Negro, rather than the white school. The language of the decision, moreover, implied that it was doubtful that any school which was set up as a segregated facility for blacks could, as a practical matter, be equal to its white opposite number. On the same day as it decided *Sweatt v. Painter,* the Court handed down a decision in *McLaurin v. Oklahoma State Regents.*[28] McLaurin had been admitted to graduate school at the University of Oklahoma, but on a "segregated" basis. He was to use separate sections of classrooms, library and cafeteria. The Court unanimously struck down these requirements.

By the end of 1950 thus, the Court had, to a considerable extent, alleviated *de jure* segregation in higher education. It had insisted on equal facilities for black students and had hinted that segregation in and of itself tended to make educational facilities unequal. Nevertheless, the process of ending segregation in education had only begun. The decisions handed down related only

27.  339 U.S. 629, 70 S.Ct. 848, 94 L. Ed. 1114 (1950).

28.  339 U.S. 637, 70 S.Ct. 851, 94 L. Ed. 1149 (1950).

to higher education, indeed graduate education, which affected a miniscule number of black students. It was at the elementary and high school level that segregation and discrimination were most harmful and where change would stimulate the greatest social resistance. It was in this context that the landmark case of *Brown v. Board of Education of Topeka* came to the Court in 1953.[29]

The facts of *Brown* were simple. Minnie Jean Brown, a six year old black child sought admission to her predominantly white neighborhood school in Topeka, Kansas. When her application was refused, her parents brought suit on equal protection grounds against the school board. Her case ultimately reached the United States Supreme Court where it was joined to the cases of three other similarly situated children from South Carolina, Virginia, and Delaware.* In each case the states involved argued that the Negro schools available fulfilled the requirements of the Equal Protection Clause of the Fourteenth Amendment in that separate but equal facilities for blacks had been provided. A showing was made, moreover, that the Negro schools were in fact equal to the white schools with relation to buildings, teachers' salaries and qualifications, curriculum, and other measurable attributes. The United States Supreme Court, thus, faced squarely the question of whether segregation, i. e., the provision of separate but equal facilities, was inherently discriminatory and a denial of equal protection of the laws.

The answer of the Court was resoundingly affirmative. In a unanimous decision, written by Chief Justice Warren himself, the Court declared unequivocally, that the mere act of separation on a racial basis was constitutionally impermissible. The Court reviewed the history of the Fourteenth Amendment in an attempt to determine whether at the time of its adoption, the

29. 347 U.S. 483, 74 S.Ct. 686, 98 L. Ed. 873 (1954).

* In each of these cases the lower courts had upheld the separate but equal doctrine, but in the Delaware case the State Supreme Court, while adhering to the doctrine, had nevertheless, ordered the admission of the plaintiff because of the superiority of the white school to the available Negro school.

Fourteenth Amendment was meant to prohibit racial segregation in the schools. The historical evidence was ambiguous and ultimately irrelevant because as the Court remarked, "We cannot turn the clock back to 1868 when the Amendment was adopted, or even to 1896 when *Plessy v. Ferguson* was written." [30] The question of school desegregation had to be considered in its present-day context, and in that context the Court had no doubt that it was an anachronism which had to be abolished.

We come then to the question presented: Does segregation of children in public schools solely on the basis of race, even though the physical facilities and other "tangible" factors may be equal, deprive the children of the minority group of equal educational opportunities? We believe that it does.

.   .   .   To separate [children] from others of similar age and qualifications solely because of their race generates a feeling of inferiority as to their status in the community that may affect their hearts and minds in a way unlikely ever to be undone.   .   .   . [31]

The Court then went on to quote from a finding in the Kansas case by a lower court which had nevertheless ruled against the plaintiffs.

"Segregation of white and colored children in public schools has a detrimental effect upon the colored children. The impact is greater when it has the sanction of the law; for the policy of separating the races is usually interpreted as denoting the inferiority of the Negro group. A sense of inferiority affects the motivation of a child to learn. Segregation with the sanction of law, therefore, has a tendency to [retard] the educational and mental development of Negro children and to deprive them of some of the benefits they would receive in a racial[ly] integrated school system." [32]

30.  Ibid., at 492.                    32.  Ibid., at 494.

31.  Ibid., at 493 and 494.

Taking cognizance of a wealth of psychological literature on the impact of segregation, the Court then went on to say that whatever the state of psychological knowledge at the time of *Plessy*, modern psychological research amply supported the belief that segregation was stigmatizing and harmful to a child. In blunt, straightforward language the Court declared

> .   .   .   Separate educational facilities are inherently unequal. Therefore, we hold that the plaintiffs .   .   .   are, by reason of the segregation complained of, deprived of equal protection of the laws.   .   .   .[33]

Thus *Plessy* and three hundred years of *de jure* segregation were laid to rest. For the first time in American history the United States Supreme Court declared that segregation, in and of itself, was a violation of the equal protection clause of the Fourteenth Amendment. It did so, moreover, not on the basis of legal precedents, but rather by taking cognizance of and accepting evidence produced by social scientists—sociologists, psychologists, and others—who found that such legal separation did indeed constitute a badge of shame for blacks in the United States.

## The Aftermath of Brown v. Board of Education: The Constitutionality of De Facto Segregation

The *Brown* decision was received tumultuously. While blacks and liberals hailed it as a long overdue triumph of democracy, reaction in the South was bitter, perilously close to violent. "Never" became the motto of many white political leaders who swore mighty oaths that southern schools would, under no circumstances be desegregated. Political doctrines unheard since pre-Civil War days were resurrected in an attempt to interpose the sovereignty of the states between their citizens and the tyranny of the federal government. Much of the protest was bluster and a ventilation of deeply felt resentment. The Civil War was not about to be refought and slowly the threat of direct op-

---

33.   Ibid., at 495.

position and uncontrolled violence faded. It was replaced by a far more effective technique—"massive resistance."

Massive resistance consisted basically of deliberate footdragging on the part of administrative officials, especially those who had responsibility for drawing school boundary lines and assigning pupils to and within schools. School boards at first refused to do anything to dismantle the dual school systems of the South. When goaded by lawsuits they reluctantly produced plans that would result in minimal integration. The United States Supreme Court in a second decision in the *Brown* case [34] had designated the United States District Courts as the agencies to oversee the integration of the schools "with all deliberate speed." It was to the District Courts, therefore, that the desegregation plans came for review. Repeatedly, unsatisfactory plans were struck down by the courts. In 1964, however, Congress passed the Civil Rights Act of 1964, Title VI of which empowered the Department of Health, Education, and Welfare to cut off federal funds to school systems practicing racial discrimination. The Justice Department, moreover, was authorized to bring suit to obtain desegregation orders against local school systems which were not complying with the mandate of *Brown*. With these additional pressures, the pace of desegregation slowly began to increase. In the first decade after *Brown* there was virtually no change in the racial composition of southern schools, but by 1971, sixteen years after the implementation decision, only 32 percent of black pupils attended schools with over 80 percent minority population. Three years earlier, 79 percent of blacks had been in such schools.[35] Substantial progress had been made in the South towards ending a century of segregated schooling.

Despite this progress, however, many authorities feel that schools in the United States are more segregated today than

34.  349 U.S. 294, 75 S.Ct. 753, 99 L. Ed. 1083 (1955).

35.  Comment "Keyes v. School District No. 1: Unlocking the North-ern Schoolhouse Doors," 9 *Harvard Civil Rights—Civil Liberties Law Review* 124 (1974).

they were twenty five years ago, and the worst offenders are no longer the southern schools but schools in large cities throughout the entire country.

> While Southern schools are now generally desegregated, well over half the black children outside the South attend schools that are at least 90 percent black. There are sizeable black majorities in the public schools in the nation's largest cities, a situation that makes desegregation politically difficult, if not logistically impossible.

> In New York, the public schools are 67 percent nonwhite. In Chicago, the figure is 70 percent; in Philadelphia, 62 percent, in Detroit, 81 percent, in Baltimore, 75 percent, and in Washington, 96 percent.[36]

School segregation in the cities cited above is not legally mandated, as was segregation in the dual school systems of the South prior to the *Brown* decision. It results instead from the traditional practice of assigning students to the schools nearest their homes. The typical residential pattern of American metropolitan areas is of older, decaying inner city districts occupied by the poor (usually black or Hispanic) and newer outlying and suburban districts occupied by the middle and upper classes (usually predominantly white). Thus, where pupils are assigned to neighborhood schools, inner city schools become overwhelmingly black or Hispanic, and outlying and suburban schools show the reverse pattern. The civil rights struggles of the 50's and 60's and the legal victories of civil rights proponents ironically may have exascerbated *de facto* school segregation by increasing white flight to the suburbs of parents who wished to avoid having their children attend schools that were substantially or predominantly black. Blacks attribute such white flight to racism and unreasoning prejudice. Whites respond that their fear is not of black children *per se* but of assaultive, disruptive children

36. *The New York Times,* July 3, 1977, p. 28.

who either cannot or will not learn and who lower the quality of the educational process for all.

Whatever the reasons, schools, outside the South, have become increasingly segregated. In 1971, when only 32 percent of blacks in the South attended predominantly (more than 80 percent) black schools, 91.3 percent of black students attended such schools in Cleveland, Ohio; 97.8 in Compton, California; 78.1 in Dayton, Ohio; 78.6 in Detroit, Michigan; 95.7 in Gary, Indiana; 86.4 in Kansas City, Missouri; 86.6 in Los Angeles, California; 78.8 in Milwaukee, Wisconsin; 91.3 in Newark, New Jersey; and 89.8 in St. Louis, Missouri.[37] What, if anything, is the significance of the *Brown* decision for schools such as these? Did *Brown* mean that racial segregation in the schools was wrong only if imposed by an affirmative action of the state (*de jure* segregation), or did *Brown* mean that any racial segregation whether *de facto* or *de jure* in the schools was intolerable and constitutionally impermissible?

The text of the *Brown* decision referred only to *de jure* segregation; the facts of the case and the decision of the Court related exclusively to school systems which were, by law, required to be segregated on a racial basis, and in striking down the doctrine of separate but equal facilities, *Brown* addressed itself to facilities that were separate because of state legislative policy. Nevertheless, many people feel that *Brown* was really about equality, about equal distribution of educational resources without regard to race. School systems that were segregated because of housing patterns were frequently just as unequal as the pre-Brown *de jure* segregated schools of the South in relation to physical plant, the qualifications of the faculty, and educational product. Students graduated from such schools, on the whole, did not demonstrate the academic competence of students graduated from white schools. Surely, it was a denial of equal protection of the laws for a black child to be required to attend an inner city, predominantly black school even if the segregation re-

37.   Comment, "Keyes v. School District," at 124.

sulted from the tradition of assigning children to neighborhood schools rather than from a state law requiring such segregation. To that end, a number of suits were mounted against school boards asking an end to the practice of assigning children automatically to their neighborhood schools and requiring that all schools in the district through use of busing where necessary, reflect the racial makeup of the entire district.

Predictably, the attempt to use busing to integrate schools on a district-wide basis met with a great deal of opposition. Some parents, both black and white, objected to transporting children, especially the younger ones, considerable distances from their homes. These objections might have been overcome in time however, since in rural districts busing has been used extensively for fifty years, with apparent success and acceptability. The more serious objection to busing was that whites who had moved to districts sufficiently affluent to provide excellent school systems, simply did not want their children to be denied the opportunity to attend those schools. Parents who had, at considerable expense, moved to the suburbs because of their fine schools were understandably furious at the thought that their children would be sent back to the inner city, to the very areas their parents had left. Thus, busing became one of the most volatile and controversial issues of the 1970's, and political leaders either opposed busing flatly or tried in some way to temporize and evade the issue. Repeated attempts were made in Congress to cut off federal funds used to bus children, and also to enact a constitutional amendment which would provide that

> No public school student shall, because of his race, creed, or color, be assigned to or be required to attend a particular school.

The amendment failed, along with a subsequent amendment which would have denied jurisdiction to the federal courts to order busing on the basis of race. During the Nixon years, however, the federal government was not aggressive in forcing the pace of school integration.

The unpopularity of busing, however, has no direct bearing on the constitutional merits of the question. Do states and localities have an affirmative duty to see to it that all schools are integrated in proportion to the population of an area? Several cases which came to the United States Supreme Court have considered this question. The earliest suits were brought against Southern school systems. In *Green v. County School Board*,[38] New Kent County, a rural district in Virginia with no residential segregation, had combined its previously segregated elementary and high schools, but had offered freedom of choice to parents as to which school a child should attend. After three years no white child chose to go to the black school which 85 percent of the black children continued to attend. The children were transported by school buses which travelled "overlapping routes throughout the county to transport the pupils to and from the two schools." A unanimous Supreme Court struck down the freedom of choice plan to achieve racial integration, holding in essence that regardless of the good faith of the school board in enacting such a plan, it simply did not meet the constitutional obligation to achieve a "racially nondiscriminatory school system."

A more complex case arose three years later in the city of Charlotte, North Carolina.[39] The Charlotte-Mecklenburg school system was a large district—550 square miles—encompassing the city of Charlotte and surrounding Mecklenburg County. In 1968, the school district had 107 schools and 84,000 students, 71 percent of which were white and 29 percent black. As of June 1969, there were 24,000 black students, 21,000 of whom attended schools within the city of Charlotte. Fourteen thousand of those 21,000—two-thirds, attended all black schools. From 1965 on, the school board had attempted to devise a plan to integrate the schools. Ultimately, two plans were devised, both of which relied on extensive busing to achieve integration throughout the

38. 391 U.S. 430, 88 S.Ct. 1689, 20 L.Ed.2d 716 (1968).

39. *Swann v. Charlotte-Mecklenburg Bd. of Educ.*, 402 U.S. 1, 91 S.Ct. 1284, 28 L.Ed.2d 586 (1971).

district of the junior and senior high schools. One plan, the Board plan, would have integrated the elementary schools by gerrymandering school districts; the other plan, the "finger" plan, would have used zoning, pairing, and grouping techniques to achieve the same results. These two plans, together with a plan prepared by the Department of Health, Education, and Welfare, had been considered and modified by the lower federal courts, and the Supreme Court accepted certiorari for the purpose of clarifying the guidelines for acceptable school desegregation plans.

The Court held, in the first place, that the "constant theme and thrust" of every holding from *Brown* I is that "state-enforced separation of races in public schools is discrimination that violates the Equal Protection Clause." The Court then went on to consider four questions related to the problem of ending such discrimination: (1) to what extent racial quotas might be used in a remedial order to correct a previously segregated system; (2) whether every all black or all white school had to be eliminated; (3) what were the limits, if any, on the rearrangements of school districts and attendance zones in a remedial plan; and (4) what were the limits on the use of busing to correct previous state-enforced discrimination?

The Court decided that it was not necessary to eliminate all one-race schools, but in a system with a previous history of segregation the burden of proof was on the school board to show that any plan for school assignments was genuinely nondiscriminatory. As an interim remedy the courts were free to order extensive busing and rezoning even if it caused considerable inconvenience to parents and students. Only if the health of the children or the quality of the educational process were significantly adversely affected could an objection to busing have validity. The Court went on to say

> Absent a constitutional violation there would be no basis for judicially ordering assignment of students on a racial basis. All things being equal, with no history

of discrimination, it might well be desirable to assign pupils to schools nearest their homes.  But all things are not equal in a system that has been deliberately constructed and maintained to enforce racial segregation.  The remedy for such segregation may be administratively awkward, inconvenient, and even bizarre in some situations and may impose burdens on some; but all awkwardness and inconvenience cannot be avoided in the interim period when remedial adjustments are being made to eliminate the dual school systems.[40]

The constitutional violation in the *Swann* case was apparently the history of legally imposed segregation, and given that history it was appropriate for the District Court to order extensive student reassignment and busing.  But what if a school district had had no history of legally required segregation?  What if segregation stemmed entirely from housing patterns within the area?  A case raising these issues, *Keyes v. School District No. 1*,[41] came to the United States Supreme Court from Denver, Colorado, a western city with no history of *de jure* racial segregation.  For a long period of time the inner city part of Denver was populated largely by blacks and Hispanics, and the schools in that area were likewise predominantly black and Hispanic. In the post-war period, however, these groups began to migrate to a middle-class, white section known as Park Hill, which by 1970 was 50 percent black.  Several Park Hill schools became predominantly black while others remained substantially white. The school board had contributed to this result by concentrating black students in a few schools in that area in order to preserve the character of the remainder.  It had done so by manipulating new school construction, deployment of mobile classroom units, boundary changes and pupil transfers.  The District Court, finding these practices constituted *de jure* segregation, ordered the School Board to desegregate the Park Hill schools, but declined

40.  Ibid., at 28.                    41.  413 U.S. 189, 93 S.Ct. 2686, 37
                                      L.Ed.2d 548 (1973).

to order the desegregation of the core (inner city) schools, the segregation of which was not a result of school board policy.

The United States Supreme Court, in a decision written by Justice Brennan, reversed the lower court in relation to the desegregation of the core city schools, holding that the manipulative practices of the school board which had resulted in the concentration of black and Hispanic students in the Park Hill schools constituted *de jure* segregation similar to that resulting from the legally mandated dual school systems of the South. The actions of the school board were shown to have been racially inspired and intended to segregate students along racial and ethnic lines. It was thus clear that minority students in the Park Hill schools had been denied equal protection of the laws, the remedy for which was clearly a reassignment of students within the Park Hill district. The situation in Park Hill, moreover, affected the status of the core city schools. These latter schools were segregated due to prevailing housing patterns which resulted in a predominantly black and Hispanic inner city population. There was no evidence of action on the part of the school board which contributed to the segregation of these schools. Nevertheless, the *de jure* segregation of Park Hill affected the situation in the core city both directly and indirectly. The gerrymandering of the Park Hill school district directly forced more blacks into the core city schools than might otherwise have been there. In addition, the fact that some schools were designed to remain predominantly white with others designated as predominantly black or Hispanic, influenced residential patterns in such a way as to continue and reinforce segregated housing. The reassignment of pupils, therefore, in Denver should be on a system-wide basis rather than confined to simply the Park Hill district where *de jure* segregation was shown to have existed.

In short, the majority of the Court held that where actions of the school board could be shown to have been motivated by an intent to segregate students along racial lines, such actions were the equivalent of *de jure* segregation just as much as if the school board had ordered the establishment of two separate racially based school systems; and the remedy for such *de jure* segregation, if necessary, could be system-wide even if *de jure* segregation had occurred in only one part of the school system. Thus, the Court decided that in both southern school districts which previously had had legally segregated school systems, and in northern school districts in which the school board had instituted policies not overtly segregative, but nevertheless designed to preserve some schools as white enclaves, the Equal Protection Clause required that pupils be reassigned throughout the system so as to achieve maximum feasible integration. In such districts the guiding principle of pupil assignment had to be the need to achieve integration, rather than the convenience of the traditional practice of assigning students to the schools nearest their homes.

Left unanswered was the question of whether such a radical departure from traditional patterns of school assignment was required in districts that had a history of neither legally mandated segregation nor manipulative practices such as existed in Denver. What was required of the thousands of communities whose schools were segregated because the outmigration of whites from older city districts to newer suburbs, and the inmigration of blacks and Hispanics from rural areas, Puerto Rico and Mexico to fill the housing vacated by whites, had resulted in segregated neighborhoods? What if a school board had in no way attempted to preserve any school or schools as a sanctuary for white students? What if, despite scrupulously racially neutral assignment policies, the schools of a city had become heavily black and Hispanic while the schools of the surrounding politically independent suburbs had remained white? Did the Constitution require pupil reassignment schemes that transcended the political boundaries of the cities? Did the Constitution require any kind of action to be taken if no evidence of *de jure* segregation was produced? Was the mere existence of predominantly black, or predominantly white, schools an indication of denial of equal protection of the laws? Was all *de facto* segregation necessarily constitutionally impermissible?

In a separate concurrence in the *Keyes* case, Justice Powell attempted to answer these questions. Powell argued that the existence of segregated schools within the district, regardless of the cause of such segregation, imposed a duty on the school board to take steps to end that segregation. The distinction between *de facto* segregation and *de jure* segregation was to him both irrelevant and untenable, resting as it did on determining the intent of actions taken by public officials. School segregation, in his view, was to a great extent the product of neither historic state-imposed *de jure* segregation, as in the South, nor deliberate covert manipulation, as in the North, but instead was the result of residential housing patterns stemming from causes beyond the control of governmental officials. If segregation was wrong, its causes were constitutionally irrelevant.

> In my view we should abandon   .   .   .   [the *de jure-de facto* distinction] and formulate constitutional principles of national rather than merely regional application.   .   .   .
>
>    .   .   .   the familiar root cause of segregated schools in *all* the biracial metropolitan areas of our country is essentially the same: one of segregated residential and migratory patterns the impact of which on the racial composition of the schools was often perpetuated and rarely ameliorated by action of public school authorities. This is a national, not a southern phenomenon. And it is largely unrelated to whether a particular State had or did not have segregative school laws.
>
>    .   .   .
>
> Public schools are creatures of the State, and whether the segregation is state-created or state-assisted or merely state-perpetuated should be irrelevant to constitional principle.   .   .   .[42]

Powell spoke only for himself. The Court majority was not willing to eradicate the distinction between *de facto* and *de jure*

42.   Ibid., at 219, 222–223, 227.

segregation. This was made clear in *Milliken v. Bradley* [43] a year later. Detroit, pursuant to the directive of the federal District Court, had proposed a plan to remedy previous *de jure* segregation in the Detroit district. While the plan was acceptable in that it provided a racial mix in the schools roughly proportionate to the racial mix of the population, the schools, nevertheless, would be predominantly black while the schools of 53 neighboring school districts were predominantly white. The District Court, therefore, ordered that the 503,000 students of neighboring suburban districts be integrated with Detroit's 276,000 pupils. The United States Supreme Court in an opinion written by Chief Justice Burger set aside the order of the District Court, holding that where no evidence of *de jure* segregation was produced, a school district could not be ordered to integrate with another. Since the white school districts in neighboring counties had not acted unconstitutionally in their pupil assignments, they could not be forced to combine their systems with that of Detroit.

> The controlling principle [is] that the scope of the remedy is determined by the nature and extent of the constitutional violation. Before . . . imposing a cross-district remedy, it must first be shown that there has been a constitutional violation within one district that produces a significant segregative effect in another. . . .

> The constitutional right of the Negro respondents residing in Detroit is to attend a unitary school system in that district. Unless petitioners drew the district lines in a discriminatory fashion, or arranged for white students residing in the Detroit District to attend schools in Oakland and Macomb Counties, they were under no constitutional duty to make provisions for Negro students to do so. . . . [44]

43. 418 U.S. 717, 94 S.Ct. 3112, 41 L.Ed.2d 1069 (1974).

44. Ibid., at 744–745, 746–747.

Burger then went on to reject the notion that desegregation required that the racial composition of each school reflect the racial composition of the whole metropolitan area and to defend the tradition of local control of education.  Justices White, Douglas, and Marshall dissented, pointing out that if schools in the Detroit area were to be truly integrated then the rejected city-suburban plan was the only feasible method of doing so. Further, since education is a state function and the state is therefore responsible for segregation in any district, the state must respond to the command of the Fourteenth Amendment. There was neither logical nor legal reason to contain the remedy within the city boundaries of Detroit.  As Marshall observed, confining pupil reassignments to the city of Detroit itself, provided no remedy for segregation because a heavily black city will produce heavily black schools.

> .   .   .   Ironically purporting to base its result on
> the principle that the scope of the remedy [should] be
> determined by the nature and extent of the constitu-
> tional violation, the Court's answer is to provide no
> remedy at all   .   .   .   guaranteeing that Negro chil-
> dren in Detroit will receive the same separate and in-
> herently unequal education in the future as they have
> been unconstitutionally afforded in the past.[45]

By denying the relief of an interdistrict remedy, the Court in *Milliken* has virtually insured that many inner city schools will remain segregated.  While integration of the schools is a goal that a majority of American people support, there is overwhelming sentiment against the use of extensive busing to accomplish this goal, and the political pressure against interdistrict busing is enormous.  Aside from the objection many parents have to their children attending school at a considerable distance from their homes, many suburban school districts owe their excellence to the extremely heavy taxes residents are willing to pay for the sake of their children's education.  If those children are ordered

45.  Ibid., at 782.

to attend an innercity school with far inferior facilities, it is understandable that the political repercussions on the officials who promulgated or implemented such an order would be disastrous. It is extremely unlikely that the Supreme Court will move any further in the direction of busing as a remedy for segregated schools. Indeed, in 1977, civil rights activists were enormously relieved when in a Dayton, Ohio case the Court affirmed city-wide busing to remedy illegal school segregation.[46] Civil rights proponents had feared that the Court would take the occasion to weaken the power of the federal District Courts to fashion integration remedies. The high court, however, contented itself with reemphasizing that evidence of illegal segregative acts had to be shown before a desegregation plan could be ordered. Barring any drastic change in the makeup of the United States Supreme Court and in the attitudes of the general public, it is likely that until housing patterns become more integrated, segregated schools will be the predominant mode of education in most of the big cities of the United States.

*Affirmative Action Programs*

If racial categories are inherently suspect under the Equal Protection Clause of the Fourteenth Amendment, can racial categories nevertheless be created for the purpose of benefiting previously discriminated against minority groups? It is this question which lies at the heart of the controversy over affirmative action programs. If we accept the rationale of Justice Harlan in *Plessy v. Ferguson* that our Constitution is color blind, then all categories based on race must surely be impermissible. Yet the real meaning of the Equal Protection Clause is not that government must treat all persons equally, but that unequal treatment, when it occurs must be rational. Are racial categories inherently unequal? Is it never rational for the government to establish a category based on race? Most people would agree that some kind of racial categories must be permissible. If a disease, for

46. *Dayton Bd. of Educ. v. Brink-*
*man*, 433 U.S. 406, 97 S.Ct. 2766, 53
L.Ed.2d 851 (1977).

example, such as sickle cell anemia were shown to be confined to blacks exclusively, then surely a screening program designed to uncover unsuspecting victims could be confined to blacks only. Such a program would treat blacks differently from whites, but would do so for the purpose of benefiting the group rather than harming them.   Does this mean that benign discrimination is permissible?   Is the kind of racial categorization forbidden by the Fourteenth Amendment only the kind that harms groups? The racial categories struck down in the *Brown v. Board of Education* case were established for the purpose of harming blacks, and in that case the Court adopted the moral tone as well as the reasoning of Harlan's dissent in *Plessy v. Ferguson.*   However, in *Swann v. Charlotte-Mecklenburg Board of Education,* the Court approved a pupil assignment scheme that was based on racial categories fully as much as was the segregated school system in Charlotte prior to the *Brown* decision.   The difference, of course, was that the racial categories in southern schools prior to *Brown* were for the purpose of segregation; the racial categories in *Swann* were for the purposes of integration.

The sins of the fathers, the Bible reminds us, are visited on later generations, and racial discrimination unfortunately is one of those sins.   If blacks and other minorities are to achieve equality of status in the United States, simply removing legal barriers to equal opportunity will not accomplish this, at least not in the short run.   An analogy has been drawn comparing the situation of blacks in the United States to runners in a race who previously have been shackled.   If the shackles are removed from the runner he is not on equal terms with those runners whose previous freedom enabled them to practice, to train, and to otherwise prepare themselves for the race.   The black runner, therefore, if he is to compete on equal terms must receive some kind of preferential treatment.   Affirmative action programs which establish quotas which discriminate in favor of minority groups are frequently justified as making up for harmful effects of past discrimination.   Thus, some university authorities, for example, have set aside a certain proportion of the places available for all entering students, exclusively for blacks, Hispanics, and in some cases women, who, it was felt, were so handicapped by previous discrimination, that they were unable to compete on equal terms with whites, or males. The result frequently has been that some whites have been denied admission who were better qualified by strictly academic criteria than some blacks or Hispanics who were admitted. Can a university establish admissions quotas based on race which supersede other standards for admission, such as test scores or grade point averages? In constitutional terms, is it rational for a state to use race as a category for admission to an academic program in such a manner that it takes precedence over other admissions categories related to academic performance?

The United States Supreme Court considered this issue in *DeFunis v. Odegaard*,[47] where the University of Washington Law School had set aside a certain number of places in its entering class for minority students. As a result of this policy, De-Funis, who was better qualified than several minority students who were admitted, was unable to gain admission. DeFunis argued that to establish an admissions system based on race was a violation of the Fourteenth Amendment, and a denial of the equal protection of the law. The University defended its admission policy on the ground that a racial category is unconstitutional only if irrational or arbitrary, and that in this case, the need to promote racial integration of the law school constituted a state interest sufficiently compelling to overcome the suspect status of a racial category. Defenders of the program also argued that the majority, i. e., whites, cannot discriminate against themselves, and therefore, a racial category enacted by whites for the benefit of blacks cannot logically be said to deny anyone equal protection of the law.[48] Nevertheless, from DeFunis' point of view, his application had been set aside in favor of the appli-

47. 416 U.S. 312, 94 S.Ct. 1704, 40 L.Ed.2d 164 (1974).

48. For further discussion of this question, see John Hart Ely, "The Constitutionality of Reverse Racial Discrimination" 41 *University of Chicago Law Review* 723 (1974).

cation of a black student who was less well qualified academically, but who was selected so that the university might compensate for past injustices to blacks, which DeFunis himself had in no way perpetrated.

The issue in the *DeFunis* case was, and is, one of the most sensitive and inflammatory of all civil rights issues. Perhaps for that reason, the United States Supreme Court, after having granted *certiorari,* sidestepped the constitutional question, and decided the case on a legal technicality, declaring that since DeFunis had been admitted to the law school pending the outcome of the litigation, the issue was moot. DeFunis was scheduled to graduate soon, and had achieved his objective—access to a law degree. No decision on the merits was required. Only Justice Douglas addressed himself to the basic issue. While recognizing the difficulties faced by previously disadvantaged minority students in competing with better prepared white students, Douglas opposed the quota system that had been established by the University. He objected in the first place to the singling out of blacks and Hispanics as the groups to be favored by the quota, since other minorities, such as the Japanese, had also been subject to previous discrimination. He also argued that a preferential admissions policy of this type, like a segregated classroom, places a stigma on the very groups it supposedly helps, in that it carries the suggestion that they are unable to achieve their goal on individual merit. Douglas suggested instead that the formal qualifications for admission be broadened to include evidence of a high degree of motivation and the ability to achieve upward mobility, as well as normal academic criteria such as entrance examinations and previous grades.

Despite the Court's discomfort, however, the issue of "reverse" discrimination simply did not go away, and three years later, in *Bakke v. Regents of California* [49] the Court was faced with the same question, this time in relation to a student seek-

49. For a good discussion of the background of the Bakke case, see Robert Lindsey, "White/Caucasian and Rejected," *New York Times Magazine,* April 3, 1977, p. 42.

ing admission to medical school.  In 1972 the Medical School of the University of California at Davis, set aside sixteen of the hundred places available in its freshman class for minority students.  Black, Chinese or Asian-American applicants who were poor or had been disadvantaged could ask to be considered for these sixteen places.  Such applicants were evaluated by criteria different from those used for ordinary candidates: they were not disqualified if they had not achieved a 2.5 undergraduate grade average, and test scores considerably lower than the minimum for regular applicants were considered acceptable.  As a result of this two-tier admission system, Bakke was denied admission although his composite admissions score was higher than that of some of the disadvantaged students who had been admitted under the special program.  Bakke challenged the program successfully in the California courts as a denial of equal protection.  The University of California appealed the decision, although there was some evidence that the Regents would not be displeased by an adverse decision at the United States Supreme Court level, given the extreme unpopularity with the public at large of such reverse discrimination policies.*  The University has defended its affirmative action program on the ground that if minority candidates were forced to compete on the merits with white applicants there would be few if any minority admissions to the Medical School, thus effectively denying blacks entry to the profession.  If it is desirable to encourage blacks to become physicians then special consideration must be given.  Bakke, of course, argues that he cannot be denied his opportunity to enter the profession of his choice simply because his skin is the wrong color.  The Court is expected to hand down its decision before June, 1978.

The *Bakke* and *DeFunis* cases illustrate the potential for conflict between the concepts of liberty and equality.  On the one hand, while blacks may have a claim to preferential treatment as compensation for past discrimination, DeFunis and Bakke

* Subsequent to Bakke's suit, California amended its constitution to forbid preferential admissions quotas based on race.

also have a claim to enter the professions of their choice on the basis of qualifications rationally related to the requirements of the profession. Even more important, society has a claim to be served by those best qualified to enter the professions. To revert to the previous analogy of the shackled runner who is newly freed: it may well be that such a runner cannot compete successfully in the race unless his opponents are handicapped, or he himself is given preferential treatment. The problem for the community, however, is that if such preferential treatment is given, the meaning of the race is changed, for the winner no longer is necessarily the individual who can run the fastest. The normal academic criteria for admission to graduate schools are supposed to insure that the brightest and most intellectually competent will be admitted to the professions. It has been argued that graduate record examinations and grade point averages do not necessarily measure intellectual competence, but even if this is true, racial or ethnic status is even less relevant as a measure of academic ability. Further, to the extent that academic achievement is downgraded as a requirement for entry into the professions, student anomie at the lower educational levels may result since an irrelevant, uncontrollable factor has been introduced as the criterion for success.

Perhaps the problem in its most basic form is that a society such as ours demands inequality. A highly developed technological society cannot apportion jobs (and their concomitant rewards) at random and without concern for the skills of those who will fill those jobs. Colleges sometimes give preference even today in admissions to the children of alumni, or big contributors, or famous people. Such policies are irrational and objectionable for precisely the reasons racial preference is objectionable, although the motive for the latter is far more worthy than that of the former.

On the other hand, our society needs peace and stability at least as much as it needs technical skills. It is essential that the United States continue to integrate all groups into the mainstream of American society. Blacks and Hispanics doubtless will achieve upward mobility even without preferential policies, as did previous immigrants into the cities, but it took the Irish a century, and the Italians only a little less to rise from the *lumpen proletariat* to the middle class.     Blacks especially, are understandably impatient, 400 years after their arrival in the New World, and more than a century after the Emancipation Proclamation.     Does the United States need an intellectually elite medical profession, or a profession representative of the racial composition of the population at large?     Will our society work better if it encourages individual competition and excellence, or emphasizes justice to groups rather than persons?     Whatever the resolution of these questions, the answers lie, not in the technical mysteries of the law, but in the social philosophy of the judges.     Thus does the law become, as Holmes said, the magic mirror wherein we see our lives reflected.

*The Concept of State Action: The Progeny of the Civil Rights Cases*

While the Bill of Rights and the Fourteenth Amendment are now interpreted to forbid racial, religious, and sexual discrimination, the protections they offer are, technically speaking, against state action, that is, the actions of *government* officials. In theory, *private* individuals are quite free to discriminate against others on racial, religious, sexual or any other grounds, limited only by the scope of the criminal law.     Thus, Mr. Jones who is white may not steal the garden hose belonging to Smith his black neighbor, but he may decline to invite Smith to swim in his back yard pool.     He may do so, moreover, even if he invites all his white neighbors and specifies that Smith is excluded because he is black.     While Smith would have a right to sue under the Fourteenth Amendment if the pool in question were municipally owned and operated, he has no recourse against Jones as long as Jones is acting in a purely private capacity.     Suppose, however, Jones were the proprietor of a large swimming pool which he operated for profit.     Could he, on racial grounds, forbid Smith the use of his pool?     Does the Constitution protect Smith from this type of discrimination?

The answers to these questions lie in a long series of decisions stemming back to the *Civil Rights Cases* of 1883. In an attempt to protect the rights of newly freed blacks, Congress in 1875, enacted a statute called the Civil Rights Act, under the terms of which the proprietors of theaters, common carriers and inns were forbidden to deny services to blacks on the basis of their color. Since under the Constitution the federal government possesses only delegated powers, Congress can act only under the aegis of some constitutional provision. In the case of the Civil Rights Act, Congress assumed that the Fourteenth Amendment provided it with power to enact a law forbidding certain types of discrimination by private individuals. The Fourteenth Amendment, of course, speaks only in terms of *state* (i. e., governmental) action: *

> . . . nor shall any State deprive any person of life, liberty, or property, without due process of law; nor deny to any person within its jurisdiction the equal protection of the laws.

Nevertheless, supporters of the Civil Rights Act apparently reasoned that it was necessary to regulate *private* discriminatory conduct in order for the purposes of the Fourteenth Amendment to be carried out, and they pointed to Section 5 of the Amendment, "The Congress shall have power to enforce, by appropriate legislation, the provisions of this article," as proof of the intent of the framers that Congress have such legislative authority.

In the *Civil Rights Cases* (a group of suits brought by private proprietors affected by the Act), the United States Supreme Court disagreed with this interpretation of the Fourteenth Amendment. Section 5 empowered Congress only to remedy discriminatory acts of the states themselves, not acts of private individuals within those states. The state legislatures, courts,

---

* The Fourteenth Amendment is also addressed to the states, not the federal government, since the Bill of Rights incorporates an identical due process clause applicable to the federal government. See Chapter 1 *supra* for a discussion of the relationship between the two due process clauses.

and executive branches were forbidden under the Fourteenth Amendment to discriminate on the basis of race, and Congress could, by legislation, prevent or remedy such unlawful discrimination, but the acts of private individuals, however discriminatory, were beyond the Congressional purview.

> .   .   .   [Section 5] does not authorize Congress to create a code of municipal law for the regulation of private rights;  but to provide modes of redress against the operation of State laws, and the action of State officers, executive or judicial, when these are subversive of the fundamental rights specified in the amendment.
>
> .   .   .
>
> .   .   .   civil rights, such as are guaranteed by the Constitution against State aggression, cannot be impaired by the wrongful acts of individuals, unsupported by State authority in the shape of laws, customs, or judicial or executive proceedings.  The wrongful act of an individual, unsupported by any such authority, is simply a private wrong, or a crime of that individual .   .   .   An individual cannot deprive a man of his right to vote, to hold property, to buy and to sell, to sue in the courts, or to be a witness or a juror; he may, by force or fraud, interfere with the enjoyment of the right in a particular case;   .   .   .   but, unless protected in these wrongful acts by some shield of State law or State authority, he cannot destroy or injure the right;  he will only render himself amenable to satisfaction or punishment;   .   .   .   [The] abrogation and denial of rights   .   .   .   for which the States alone were or could be responsible, was the great seminal and fundamental wrong which was intended to be remedied.   .   .   .   [50]

50.  *Civil Rights Cases*, 109 U.S. 3 at
11, 17–18, 3 S.Ct. 18, 21, 26, 27 L.Ed.
835 (1883).

The logic of the Court was faultless. The wording of the Fourteenth Amendment did indeed refer to state action only. The problem, however, then as now, was to determine what precisely constituted state action, and what constituted private action. Was the dividing line between the two as crystal clear as the Court seemed to assume? In the instant case, for example, if a railroad had been granted a monopoly of rail facilities by the state, and then proceeded to deny service to blacks because of their color, even though the railroad was a private corporation, could such discrimination have occurred without the support by state authority "in the shape of laws, customs, or judicial or executive proceedings."? At the very least, the state by continuing to protect the railroad in its monopoly, was tolerating the discriminatory actions complained of; at worst it was denying to black citizens the equal protection of the law by failing to forbid such discrimination through appropriate legislation. Justice Bradley, in writing for the majority, recognized the problem but assumed apparently that the states could or would cope adequately with the problem under their own laws or constitutions.

> . . . Innkeepers and public carriers, by the laws of all the States, so far as we are aware, are bound, to the extent of their facilities, to furnish proper accommodations to all unobjectionable persons who in good faith apply for them. If the laws themselves make any unjust discrimination, amenable to the prohibitions of the Fourteenth Amendment, Congress has full power to afford a remedy under that amendment and in accordance with it.[51]

Justice Harlan objected vigorously to what he saw as the glibness and superficiality of the majority opinion. Since the purpose of the Amendment was to remove the disabilities imposed on former slaves by virtue of their condition, realistically it was necessary for Congress, in order to accomplish the Amendment's

51. Ibid., at 25.

purposes, to be able to combat racial discrimination at all levels, the more so when the types of conduct prohibited by the statute in question were quasi-public in nature. To end discrimination against blacks, Harlan said

> . . . Congress . . . under its express power to enforce [the Fourteenth] Amendment, by appropriate legislation, may enact laws . . . of a direct and primary character, operating upon States, their officers and agents, and also, upon, at least, such individuals and corporations as exercise public functions and wield power and authority under the State.[52]

Harlan argued further that the activities in question—running railroads, inns and theatres—since all were dependent to one degree or another on privileges granted by the state, were in fact quasi-public rather than private activities.

> [A]s to public conveyances . . .. railroads . . . are none the less public highways because controlled and owned by private corporations; . . . that no matter who is the agent, and what is the agency, the function performed is *that of the state* . . .
>
> As to inns. . . .
>
> These authorities are sufficient to show that a keeper of an inn is in the exercise of a quasi public employment. The law gives him special privileges and he is charged with certain duties and responsibilities to the public. The public nature of his employment forbids him from discriminating against any person asking admission as a guest on account of the race and color of that person.
>
> As to places of public amusement. [W]ithin the meaning of the act of 1875, [they] are such as are established and maintained under direct license of the

---

52. Ibid., at 36.

law. . . . A license from the public to establish a
place of public amusement, imports, in law, equality of
right, at such places, among all the members of that
public. . . .[53]

Harlan agreed with the majority that only discriminatory
*state* action was prohibited by the Fourteenth Amendment.
Where he disagreed was in what constituted state action. He
did not deny that discrimination could occur in a purely private
context, but the mere fact that a private individual was the
agent of discrimination did not mean that the discrimination
was private in nature.

> . . . I agree that if one citizen chooses not to hold
> social intercourse with another, he is not and cannot be
> made amenable to the law for his conduct in that regard;
> for even upon grounds of race no legal right of a
> citizen is violated by the refusal of others to maintain
> merely social relations with him . . . . . . .
> The rights which Congress, by the act of 1875, endeav-
> ored to secure and protect are legal, not social, rights.
> The right, for instance, of a colored citizen to use the
> accommodations of a public highway . . . is no
> more a social right than his right, under the law, to use
> the public streets of a city, or a town, or a turnpike
> road, or a public market, or a post office, or his right
> to sit in a public building with others, of whatever race,
> for the purpose of hearing the political questions of the
> day discussed. . . .[54]

Harlan's dissent implied that without a broad definition of
"state" action it would be impossible to remove from blacks the
disabilities imposed on them by racial discrimination. He was,
of course, correct in his assessment of the situation. For more
than half a century the courts clung stubbornly to a narrow and
restrictive view of state action. It was only after World War II
that the United States Supreme Court began to reexamine the

---

53.  Ibid., at 37–38, 40–41.          54.  Ibid., at 59–60.

concept of state action.   In *Shelley v. Kraemer*,* [55] the Court considered the cases of two black petitioners from Missouri and Michigan who had purchased houses from white owners.   The properties in question were encumbered by restrictive covenants which provided that for a specified time (in one case fifty years from 1911) the property could be sold only to Caucasians. When the property was sold by white owners to the black petitioners, several of the owners of the adjoining properties who were parties to the restrictive covenant sued to prevent the blacks from taking possession and to divest them of title.   The state courts upheld the legality of the restrictive covenant and granted the white property owners the relief sought.   The United States Supreme Court reversed the state court's decision, holding that the Equal Protection Clause prohibits judicial enforcement of a racially discriminatory restrictive covenant. Basing its decision on much of the reasoning and dicta of the *Civil Rights Cases,* the Court upheld the legality of restrictive covenants, arguing that the covenants themselves were purely private conduct not covered by the restrictions of the Fourteenth Amendment.

> Since the decision of this Court in the *Civil Rights Cases,* the principle has become firmly imbedded in our constitutional law that the action inhibited by the first section of the Fourteenth Amendment is only such action as may fairly be said to be that of the State.   That Amendment erects no shield against merely private conduct, however discriminatory or wrongful.[56]

The enforcement of such covenants, however, was another matter entirely.   To use the courts to enforce racial discrimination was state action within the meaning of the Fourteenth Amendment and hence constitutionally impermissible.   Again quoting the *Civil Rights Cases,* the Court cited the opinion of

* With *McGhee v. Sipes, et al.*          56.   Ibid., at 13.

55.   334 U.S. 1, 68 S.Ct. 836, 92 L.Ed.
      1161 (1948).

the majority that state action included "State authority in the shape of laws, customs, or judicial or executive proceedings." [57] While nothing in the Constitution forbade white property owners from binding themselves with racially discriminatory covenants, those covenants could have no more status than that of gentlemen's agreements because the power of the state could not be used to enforce such covenants.    Thus, the United States Supreme Court recognized that in the real world, state action and private action were not two entirely different easily distinguishable phenomena, but were in many cases, not only intertwined, but interdependent.    Private discrimination that was not forbidden was, at the very least, tolerated by the state, and in many cases depended on the cooperation of the state for its implementation, as in *Shelley*, for example, where without the cooperation of the courts, the effectiveness of restrictive property covenants obviously was greatly reduced.    The question that remained unresolved after *Shelley*, thus, was to what extent must state action be mixed with private action in order for the latter to fall under the prohibitions of the Fourteenth Amendment.

This issue was addressed in *Burton v. Wilmington Parking Authority*.[58]    The Wilmington Parking Authority was a public corporation created by the state of Delaware for the purpose of providing parking facilities in the city of Wilmington.    In order to increase its revenues the Authority had entered into leases with several business establishments, renting them space adjacent to the parking facilities.    Among these tenants was the Eagle Coffee Shop, a restaurant, which refused to serve blacks. Was the refusal of the Eagle Coffee Shop to serve black patrons private action not covered by the Fourteenth Amendment, or was it state action forbidden by the Amendment?    The Authority argued that it was not a public agency within the meaning of the Fourteenth Amendment.    Only 15 percent of the total cost of the facility had come from public funds.    More than two-thirds of its income was derived from commercial leasing rather

---

57.   Ibid., at 14.

58.   365 U.S. 715, 81 S.Ct. 856, 6 L. Ed.2d 45 (1961).

than from parking fees, and the only connection that the restaurant had with the Authority was the payment of rent which helped the Authority defray the costs of an otherwise unprofitable enterprise.  In short, the fact that the restaurant (a private facility) happened to have as landlord the Authority (a public corporation created by Delaware) did not make it a state agency subject to the restrictions of the Fourteenth Amendment.

A majority of the United States Supreme Court refused to accept these arguments.  Despite mixed funding the prestige and authority of the state were directly involved in the parking authority and therefore in the operation of the restaurant.  For a restaurant on public premises to discriminate was state action within the meaning of the Fourteenth Amendment, because the state was inextricably involved in the operation.

> .   .   .  By its inaction, the Authority, and through it the State, has not only made itself a party to the refusal of service, but has elected to place its power, property and prestige behind the admitted discrimination.  The State has so far insinuated itself into a position of interdependence with Eagle that it must be recognized as a joint participant in the challenged activity, which, on that account, cannot be considered to have been so "purely private" as to fall without the scope of the Fourteenth Amendment.[59]

The facts in *Burton* were relatively unambiguous since the Parking Authority was admittedly an agency of the state of Delaware, albeit not in the same precise fashion as a normal executive department.  It was thus relatively easy for the Court to conclude that actions of a lessee of the Authority were state action rather than private action.  But what if the discriminatory action were taken by a private individual whose connection with the state was far more tenuous?  In 1831, Stephen Girard left money to establish and operate a school in Philadelphia for white male orphans who were fatherless.  The school was called

59.  Ibid., at 725.

Girard College and was administered by a state agency, the Board of Directors of City Trusts. In 1957, suit was brought alleging that the participation of the state in the administration of the school was forbidden by the Equal Protection Clause of the Fourteenth Amendment inasmuch as the school served only white males. The United States Supreme Court, per curiam, agreed that state action was involved even though the participation of the Board was limited to acting as a fiduciary agent for a private individual.[60] The state court then ordered that private individuals be substituted for the public trustees, and the United States Supreme Court denied certiorari to review this action, leaving unresolved the question of whether the College could be limited to serving white males, even if its auspices were entirely private.[61] *

The latter issue was addressed nine years later in *Evans v. Newton*.[62] One Senator Bacon had left land in 1911 to the city of Macon, Georgia, for the establishment of a park to be used by white people only. When pressure generated by the civil rights movement of the 1960's led the city of Macon to open the park to blacks as well, Bacon's heirs and some others sued to remove the city as trustee. Black citizens objected to the city's removal, and the city thereupon resigned as trustee. The Georgia courts accepted the city's resignation and appointed private trustees to carry out the original terms of the will. The question presented to the United States Supreme Court was whether the operation of a segregated public park in these circumstances was permissible under the Fourteenth Amendment.

In an opinion written by Justice Douglas, the Court held that the park could not be operated as a segregated facility. Al-

60.   *Com. of Pennsylvania v. Board of Directors, City Trusts*, 353 U.S. 230, 77 S.Ct. 806, 1 L.Ed.2d 792 (1957).

61.   357 U.S. 570, 78 S.Ct. 1383, 2 L. Ed.2d 1546 (1958).

* In 1968 the United States Supreme Court ordered the integration of the school. In 1973 the admissions policy was changed again to admit motherless boys.

62.   382 U.S. 296, 86 S.Ct. 486, 15 L. Ed.2d 373 (1966).

though no public officials were involved directly in the operation of the park, nevertheless, the park was by its nature so public in character that those who ran it, even though private individuals, became agents of the state by virtue of the fact that they were performing functions that were governmental in nature. The city maintained and policed the park, and the mere replacement of public trustees by private trustees, did not make the board any less municipal in function. While a school could be operated for the use of one race only, assuming that the state was in no way implicated in its operation, a park was of a different nature, and could not be disassociated from the municipality of which it was a part.

Three justices dissented. Black objected to the United States Supreme Court's reaching the merits of the case. He argued that if the trustees could not operate the park as Bacon intended, the bequest should have been permitted by the state courts to revert to Bacon's heirs. More significantly, Harlan and Stewart dissented on the ground that the decision as to the "public" character of the park rested entirely on the assumption that the city patrolled, maintained and was otherwise involved in the administration of the park. No evidence of this, however, appeared in the record. Moreover, if parks were to be considered so public by their nature that under no circumstances could they be operated as segregated facilities, by what reasoning could segregated schools be permitted? How could the majority argue that privately operated segregated schools were permissible under the Fourteenth Amendment, but privately operated segregated parks were not?

Harlan complained that the majority decision in *Evans* had opened a Pandora's box which would convert all private action into state action. Did *Evans v. Newton* mean that no private bequest which excluded beneficiaries on racial (or presumably religious or ethnic) grounds would be permissible inasmuch as the authority of state was involved if only in the probate of the will? Were homes for the aged, hospitals or universities (which frequently received bequests for the benefit of specific ethnic or

religious groups) less public in character than parks?   If so,
why?  *Evans v. Newton,* like the *DeFunis* and *Bakke* cases, suggests the potential for conflict between constitutional principles
that may result when any one principle is pushed to its outer-
most limits: the conflict between assuring equal treatment to all
status groups—social, ethnic, sexual, religious—and the liberty
of private individuals to choose their associates, the mode of education of their children, the professions they will enter, the
way they leave their money.

In 1964, some of the problems raised by the *Civil Rights Cases*
and the *Burton v. Wilmington Parking Authority* case, were resolved by Congress which, following the lead of the courts, made
certain types of private discrimination *statutorily* illegal.   The
Civil Rights Act of that year (also called the Public Accommodations Act) guaranteed to all persons equal access, without discrimination or segregation, to all types of facilities or businesses which offered service to the public: hotels, motels,
restaurants, catering establishments, sporting arenas, gasoline
stations, bars and barber shops.   Boarding houses with fewer
than five rooms for rent and private clubs were excluded.
While the constitutional authority for the Act was both the power of Congress to regulate interstate commerce, and the enforcement powers specified in Section 5 of the Fourteenth Amendment, in *Heart of Atlanta Motel v. United States,*[63] a suit which
challenged the constitutionality of the Act, the Court declared
the commerce power alone to be sufficient, and did not consider
the Fourteenth Amendment grounds at all.

The Civil Rights Act of 1964 relieved the Courts of the burden
of determining the dividing line between state and private action
in many types of cases.   *Lombard v. Louisiana,*[64] a 1963 case,
for example, involved blacks who, when denied service at a lunch
counter, refused to leave the premises.   No city ordinance required that the lunch counter be segregated, but the owners, unwilling to serve blacks, called the city police to evict the protes-

**63.**  379 U.S. 241, 85 S.Ct. 348, 13 L.     **64.**  373 U.S. 267, 83 S.Ct. 1122, 10 L.
Ed.2d 258 (1964).                              Ed.2d 338 (1963).

ters. On appeal, the United States Supreme Court held that the use of the police constituted state action even though there was no discriminatory municipal legislation involved, since state action could be taken through the executive branch (the police) as authoritatively as through the legislature. But what if the police had been called to eject blacks from a private home where they were not wanted? Would that have constituted impermissible state action? No, said Justice Douglas in a separate concurring opinion, because in a home one had an expectation of and right to privacy which the Bill of Rights protects, but the proprietor of a restaurant had no such inherent right. By opening the doors of his business to the public, he had moved into the public domain and relinquished his right to privacy.

It was necessary for *Lombard* to be decided on constitutional grounds—as a denial of equal protection under the Fourteenth Amendment—because at the time there was no *statutory* prohibition against the proprietor's actions. After the passage of the Civil Rights Act of 1964 and the United States Supreme Court's declaration of its validity, there was no longer a constitutional issue in such cases, merely a question of whether the Act had been violated, a much easier issue to adjudicate.

The Civil Rights Act of 1964 did not, however, address itself to discrimination in housing. One of the most troublesome problems for blacks has been the refusal of white property owners to rent or sell housing to them. Some states had attempted to eliminate such discriminatory practices by passing open occupancy laws which made such refusal to rent or sell illegal. In California, two such laws were passed, the Unruh Civil Rights Act of 1959 and the Rumford Act of 1963. These laws proved to be very unpopular, and in 1964 by a huge margin, California voters, in a referendum, approved Proposition 14, an amendment to the state constitution, which in effect, repealed the laws and provided that property owners had "absolute discretion" to rent or sell property to persons of their choice. California, thus, adopted as part of its constitution what some saw as a virtual license for private individuals to discriminate. Was Proposition

14 a statement of neutrality by the state, or was it encouragement for discrimination? Was any resulting discrimination state action or private action? Did the fact that this "license" was the result of a referendum by the electorate at large make any difference?

In 1967, suit was brought by a Mr. and Mrs. Mulkey who charged that they had been denied the rental of an apartment solely because they were black. The landlord in question, Reitman, defended himself by citing Proposition 14 which had since become Article I, Section 26 of the Constitution of the State of California. The Mulkeys thereupon alleged a denial of equal protection of the law by the state. The California Supreme Court upheld the Mulkeys' claim, and on appeal to the United States Supreme Court the judgment was affirmed.[65]

The majority of the Court, in an opinion written by Justice White, virtually ignored the unique circumstances under which the California constitution was amended, apparently assuming that a popular referendum had no greater legitimacy than any other method of changing California's constitution. White held, moreover, that given the fact that Proposition 14 was placed on the ballot specifically because of opposition to earlier fair housing laws, its undeniable intent was to permit discrimination, and by thus creating a climate favorable to discrimination, California was denying racial minorities equal protection of the laws.

> The California court could very reasonably conclude that § 26 would and did have wider impact than a mere repeal of existing statutes. . . . Private discriminations in housing were now not only free from Rumford and Unruh but they also enjoyed a far different status than was true before the passage of those statutes. The right to discriminate, including the right to discriminate on racial grounds, was now embodied in the State's basic charter, immune from legislative, ex-

65. *Reitman v. Mulkey*, 387 U.S. 369, 87 S.Ct. 1627, 18 L.Ed.2d 830 (1967).

ecutive, or judicial regulation at any level of the State government.   .   .   .[66]

Douglas went further and argued that by permitting private real estate brokers to discriminate, the state was, in effect, turning over the power to create zoning regulations for many neighborhoods to private individuals.

Real estate brokers   .   .   .   are largely dedicated to maintenance of segregated communities.   .   .   .

Proposition 14 is a form of sophisticated discrimination whereby the people of California harness the energies of private groups to do indirectly what they cannot under our decisions allow their government to do.[67]

Harlan, Black, Clark, and Stewart dissented, contending that Section 26 was no more than a statement of neutrality by the state in relation to private action. The constitutional section in question was simply permissive and despite the context in which it had been adopted, i. e., the unpopularity of the Unruh and Rumford Acts, it was unfair to conclude that the State was encouraging discrimination. Reitman's action, moreover, was private action in which the State had taken no part, and therefore, precedents such as *Lombard v. Louisiana, Evans v. Newton,* and *Burton v. Wilmington Parking Authority* were inapplicable, inasmuch as in these cases some agent of the state had been directly involved. In *Lombard* the sheriff had been called; in *Evans* the city was the official supervisor of the park; and, in *Burton,* a state agency was the landlord of the offending restaurant. In *Reitman,* however, no state official or agency had played any part, and therefore, no state action in the meaning of the Fourteenth Amendment, had occurred.*

66. Ibid., at 376–377.

67. Ibid., at 381, 383.

* What would become of the dissenters' rationale if Mulkey had illegally moved into the apartment and Reitman called upon the police to evict him?

The dissenters then went on to point to the basic conflict suggested by the *Evans* and *Girard College* cases: the conflict between liberty of private action and equal protection.

> A moment of thought will reveal the far-reaching possibilities of the Court's new doctrine, which I am sure the Court does not intend. Every act of private discrimination is either forbidden by state law or permitted by it. There can be little doubt that such permissiveness—whether by express constitutional or statutory provision, or implicit in the common law—to some extent "encourages" those who wish to discriminate to do so. Under this theory "state action" in the form of laws that do nothing more than passively permit private discrimination could be said to tinge *all* private discrimination with the taint of unconstitutional state encouragement.[68] *

*Reitman* considerably enlarged the area of private conduct considered tinged by state action, but left open the question of how far the reach of the state could extend in regulating private discriminatory conduct. Five years later, in *Moose Lodge v. Irvis*,[69] the Court gave a partial answer to the question. Irvis, a black, was a guest of a member of the Moose Lodge, a private club. He was denied service by the club because he was black,

---

68.  Ibid., at 394–395.

* As it did subsequent to the sit-in cases (*Lombard v. Louisiana* et al.) Congress alleviated the problems of the courts in determining the extent of state involvement in private discriminatory action, by making such action *statutorily* illegal. The Fair Housing Act of 1968 made it unlawful to discriminate on the basis of race or color in the sale or rental of private housing, except for transactions involving single family homes sold or rented by the owner and not involving the services of a real estate broker; or the sale or rental of non-commercial housing owned, operated or supervised by religious organizations or *bona fide* private clubs for the benefit of their members. The federal statute specifically invalidated any state law or policy which permitted discriminatory housing practices.

69.  407 U.S. 163, 92 S.Ct. 1965, 32 L.Ed.2d 627 (1972).

and he sued on the ground that since the club had been granted a liquor license by the state of Pennsylvania, its refusal to serve him was state action within the meaning of the Fourteenth Amendment and constituted a denial of equal protection of the laws. The majority of the Court held that the Moose Lodge was a private club in a private building and its activities did not fall under the prohibitions of the Fourteenth Amendment, the granting of the liquor license notwithstanding.

> The Court has never held  .  .  . that discrimination by an otherwise private entity would be violative of the Equal Protection Clause if the private entity received any sort of benefit or service at all from the State, or if it is subject to state regulation in any degree whatever. Since state-furnished services include such necessities of life as electricity, water, and police and fire protection, such a holding would utterly emasculate the distinction between private as distinguished from state conduct set forth in the *Civil Rights Cases*.
> .  .  .[70]

The dissenters, Justices Douglas, Marshall, and Brennan conceded that the Lodge was not open to the public at large, nor did it perform a function or service that would otherwise be performed by the state. Nor, did they contend that the mere granting of the liquor license by itself converted the otherwise private social club into an agency of the state. They were troubled by the fact that in Pennsylvania liquor licenses were not freely available, and that in Harrisburg where the Moose Lodge was located, the quota for club licenses had been full for many years. Club licenses, moreover, permitted the sale of liquor during certain times of the week when public facilities such as bars and restaurants could not serve patrons. Thus, if a black wished to obtain liquor during these prohibited periods, his only recourse was to a private club, and the possibility of establishing a private club was precluded by the fact that no more liquor li-

70.   Ibid., at 173.

censes were available. The liquor license, furthermore, was not intended simply to produce revenue. It was actually a regulatory device used to control

> . . . a wide variety of moral conduct such as the presence and activities of homosexuals, performance of a topless dancer, lewd dancing, swearing, being noisy or disorderly. . . .[71]

and as such for the dissenters, it was the factor that converted private to state action.

As the justices of the United States Supreme Court would no doubt agree, the line between state action and private action is far from obvious. In every case, from *Shelley v. Kraemer* through *Girard College* to *Evans v. Newton* and *Reitman v. Mulkey,* the state played some role in private conduct that discriminated against blacks. Even in *Moose Lodge* the dissenters had considerable logic on their side. Yet as Justice Harlan pointed out in *Reitman,* if every action that is permitted by the state, or in which the state is involved through the provision of basic services or routine regulation becomes, *ipso facto*, state action, then there is no such thing as private action. If private action is abolished, then a good measure of personal liberty will have been destroyed, for blacks no less than for whites, along with much of society's leavening process, considerable joy of living, and the *raison d'etre* of the founding of the American republic. To deny the role of the state in making possible much private discriminatory conduct would be antithetical to democratic ideals, but to preclude the possibility of private action is to make the remedy as socially destructive as the disease. In *Moose Lodge,* the Court seemed to be responding to the need to draw a line, even if arbitrarily, between conduct sanctioned by the state, and conduct that is purely private and toward which the state must remain neutral.

---

71.   Ibid., at 188.

*Sexual Discrimination*

In many respects, women have always been treated differently under the law from men, but it is only within the last decade that the unreasonableness of sexual discrimination has become an issue of major concern before the United States Supreme Court. There were feminists and fighters for women's rights even in colonial times, and a substantial women's rights movement developed in the 1840's which addressed itself to the suffrage question as well as women's rights in marriage, in relation to their children, and their ability to hold property. In 1920, the Constitution was amended to forbid voting restrictions based on sex and, perhaps as a result of its success in achieving the vote, the women's rights movement became all but dormant for almost half a century. Spurred by the civil rights ferment of the 1960's, however, the issue of women's rights reemerged, this time in the courts as well as in the legislatures.

The problem for the courts in determining whether there has, in fact, been a denial of equal protection of the laws to women lies in the view that the judges (and society) hold of women's proper place in society. Since the Fourteenth Amendment does not forbid unequal treatment, but only irrational unequal treatment, the question of what is rational relates directly to the accepted social view of woman's role. If the proper place of woman is in the home, then it is appropriate for the courts to see that she is protected and cared for while performing her duties in the home; at the same time, if her proper place is in the home, it is quite reasonable for statutes to discourage or even prohibit her from engaging in activities properly reserved for males who must undertake the burden of her support. In 1873, a woman's role was described by three justices of the United States Supreme Court:

> . . . The constitution of the family organization, which is founded in the divine ordinance, as well as in the nature of things, indicates the domestic sphere as

that which properly belongs to the domain and functions of womanhood.  .   .   . [72]

In an era which antedated the development of effective contraceptives and labor saving household appliances, woman's place,
for the vast majority of women *had* to be the home.  Someone
had to care for the children, clean, cook and do all the other domestic chores that are necessary for the maintenance of life and
a decent standard of comfort.  For many a woman, child bearing years were long and ended frequently only with menopause,
or the death of her mate.  Not only was her place in the home,
but the woman who was forced out of her home in order to enter the labor market was considered most unfortunate, as indeed
in most cases she was.  Far from being liberated, she was en-
slaved by a second job laid on top of her primary full time domestic duties.  The results often were disastrous for the woman, for her family, for society at large.  Small wonder then that
the initial efforts of many reformers were directed toward *unequal* treatment for women—towards laws that would single
women out for special protection designed to meet their special
needs.

In 1903, the Oregon state legislature passed a law limiting the
hours of work for women in factories and laundries to ten per
day.  The law was challenged both as a violation of women's
rights to make contracts (to work more than ten hours a day)
and as a denial of equal protection of the laws (to men) in that
women were singled out for special favor.  The National Consumer's League (a spiritual ancestor of Ralph Nader's public interest groups), appeared as *amicus curiae* before the United
States Supreme Court in defense of the statute.  Louis Brandeis,
attorney for the League, filed a brief which became famous by
defending the statute, not in terms of the legal precedents bearing on contractual relationships, but in terms of the law's social

---

72. *Bradwell v. Illinois*, 83 U.S. (16
Wall.) 130, at 141, 21 L.Ed. 442
(1873) as quoted in Norman Dorsen
and Susan Deller Ross, "The Necessity of a Constitutional Amendment," 6 *Harvard Civil Rights—
Civil Liberties Law Review* 216
(1971).

utility and appropriateness.  Since women were as a group phys- ically weaker than men, and since the health of women of child bearing age was important for both present and future genera- tions, Brandeis argued that the state had a legitimate interest in singling out women for special protection.  While it might not be necessary to regulate the working conditions of male work- ers, it was reasonable for the state to concern itself with the number of hours mothers and potential mothers worked.  The Court, in *Muller v. Oregon,* accepted his argument and upheld the validity of the Oregon statute, noting that "woman's physical structure, and the functions she performs in consequence there- of, justifies special legislation restricting or qualifying the con- ditions under which she should be permitted to toil." [73]

*Muller* established the pattern for much legislation for women in the United States.  On the whole, this legislation was pater- nalistic and designed to protect a group which the courts saw as not necessarily inferior, but less able to cope with society and, therefore, worthy of special protection.  The problem was, of course, that in the very act of helping women, the courts were defining and imposing a role on women that an increasing num- ber of women did not wish to accept.  Even during the nine- teenth century some relatively affluent and well-educated wom- en wished to function outside their homes on equal terms with men, and in the twentieth century as contraceptives became available along with mechanical equipment such as the washing machine and the vacuum cleaner, many women had years free from child-bearing and time not needed for domestic chores. What seemed reasonable protection in 1908 became restrictive and stigmatizing fifty years later.

An example of the stigmatizing effect of discriminatory treat- ment based on paternalism was the fact that many states im- posed little or no obligation on women to serve on grand or petit juries.  While jury service is not an activity most citizens em- bark upon with enthusiasm and joy, nevertheless, to be barred

73.  208 U.S. 412 at 420, 28 S.Ct. 324,
326, 52 L.Ed. 551 (1908).

or discouraged from jury service can readily be construed as a mark of inferiority. In *Hoyt v. Florida*,[74] the fairness of different treatment for men and women in regard to jury service was argued before the United States Supreme Court. A Mrs. Hoyt was charged with the murder of her husband. He had been unfaithful to her, and when he rejected her efforts at reconciliation, she killed him with a baseball bat. She was convicted of the crime by an all male jury and appealed her conviction on the ground that Florida's method of choosing jurors discouraged women from serving on juries, thus denying her equal protection of the laws.*

Florida law provided that while women were not to be called for jury service save at their own request, men were called routinely without having to volunteer. Men were heavily overrepresented in the venires from which jurors were drawn. The question presented to the Court was whether a method of jury selection that was different for men and women was permissible under the Fourteenth Amendment. The Court held that it was, since Florida's regulation was based on the assumption that women had special responsibilities which might not be consistent with jury service. Since the regulation appeared to have been made in good faith to accommodate women rather than to discriminate against them, the Court held that the Florida law was not unconstitutional.

The reasoning of the Court, however, was somewhat ingenuous. While it is true that mothers of young children, for example, might find it extremely difficult to serve on juries, many men had similar problems. Physicians, small business men, and hourly laborers, to mention but a few, frequently found jury service extremely onerous. Yet Florida did not forbear to call

74. 368 U.S. 57, 82 S.Ct. 159, 7 L. Ed.2d 118 (1961).

* Though Hoyt's claim was that she was denied equal protection of the laws as a *defendant* rather than as a woman, the arguments presented related to the question of whether Florida had done an injustice to all women because they were not given equal civic responsibility, as well as to Hoyt herself because she was denied a possibility of a jury representative of the community.

such men or grant them automatic exemption. They were called and when necessary given exemption by the presiding judge on a case by case basis. There was no evidence, moreover, that more women than men found jury service difficult, since statistically most women enjoyed approximately thirty-five years of adult life free from the burdens of caring for young children. On what basis then, was it permissible for the state legislature to establish different policies and procedures for the recruiting of male, as opposed to female, jurors? In 1975, the Court agreed to reconsider this issue. In *Taylor v. Louisiana*,[75] one Billy J. Taylor, a male, was convicted of kidnapping and sentenced to death by a jury chosen from a venire that was disproportionately male because of a Louisiana statute which excluded women from jury service unless they had previously filed a statement with the local court clerk indicating their willingness to be called for jury duty. Taylor claimed he was denied his Sixth Amendment right to a "fair trial by a jury of a representative segment of the community." *

In considering Taylor's claim, the Court conceded immediately that Taylor was entitled to a jury drawn from a fair cross-section of the community. Under the circumstances then, the essential question was whether a jury selection process that tended to skew the pool of potential jurors so that it included more males than females, was permissible under the Fourteenth Amendment. Louisiana cited *Hoyt v. Florida* in defense of its selection process but the Court disagreed, holding that whatever the position of women was earlier in history or at the time of the adoption of the Sixth and Fourteenth Amendments, their po-

---

75. 419 U.S. 522, 95 S.Ct. 692, 42 L. Ed.2d 690 (1975).

* Again, although Taylor's claim was based on Sixth Amendment grounds, rather than Fourteenth Amendment — equal protection grounds, the Court had to consider the rationality of treating women differently from men, and both the arguments and the decision bore directly on the validity of a sexual classification in regard to jury selection.

sition had changed sufficiently that hardship cases among women could be handled on an *ad hoc* basis as they were for men.

> . . . It is untenable to suggest these days that it would be a special hardship for each and every woman to perform jury service or that society cannot spare *any* women from their present duties. . . . [76]

In *Taylor,* thus, the Court recognized and confronted the central problem of sex discrimination cases: an assessment of the proper role of women in society. The Court decision implied strongly, that sex, like race, was a suspect classification and that the burden of proof rested on the state to justify different treatment for men and women.

The *Taylor* decision, and its reassessment of women's role in society did not come as a surprise to observers of the Court. In the five years preceding *Taylor,* the Court had handed down several decisions favorable to women's rights. In *Reed v. Reed,*[77] the adoptive mother of a minor child had applied for appointment as administrator of her son's estate. The child's adoptive father, who had been separated from the mother for some time prior to the child's death, then filed a competing petition which was granted because Idaho law automatically granted preference for men over women when persons of the same entitlement applied for appointment as administrator of an estate. The United States Supreme Court held that such discrimination was irrational and therefore prohibited by the Equal Protection Clause of the Fourteenth Amendment. The Court rejected Idaho's argument that the measure was a reasonable one designed to reduce the work of the probate courts by eliminating one source of controversy. Chief Justice Burger, for a unanimous court went on to say that

> . . . Having examined the record and considered the briefs and oral arguments of the parties, we have concluded that the arbitrary preference established in

---

76. Ibid., at 534–535.

77. 404 U.S. 71, 92 S.Ct. 251, 30 L. Ed.2d 225 (1971).

favor of males by Section 15–314 of the Idaho Code
cannot stand in the face of the Fourteenth Amendment's command that no State deny the equal protection of the laws to any person within its jurisdiction.
. . . To give a mandatory preference to members of either sex over members of the other, merely to
accomplish the elimination of hearings on the merits, is
to make the very kind of arbitrary legislative choice
forbidden by the . . . Amendment; . . .[78]

Two years later in *Frontiero v. Richardson*[79] the Court considered the case of a female member of the armed forces who
wished to claim her spouse as a dependent for purposes of obtaining increased quarters allowances and medical and dental
benefits. While male servicemen could claim their spouses as
dependents without regard to whether their wives were, in fact,
dependent upon them for support, female service personnel were
precluded from claiming such dependency unless their husbands
actually did receive more than one half their support from them.
Frontiero contended that since classifications based on sex, like
those based on race, were inherently suspect, the armed forces
could not treat her differently from a male serviceman. The
Court agreed, pointing out that

. . . throughout much of the nineteenth century
the position of women in our society was, in many respects, comparable to that of blacks under the pre-Civil
War slave codes. Neither slaves nor women could hold
office, serve on juries, or bring suit in their own names,
and married women traditionally were denied the legal
capacity to hold or convey property or to serve as legal
guardians of their own children. And although blacks
were guaranteed the right to vote in 1870, women were

78. Ibid., at 74, 76.  79. 411 U.S. 677, 93 S.Ct. 1764, 36 L.Ed.2d 583 (1973).

denied even that right  .  .  .  until adoption of the
Nineteenth Amendment half a century later.[80]

The Court rejected the government's argument that it was
easier simply to presume that men's wives would be dependent
upon them and women's husbands would not.  No evidence had
been introduced by the army to support the contention that it
was actually cheaper to grant increased benefits to all men rather
than to require the same proof of dependency for male servicemen as for female service persons.  Both *Reed* and *Frontiero*
were 8–1 decisions with only Justice Rehnquist dissenting.  In
*Frontiero*, however, Justices Powell and Blackmun, as well as
Chief Justice Burger concurred in the judgment but rejected
the notion that sex is a suspect classification.  They argued that
*Frontiero* should have been decided on the basis of *Reed,* with
the judgment as to the necessity for equal treatment of men and
women left to the legislative forum.

Closely related to the issues in *Frontiero* was the question
presented by *Weinberger v. Wiesenfeld*.[81]  The Social Security
Act provided for the payment of benefits to the wife, but not the
husband, of a deceased wage earner with minor children.  Wiesenfeld contended that in effect, this reduced the value of the
contributions made by female wage earners since the benefits to
her dependents were less than the benefits available from the
contributions of male wage earners.  The United States Supreme
Court agreed.  While it was true that men were more likely
than women to be the primary supporters of their families, the
distinction "that male workers' earnings are vital to the support
of their families, while the earnings of female wage earners do
not significantly contribute to their families' support," [82] was a
generalization which was constitutionally impermissible.  A father, no less than a mother had a right to care for, raise, and
manage his children, which interest could not be set aside, for

---

80.  Ibid., at 685.

81.  420 U.S. 636, 95 S.Ct. 1225, 43
     L.Ed.2d 514 (1975).

82.  Ibid., at 643.

administrative convenience based on an "archaic and overbroad generalization."

In only one significant case in the 1970–1975 period did the Court rule against the interests of women. *Geduldig v. Aiello* [83] challenged the exclusion of pregnancy as a comprehensible disability from California's disability insurance scheme. The insurance system was designed to be self-supporting at a one percent annual level of contribution. Certain disabilities, such as alcoholism and drug addiction as well as pregnancy, were excluded for financial reasons. Carolyn Aiello charged that it was a denial of equal protection of the laws to exclude pregnancy, a disability exclusive to women, when all types of exclusively male disabilities were covered. The United States Supreme Court disagreed. It was not incumbent upon the state to either raise contributions or lower benefits simply in order to cover a particular type of disability which was very expensive, even though that disability happened to be confined to women. There was no evidence in the Court's opinion that the state acted for reasons other than fiscal necessity.

While the state may have been motivated by purely fiscal concerns, critics of the decision nevertheless questioned why *pregnancy* should have been eliminated to balance the budget? Why not cancer, or heart disease or gall bladder operations? Should it not have been constitutionally impermissible to select a disability which affected women exclusively? While the Court did not explain its decision, several reasons for their willingness to accept the California scheme suggests themselves. The most obvious of these is that pregnancy is not usually considered a disease, and disability schemes are designed to deal with time lost due to illness. (Some support for this point of view can be deduced from the fact that the California scheme did pay benefits for disability due to abnormal pregnancy; only normal pregnancies were excluded from benefits.) The incidence of pregnancy, moreover, is quite high in an adult group of child bearing age,

83.  417 U.S. 484, 94 S.Ct. 2485, 41 L.Ed.2d 256 (1974).

compared to the incidence of cancer, heart disease, or any other major disease. In addition, coverage for normal pregnancy substantially increases the expense of disability insurance, and the temptation of administrators to save money by eliminating a condition that is not an illness (though admittedly a disability) is very great.

Ironically, it is child-bearing, the only biological function absolutely unique to women, that has led to two further setbacks for the women's rights movement. The case of *General Electric Co. v. Gilbert* [84] was the counterpart in the private sector of *Geduldig v. Aiello.* The General Electric Company provided for its employees a disability plan which, like the California plan in *Geduldig,* excluded pregnancy related disabilities, and included many disabilities suffered exclusively by men. Since General Electric was a private employer, rather than an agency of the state, suit could not be brought under the Equal Protection Clause directly, but instead was instituted under Title VII of the Civil Rights Act of 1964. Title VII forbade discrimination based on sex in employment, and mandated equal pay for equal work. The plaintiff, Martha V. Gilbert, who had been denied disability benefits while absent from work due to pregnancy, argued that the General Electric plan discriminated against women and, in effect, reduced the compensation of women because the plan was not worth as much in financial terms to women as it was to men. The Equal Employment Commission, moreover, had issued guidelines which provided that pregnancy related disabilities should be covered by disability and sick leave plans.

The United States Supreme Court rejected these arguments and held, as in *Geduldig,* that the exclusion of pregnancy was not in itself evidence of discrimination against women and merely removed one physical disability (among others) from coverage. There was no evidence that the exclusion was designed to discriminate against women. Pregnancy was selected for exclusion because it was significantly different in other ways from

84.   429 U.S. 125, 97 S.Ct. 401, 50 L.
Ed.2d 343 (1976).

the typical covered disease or disability. There was no evidence, moreover, that the disability benefit was less valuable to women than to men. In short, the Court accepted the employer's argument that for financial reasons, pregnancy as an atypical disability, had been selected along with certain other conditions for exclusion, and the fact that its impact was solely on women was purely incidental. Since the intent, therefore, was nondiscriminatory, there was no violation of the Civil Rights Act.

Using similar reasoning, the Court ruled in June 1977, that no state was required to spend Medicaid funds for elective abortions, and that cities and towns that had public hospitals were not constitutionally required to provide, or even permit, elective abortions in those hospitals. In *Poelker v. Doe* [85] the question before the Court was whether the Social Security Act or the Constitution permitted states to bar nontherapeutic abortions for indigent women. The plaintiffs, who had been denied abortions, claimed that by funding medical services for pregnancies that went to term, but denying funds for pregnancies that were interrupted by elective abortions, the states were denying women liberty without due process of law inasmuch as in 1973 the United States Supreme Court had declared that women had a right to have elective abortions, at least during the first six months of pregnancy.[86] The Court rejected these arguments, holding that the states had a right to make reasonable plans for the expenditure of Medicaid funds or the use of public hospitals. Since the states had a valid interest in encouraging childbirth, it was reasonable for the states to fund pregnancy and childbirth services but to deny funds for abortion. The fact that such denial impinged on a woman's freedom to choose whether or not to have a child was incidental and subservient to the interest of the state in promoting a valid public policy.

Both the *Poelker* and *General Electric* decisions were greeted with dismay by supporters of women's rights. From their point of view, the Court was willing to accept any rationalization how-

85. 432 U.S. 519, 97 S.Ct. 2391, 53 L.Ed.2d 528 (1977).

86. *Roe v. Wade*, 410 U.S. 113, 93 S.Ct. 705, 35 L.Ed.2d 147 (1973).

ever slim, for the denial of equal protection to women. For the Civil Rights Act, and the Due Process and Equal Protection clauses to be meaningful, public or private policy that was discriminatory should be justified for only the most imperative reasons, not merely the convenience of the agency involved. The reasons offered for the discriminatory policies in *Geduldig, Poelker,* and *General Electric* hardly reached that level of seriousness.

Worse yet, these three cases ignored the 1970–1975 precedents which interpreted the Equal Protection Clause so as to protect women's rights. With the exception of the 1970–1975 period, the courts had generally refused to use the Equal Protection Clause for the protection of women, and indeed it was the unsympathetic attitude of the courts toward women which gave rise to the movement for an Equal Rights Amendment. Since 1970, a constitutional amendment designed to protect the civil rights of women has been under consideration. The text reads:

> Equality of rights under the law shall not be denied or abridged by the United States or by any State on account of sex. Congress and the several States shall have the power within their respective jurisdictions, to enforce this article by appropriate legislation.

A very extensive campaign was mounted by women's groups and their sympathizers to obtain the adoption of this amendment, and by 1977 thirty-five states had approved the amendment, which needed the approval of three more states to go into effect.[87] *

---

87. For an excellent discussion of the necessity for ERA see, "Equal Rights for Women: A Symposium on the Proposed Constitutional Amendment," 6 *Harvard Civil Rights-Civil Liberties Law Review* 215 (March 1971).

* When the proposed amendment was passed by Congress in 1970, seven years was specified by the Con-gressional resolution as the time period for ratification by the states. By 1977, three additional states were needed for ratification and several states which had ratified ERA, rescinded their ratification. ERA's supporters thus had two legal questions to resolve. (1) Since it was *Congress* that specified the seven year time period, could Congress, if

The notion that sex is a suspect classification and that women's rights should be protected from arbitrary and discriminatory governmental actions appears to have widespread support. There is not nearly so broad a consensus, however, that an Equal Rights Amendment to the Constitution is the proper way to secure these rights. Questions have been raised in relation to ERA by those who support its goals, but are dubious as to the wisdom of the Amendment itself. Critics ask if ERA is necessary, or whether women's rights might not be protected as effectively under the Equal Protection clause of the Fourteenth Amendment. Does ERA create rigidities which might be harmful to women (e. g., forbidding special benefits or protective legislation) while not accomplishing anything more than do the existing constitutional guarantees?

ERA protagonists respond that the Equal Protection Clause is a weak reed on which to rely. They point to the historical record of the courts in failing to recognize or correct injustices against women under the Equal Protection Clause, and to the most recent decisions of the Court relating to abortion and pregnancy benefits as cases in point. ERA would, they argue, provide an authoritative declaration of public policy which would remove from the area of discretion exercised by judges in all courts, local and national, the policy decision as to whether women are entitled to be treated in the same manner as men. If such equality of treatment imposes burdens and obligations on women that heretofore they have not shared, such as conscription into the Armed Forces, or child support or alimony payments where financially feasible, this is an acceptable price to pay for first class citizenship and a full role in society. Generally, the biological differences between men and women in the modern world are not such as to justify preferential or protective legislation for women which in the past was used to justify public policies that resulted in diminution of career opportunities and earning power as well as status and prestige for many women.

it wished, extend that time period? and (2) Could a state that had approved the amendment subsequently change its mind and rescind that approval?

Even if ERA is finally ratified, however, will it be as effective in protecting women's rights as its supporters claim it will? Critics suggest that if the courts have not been willing to grant women equality of treatment under the existing Equal Protection Clause, ERA will not be any more effective in obtaining such rights. In the pregnancy cases, for example, *Geduldig v. Aiello* and *General Electric v. Gilbert,* the Court supported the policies of California and General Electric, not because they declared sexual discrimination to be constitutionally permissible, but because they did not view the policies in question as *being discriminatory*. If it was not discriminatory for California to exclude normal pregnancy from disability benefits under the Equal Protection Clause, why should it be necessarily any more discriminatory if considered in the light of ERA? If the courts, in other words, do not see a particular policy as sex discrimination, how will an amendment to the Constitution that forbids sex discrimination help matters? It is virtually impossible for men and women in all circumstances to be treated identically by the law. If they are not treated identically then the legal standard, whether under ERA or the Equal Protection Clause has to be of reasonableness. If the standard is reasonableness, then in what manner is ERA superior to the Equal Protection Clause?

Proponents of the ERA would respond that ERA's superiority over Equal Protection is that it forces the courts to consider sex categories as suspect groups. It forces the courts to place the burden of proof of justifying such groupings on the state or private individual who discriminates. Opponents of ERA would respond, possibly, that the courts in the 1970–1975 cases favorable to women did precisely that under the Equal Protection Clause and can be expected to do so as long as the strong push toward egalitarianism in society continues. If the push were to subside, the mere presence in the Constitution of a formal amendment guaranteeing sexual equality would be of no avail. Like the existing Due Process and Equal Protection Clauses, its protection would be interpreted away. Moreover, say the critics, the arguments raised by Brandeis in the *Muller* case are still valid.

Women are physically weaker (as a group) and different from men, and there may well be public health considerations that necessitate protective legislation for women. If for example, it were found that working in a particular industry greatly increased the risk of fetal abnormality, would a law forbidding such work to women be valid under ERA? If it were, how would ERA differ from the Equal Protection Clause? ERA's supporters reply that in today's world there are few, if any, jobs that are hazardous to women that are not equally hazardous to men, and that those concerned with industrial health and safety should be working for legislation to protect all workers rather than just women.

It is not clear that ERA is necessary. Certainly if the pattern established by *Frontiero, Taylor,* and *Reed* becomes the dominant mode of judicial reasoning of the United States Supreme Court, it is hard to see the superiority of ERA over existing constitutional protections. This assumes, however, that *Geduldig, General Electric,* and *Poelker* are aberrations, deviations from the main stream signifying nothing more than the Court's concern for fiscal imperatives. If, however, *Geduldig et al.,* signal a return to the days when women were considered by the courts to be something less than first class citizens, ERA is essential for the protection of women's rights. While the courts do indeed follow the election returns, sometimes they don't follow fast enough, and they need a push. Maybe ERA is that push.

# Chapter VI

## PRESSURE GROUPS, LAWYERS, AND
## THE SUPREME COURT

"At its best the Court is a great teacher, illuminating issues and then drawing support for further steps from the more sensitive public attitudes it has helped to create."

Anthony Lewis,
*Gideon's Trumpet*

"Their power is enormous, but it is the power of public opinion."

Alexis de Tocqueville,
*Democracy in America*
(referring to justices
of the United States
Supreme Court).

Students of constitutional law soon come to realize that the most significant decisions of the United States Supreme Court have not been legal decisions so much as they have been essays in social and political philosophy. In the interpretation of gloriously imprecise phrases such as "due process," "equal protection," and "interstate commerce" the Court has shaped the society of which it was a part, and marked itself as a *political* or policy making branch of government. As such, the democratic ethic requires that it be accessible and responsible to the constituency for which it makes policy, if not directly as are the legislative branches, then indirectly, in ways idiosyncratic to its own peculiar nature.

While the fact that its members are appointed for life would appear to insure total insulation of the court from the pressures of interest group politics, in fact this is not so. The Court is very much affected by the concerns of the public at large, and

278

there have been very few occasions in its history when the Court has been seriously out of step with public opinion.* How political pressures penetrate the shield of the security afforded by lifetime appointments is a fascinating study. An examination of the Court and its procedures suggests that it is through influencing the *agenda* of the Court, that interest groups are able to assert their claims. Since the Court is almost totally free to pick and choose those cases it wishes to hear from a very large group of appeals, it is quite possible for the Court to emphasize some issues and ignore others. The successful interest group is the one that can persuade the justices that the issue it is raising is more important than the questions raised by some other group. In choosing between competing sets of litigants, all clamoring to be heard, the Court chooses between competing sets of interests that the litigants represent. In making these choices, the justices, in their own way are responding to the clash of *political* interests in the country at large.

The constitutional and statutory rules regulating the Court's operations make this possible. In the first place, because of constitutional limits on its functions, the Court can speak *only in the process of deciding a case. It does not render advisory opinions.* This means that if the Court has something to say, it must wait until a suitable vehicle in case form happens to present itself. It also means that if any individual or group in the United States wishes to elicit from the Court an authoritative statement or definition of constitutional rights, it may approach the Court only by litigating a suitable case. In short, no matter how brilliant, how wise, how urgent the opinions of the justices may be, they will remain forever unheard and unsaid unless a case presents itself wherein these thoughts may be appropriately included. No law, no matter how outrageous, or how patently contrary to the Constitution, is unconstitutional until the justices declare it to be unconstitutional; and they cannot

---

* Historians would probably single out the *Dred Scott* decision on the eve of the Civil War, and the anti-New Deal decisions of 1932–1936, as being particularly unresponsive to the opinions of the dominant political groups of the day.

so declare it until it is challenged by a case or controversy that the procedural rules of the Court permit it to hear.

Secondly, Congressional statutes regulating the Court's appellate functions have insured that the case load of the Court is almost entirely discretionary; that is, the Court has the power, in over 90 percent of cases requesting review, to decide which ones it wishes to hear.* Furthermore, the number of cases that the Court hears is miniscule compared to the number of cases it *could* theoretically hear, and is a small fraction of even those cases requesting a hearing. For most litigants, thus, the Supreme Court as a court of last resort does not, in reality, exist. The Court itself recognizes that its function is far more subtle and complex than that of the ordinary appellate court. As Justice Frankfurter once said, "After all, this is the Nation's ultimate judicial tribunal, not a super-legal-aid bureau."[1] The Court, in deciding which cases to hear, is not primarily motivated by the justice or injustice of the lower court's verdict, or by the fate of the defendant should the review not be granted. Its chief motivation is presumably that the question to be decided is of national significance. The Court's formal rules of procedure provide some guidance: for example, cases must arise under the laws or Constitution of the United States and present a federal question for decision; litigants must have suffered a personal injury or damage in order to have standing to sue; and must have exhausted all previous remedies. In the last analysis, however, the rules of procedure are only guidelines to be more or less flexibly applied; the Court hears what it thinks is important for the Court to hear, and the definition of "importance," like the definition of "national significance," is determined by the justices themselves.

While the members of the Court make the final determination as to which cases will be heard in a given term, it is worth not-

---

* Very few cases come to the United States Supreme Court on original jurisdiction. The great bulk of its significant case load comes on appeal from the state and lower federal courts.

1. *Uveges v. Pennsylvania*, 335 U.S. 437 at 449–450, 69 S.Ct. 184, 190, 93 L.Ed. 127 (1948).

ing that almost all the important cases decided by the Court (especially in recent years) have been shaped to some extent by judicial pressure groups.* Consider, for example, the successful effort to strike down *judicially* the Connecticut statute that made the use of contraceptives a crime. For almost fifty years the Planned Parenthood forces attempted to have the Connecticut state legislature repeal this absurd and unenforceable law only to be defeated by the potential political power of the Catholic Church at the polls. Regardless of their personal sentiments, legislators were unwilling to repeal the statute for fear of not being reelected. Finally, after years of litigation, the Planned Parenthood League of Connecticut achieved its goal when the United States Supreme Court declared the Connecticut birth control law unconstitutional.

In *Griswold v. Connecticut* [2] (the Connecticut birth control case), the appellant Griswold was the director of the Planned Parenthood League of Connecticut, and the allegedly illegal acts charged were committed at her direction while acting in her official capacity; PPLC retained the attorneys who defended her and paid for the entire course of litigation; Planned Parenthood of America, of which PPLC was an affiliate, also entered a brief *amicus curiae* (friend of the Court) at the Supreme Court level. The *Griswold* case, in short, reached the United States Supreme Court for adjudication only because of the activities of a group which (at least at that point in its history) existed in large part specifically for the purpose of challenging restrictive legislation in the courts.

*Griswold* and Planned Parenthood is perhaps an extreme example, but dozens of others come to mind. The American Jewish Congress has been involved in almost all cases where church-state relations have been challenged; the NAACP has been active in segregation cases; and the ACLU has argued in

---

* A judicial pressure group is a voluntary association of individuals joined by some common interest whose advancement they seek through the courts.

2. 381 U.S. 479, 85 S.Ct. 1678, 14 L. Ed.2d 510 (1965).

scores of civil liberties cases. Pressure group involvement can take many forms, but probably the most frequent is the presentation of an *amicus curiae* brief at the United States Supreme Court level, or the providing of counsel or money to defray expenses at any level of a case. Sometimes a group may provide the litigants (as in Griswold) or even witnesses. Although the American Civil Liberties Union (ACLU) and the National Association for the Advancement of Colored People (NAACP) are currently the most active and well-known judicial pressure groups, not all such judicial pressure groups represent liberal points of view. Many conservative groups on occasion provide either counsel, financing, or *amicus curiae* briefs for cases in which they are interested. Administrative officials, moreover, frequently band together and act in a manner very similar to the ACLU; for example, in the *Miranda* [3] case, involving police procedure, the attorneys general of many states filed briefs *amicus curiae* in opposition to the position taken by the ACLU briefs *amicus curiae*.

Thus, the contribution of judicial pressure groups (whether permanent or *ad hoc*), is to shape the case load of the Court by making it possible for certain cases to reach the highest appellate levels, and to influence the thinking of the justices themselves by the arguments made before the Court. The attempt to influence the courts, and the United States Supreme Court in particular, in this way is peculiarly available to small and unpopular minorities who find it relatively easy to form effective judicial pressure groups. Even a single private attorney may play such a role, and an examination of the principal criminal procedure cases heard by the Warren Court yields some fascinating insights.

Defendants like Ernesto Miranda, Wilbert Rideau, Michael Vignera, et al., collectively present a picture of what most people consider the dregs of society. Miranda, charged with rape, was an unemployed, semiliterate, mentally dull truck driver, with a

---

3. 384 U.S. 436, 86 S.Ct. 1602, 16 L.
Ed.2d 694 (1966).

long criminal record going back to his childhood; Rideau was black, uneducated, and accused of a particularly cold-blooded series of killings; Vignera committed a robbery that netted him only ninety-three dollars and handled himself so stupidly afterward that he virtually insured his arrest and conviction. In all of these cases, the defendants were almost certainly guilty of the crimes with which they were charged but the proceedings by which their convictions were obtained were in some respect faulty. Miranda's confession appeared to have been coerced; Rideau was subjected to unwarranted prejudicial pretrial publicity; Vignera was unaware of his right to counsel. Each of their convictions was appealed and ultimately was reviewed by the United States Supreme Court.

The attorneys who represented these defendants and others like them were a picture of the elite of our society: well-to-do, sometimes prominent parents; ivy league colleges and law schools; prestigious and usually lucrative law practices, etc. Victor M. Earle III, for example, who was Vignera's attorney,* is the son of a Princeton-educated stockbroker father; an alumnus of Williams College and Columbia Law School; was at the time of his involvement with Vignera associated with Cravath, Swayne and Moore, a leading Wall Street law firm; and in a previous Supreme Court appearance had faced opposing counsel in the person of none other than Richard M. Nixon.

As a group, the defendants and attorneys described above came from opposite ends of the social spectrum. It is true, that not all defendants were poor, black, and under-educated. Some were white and rich, like Sam Sheppard. Neither were all attorneys who appeared before the Supreme Court in criminal procedure cases from Ivy League colleges and prestigious law firms that provided them with excellent incomes. Some attorneys had

---

* *Vignera v. New York*, 384 U.S. 436, 86 S.Ct. 1602, 16 L.Ed.2d 694 (1966) was a companion case to *Miranda v. Arizona*, and it was the substance of Mr. Earle's brief on behalf of Vignera that was eventually adopted as the Court's majority opinion in *Miranda*, including the famous warnings.

attended local law schools and lived on modest salaries from legal defender groups.

On the whole, however, the picture is true. Those who have appeared as defendants or petitioners in United States Supreme Court criminal procedure cases have been of very low socio-economic status. The lawyers who represented them were, on the other hand, a highly elite group. In some respects, perhaps, this is not surprising. We expect that nasty brutish crimes will be committed by nasty brutish people, just as we expect that the cream of the legal profession will practice before the bar of the United States Supreme Court. The interesting question is, however, how does this come about? How does a defendant like Vignera get an attorney like Earle? Even more interesting, is why—Why do attorneys like Earle take cases like these? Why do they become involved with men who, on the whole, are not only born losers, but are extremely unlikely to be rehabilitated or reformed in their behavior patterns?

How these attorneys came to be involved in these cases is relatively easy to determine. Some attorneys were affiliated with, or volunteered their services to, legal defender groups such as the American Civil Liberties Union or the NAACP Legal Defense Fund. Some were employed by the Legal Aid Society. Some were appointed by the court, either at the trial level or on appeal—sometimes even by the United States Supreme Court itself, frequently after they had made their availability known to the court. Occasionally, attorneys were recommended to the client by a friend, another attorney, an employer or even a community figure such as a priest. Some lawyers handled the case from beginning to end; others came in at some point in the appellate process.

To say that these attorneys were either court appointees or associated with legal defense groups, however, is not to explain very much. It only begs the real question of why this type of lawyer was associated with such organizations. While some attorneys took such cases in the same spirit as physicians who serve without pay in clinics for the poor, and some no doubt wanted the prestige, fun and excitement that goes with an opportunity to appear before the United States Supreme Court, many attorneys took these cases out of concern for the principle of law involved as distinguished from the interests of the client.[4] Many attorneys perceived themselves in the role of defenders of a system of law and government that they viewed as threatened by inadequate, incompetent, or immoral government officials.

As an example, in the case of *Aguilar v. Texas*, the defendant was arrested on an affidavit from police officers which simply stated that they had "reliable information" from a credible person that narcotics were kept in Aguilar's home. No further information was given to the magistrate issuing the search warrant as to the nature of either the informant or the source of his information. Clyde W. Woody, attorney for Aguilar, commented:

> It was necessary to fully apprise the Court of Criminal Appeals as well as the trial courts of the State of Texas of the real meaning of the Fourth and Fifth Amendments of the Constitution of the United States. In my opinion the Courts of this state, as well as the citizens of the State of Texas, were the victims of a fraud being perpetrated under the guise of law enforcement. The function of the arrest and search warrant in Texas prior to *Aguilar* has been utilized as a writ of assistance which in my opinion would bring discredit and lawlessness to the Courts and cause the citizens to lose respect for the Constitution as well as the Judiciary. It was obvious that the executive branch in Texas had already succeeded in bringing discredit upon themselves.[5]

4. Alexander B. Smith and Harriet Pollack, "Rich Lawyer/Poor Client," *Student Lawyer* (September 1973) pp. 22–25, 62–63.

5. Ibid., p. 62.

In a similar vein, Gretchen White Oberman (then a Legal Aid attorney), discussed *Sibron v. New York*,[6] a case involving the New York State "stop and frisk" law which lowered the standards for police searches and seizures of suspected persons.

> The Legal Aid Society is assigned to hundreds and thousands of cases at the trial level and this was one of the many. The trial attorney saw the legal potential and asked Mr. Finkel of the Appeals Bureau to handle it personally on appeal  .   .   . Mr. Finkel had it in the Appellate Term and the New York Court of Appeals. I had handled *People v. Rivera,* the first stop and frisk case in the New York Court of Appeals a couple of years before and Mr. Finkel, knowing my commitment to the privacy principle of the Fourth Amendment asked me to collaborate with him on the jurisdictional statement to the Supreme Court, and on the brief and argument when the case was taken by the Court for review.

> Our work together was a true labor of love. We believed every word we wrote in the brief and every statement we made orally before the Court. I would have done the same thing without salary from the Society because I believed that the issue involved was important to the law and ultimately to the entire social fabric of the country.[7]

Many attorneys, however, are reluctant to admit to taking a case for the satisfaction of an ideological consideration rather than to meet the needs of the client. The ethics of the legal profession dictate that a lawyer's first concern must be for his client, and any other consideration permitted to intrude itself into the case might lead to a conflict of interest. Thus, Victor

6.  392 U.S. 40, 88 S.Ct. 1889, 20 L.
Ed.2d 917 (1968).

7.  Smith    and    Pollack,    "Rich
Lawyer/Poor Client," p. 62.

M. Earle III, explained carefully why he undertook to defend Michael Vignera:

> Understand that the principle [activating me] is free service for the indigents, not the particular legal or constitutional issue involved. As it happened, I believed strongly that the police needed to be controlled in their interrogations, and my brief contained the four-part warning which the Court adopted in its *Miranda* opinion.[8]

Doubtless Mr. Earle was concerned for Vignera. It is not easy however, to write a brief good enough for the United States Supreme Court to use as the substance of its decision. Such a brief requires more than a casual effort; such an effort requires more than a casual commitment.

Many people are shocked by the notion that the United States Supreme Court is influenced by pressure groups; yet they should not be. In the long run, the likelihood of success of these groups depends on the receptivity of public opinion. The Supreme Court may not follow the election returns quite as faithfully as the legislative and executive branches do, but follow them they must, because the law basically is not the watchdog of society; it is its reflection. If Planned Parenthood, or the NAACP or Citizens for Decent Literature or even Victor M. Earle III spoke only for themselves, the Court would not hear the cases in which they were involved, nor be influenced favorably if it did. It is only when the Court perceives these claims as a *reflection* of substantial attitudinal changes in society, that it is willing to give legal relief.

In giving this relief, the Court helps to maintain the balance between the right of the majority to govern, and the need of minorities for protection from those in power. Democracy is more than majoritarianism. It is limited government. And the function of the Court is to set the limits.

8.    Ibid.

\*

# TABLE OF CASES

The principal cases are in italic type. Cases cited or discussed are in roman. References are to Pages.

*

# INDEX

References are to Pages

**ABORTION**
See Discrimination, Sexual

**ACTIVISM, JUDICIAL**
See Supreme Court, Role of

**ADVISORY OPINIONS**
See Supreme Court

**AFFIRMATIVE ACTION PRO-
GRAMS**
See Discrimination

**AMERICAN COURTS**
See Courts, American

**AMERICAN DEMOCRACY**
See Democracy

**ARREST**
"Probable cause" requirement, 142–
143

**ASSEMBLY**
See Freedom of Assembly

**BLACKS**
See Discrimination

**BRANDEIS BRIEF**
See Discrimination

**BURGER COURT**
Comparison with Warren Court, 151–
157

**BUSING**
See Discrimination, Blacks

**CIVIL DISOBEDIENCE**
See Freedom of Assembly

**CIVIL LIBERTIES**
Defined, 8

**CIVIL RIGHTS**
Generally, 1–2, 8–9
Defined, 8

**CIVIL RIGHTS ACTS (1875 AND
1964)**
See Discrimination, Private action or
conduct

**CLEAR AND PRESENT DANGER
STANDARD**
See Freedom of Speech, Communism

**COMMUNISM**
See Freedom of Speech

**CONFESSIONS AND RIGHT TO
COUNSEL**
Generally, 169–180
*Escobedo* decision, 173–174
Exclusionary rule, 172
*Miranda* decision,
    Generally, 175–180
    Narrowing of scope,
        Cross-examination of defendant,
        177
        "Not in custody" confession, 179
        Second interrogation directed to-
        ward unrelated crime, 178
Physically coerced confessions, 170–
171
Psychologically coerced confessions,
171–172
Self incrimination, 169–170, 174

**COUNSEL**
See generally Confessions and Right
to Counsel; Fair Trial and Right
to Counsel